Guns & Babies

By: J. David Nelson

For Julie, who has made the ideological, political, moral and ethical journey of this life with me, and has offered course correcting input when I have gone astray.

For Suzanne, brilliant editor-in-chief, who, as always, did such a stellar job with editing and presentation critiques.

For Will, who provided a very perceptive analysis of the concept presentations and conclusions.

For Lloyd, who carefully reviewed multiple drafts of the manuscript and offered invaluable critiques of the presentation, analysis and conclusions.

For Bob, who provided perceptive insight on key content clarification as well as very valuable editing.

GUNS & BABIES

TABLE OF CONTENTS

SETTING THE STAGE

BOOK I – BABIES

BOOK II – GUNS

BOOK III – AMERICA THE BEAUTIFUL

SETTING THE STAGE

Are there any issues that are more inflammatory in American politics and public life than gun rights and abortion? These two issues have been raging in public debate and have animated and divided the citizens of this great country for the last half century. However, the divide among the electorate was first precipitated by another series of events which began around the time of my earliest personal engagement with social and political issues, which was about 1960.

The first Presidential election that I have a recollection of is the election of John F. Kennedy. Growing up in a small town in Mississippi, I remember the concern over what the implications of electing a Catholic president might be. Soon after his election in 1960, the commitment of President Kennedy to racial equality and desegregation made him persona non-grata in the southern states, that is, to the white citizenry who controlled every aspect of state and local government in those states. On the day of his assassination in 1963, I was a high school sophomore. We were dismissed from school early that day, and as I walked toward home with one of my classmates, he made a remark that I remember as clearly as I remember the shocking news of the fate of President Kennedy. He said, "I am sorry for him and his family, but I am glad he is out of there."

However, what no opponent of desegregation could anticipate at the time of President Kennedy's assassination, was that his tragic death would be the catalyst for the passage of the Civil Rights Act of 1964, which he had only begun to promote. When Vice President Lyndon Johnson, formerly the Democratic Majority Leader of the U.S. Senate from the State of Texas, was sworn in as President, the states who were harboring segregation and even those elsewhere who were not interested in racial equality, breathed a collective sigh of relief. Not one of them expected that President Johnson would take up the cause of racial equality and desegregation. Most certainly, they did not expect that he would engage in that cause with such vigor and determination. But that he did, relying on his years of experience in political arm twisting and on the nation's need to establish a legacy for its fallen President. Racial equality, codified by the Civil Rights Act of 1964, along with Medicare and Medicaid, were the hallmarks of President Johnson's "Great Society." The Civil Rights Act of 1964 ended segregation in public places and banned employment discrimination on the basis of race, color, religion, sex or national origin.

What needs to be remembered is that prior to the time of John Kennedy's election in 1960, the southern states were solidly democratic states. That stemmed back to days of the Reconstruction following the Civil War. Abraham Lincoln had been, of course, a Republican. An interesting quirk in the election involved Mississippi and Alabama. Uncommitted Democratic electoral college delegates were elected in Mississippi and four of the five electoral college delegates elected in Alabama were also uncommitted, the other being committed to Kennedy. Those uncommitted delegates voted for Virginia Democratic Senator Harry Byrd in the electoral college.

The following map from Wikipedia, *1960 US Presidential Election*, shows the results of the 1960 election.

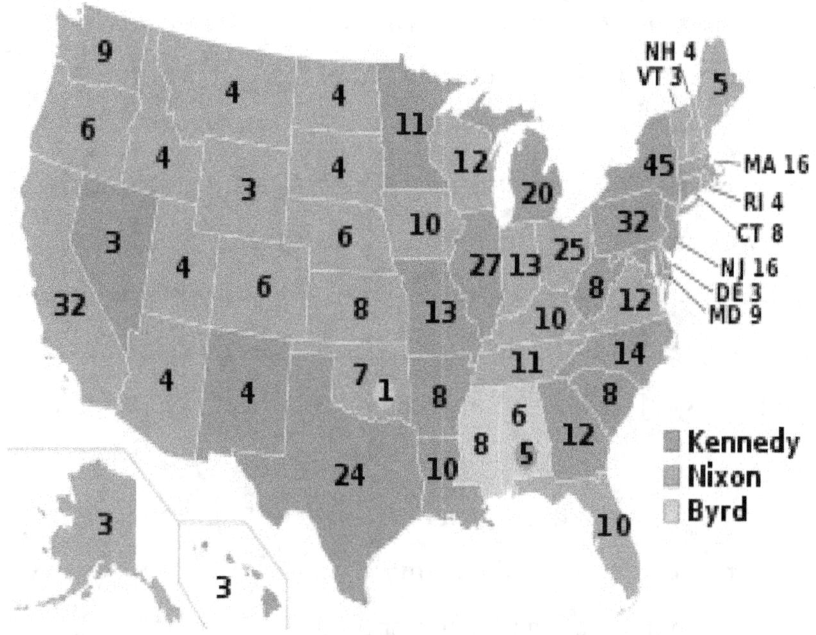

https://en.wikipedia.org/wiki/1960_United_States_presidential_election

If the vote for uncommitted delegates in Mississippi and Alabama in 1960 constituted a minute crack in the dam, the crack in the dam fully developed in the election of 1964. Although Johnson carried 44 states and the District of Columbia in the election of 1964, and Goldwater won his home state of Arizona and only five others, it is the identity of the five others that is the heart of the story. Louisiana, Mississippi, Alabama, Georgia and South Carolina all voted for Barry Goldwater. Most of these states had not voted for a Republican presidential candidate since the end of Reconstruction in 1877. Along with Johnson's landslide victory, many conservative Republican Congressmen were defeated. The large Democratic majority elected to both houses of Congress heralded the passage of major Great Society legislation, such as the Voting Rights Act and the Social Security

Amendments of 1965. However, Goldwater's unsuccessful bid for the Presidency heralded the long-term realignment of the voters of the southeastern states.

The election of 1964 is the first election that I paid close attention to. Although I was only 15 at the time, I remember listening to speeches from the candidates before the election and watching Walter Cronkite on CBS and listening to the radio as the results of the election came in. If I had been of voting age, I most certainly would have voted for Barry Goldwater.

The great divide among the American citizenry fomented by the fires of the desegregation and racial equality controversy, was made even worse by another monumental challenge imposed on this country, the Vietnam War. By the time of the 1964 election, the war was raging. Among the political strategies devised and implemented by Johnson was to goad Goldwater into making a strong public expression of support for the war, which Johnson followed up with an expression of the country's need to extricate itself from the war.

The 1964 election also saw the emergence of a very divisive personality on the national political scene. George Wallace served two nonconsecutive terms and two consecutive terms as the Democratic Governor of Alabama. He sought the Democratic Party nomination for the U.S. Presidency for three elections, 1964, 1972 and 1976. For the 1968 election, he was the American Independent Party candidate. In his 1963 Inaugural Address as Governor of the State of Alabama, Wallace declared "segregation now, segregation tomorrow, segregation forever". He will likely be most remembered for standing in front of the

University of Alabama in an attempt to stop the enrollment of black students.

The George Wallace controversy was only one of the extraordinary aspects of the 1968 election, which included:

(a)   the assassination of civil rights leader Martin Luther King, Jr. and subsequent race riots across the nation;

(b)   the assassination of presidential candidate Robert F. Kennedy;

(c)   widespread demonstrations against the Vietnam War on university and college campuses; and

(d)   violent confrontations between police and anti-war protesters at the 1968 Democratic National Convention.

On November 5, 1968, the Republican nominee, former Vice President Richard Nixon won the election over the Democratic nominee, Vice President Hubert Humphrey. Primarily because of the raging Vietnam War, President Johnson had decided not to run for re-election. Nixon ran on a campaign that promised to restore "law and order." Some consider the election of 1968 as the realigning election that permanently disrupted the New Deal Coalition that had dominated presidential politics for 36 years. It was also the last election in which the two opposing candidates had both served as Vice President.

The 1968 presidential election featured the strong, third party candidacy of George Wallace as the American Independent Party candidate. Because Wallace strongly opposed desegregation, he proved to be a formidable candidate in the South. He accomplished what has not been accomplished by any independent candidate since. He won electoral votes. As a matter of fact, he won the electoral votes for the states of Arkansas, Louisiana, Mississippi, Alabama and Georgia, along with one electoral vote from the state of North Carolina, for a total of 46. Despite the surprisingly strong showing for Wallace, I distinctly remember, though 52 years of water has flowed under the bridge since then, CBS News journalist Roger Mudd commenting on the election results and referring to the candidacy of George Wallace as remaining "as Southern as grits and gravy." Although I would have voted for Richard Nixon, and not George Wallace, if I had been of voting age at the time, I nevertheless remember feeling insulted, doubtless along with by this comment

In the 1960's, Congress came under increasing pressure to lower the voting age from 21 to 18. This was due in large part to the Vietnam War in which so many young men died. The slogan "old enough to fight, old enough to vote," emerged from the public fray over the Vietnam War. Finally, in 1970, Senator Ted Kennedy and others pushed a bill through Congress which amended the Voting Rights Act of 1964 by lowering the voting age to 18 in all federal and state elections. President Nixon signed the bill into law in 1970, while expressing serious concerns about the constitutionality of the law. Due to subsequent court battles over the constitutionality of the law, the Twenty Sixth Amendment to the Constitution was ratified in 1971, guaranteeing the right to vote to all persons 18 or older in all federal, state and local elections.

I was 19 at the time of the 1968 election and, so, the 1970 Amendment to the Voting Rights Act and 26th Amendment in 1971 came too late for me. However, I remember closely following the primaries and I was glued to the TV set for the conventions of both the parties. It was our Constitution in action. I was between my sophomore and junior years in college and working at a summer internship for the US Army at the Redstone Arsenal in Huntsville, Alabama. My wife and I watched the conventions on our tiny black and white TV in the sweltering heat of the Alabama summer nights. It was about the only entertainment we could afford on our college student budget. Without a doubt, if I had been of voting age, I would have enthusiastically cast my vote for Richard Nixon in the 1968 election.

Wallace survived an assassination attempt in Laurel, Maryland in 1972, but was rendered a paraplegic and was confined to a wheelchair until his death in 1998.   He eventually admitted the error of his position on segregation.

As I already mentioned, Wallace sought the nomination of the Democratic Party as its presidential candidate for the 1964, 1972 and 1976 elections. Let me say that again - the *Democratic Party*. The 1972 and 1976 attempts were after his strong showing as an Independent candidate in 1968. There was still hope among many in the South that the Democratic Party, the party that had been highly favored in the South for so many years, would revert to its former ways and save them from the ravages of desegregation. That hope was soon dashed for good.

In the 1971 *Swann v. Charlotte-Mecklenburg Board of Education* decision, the Supreme Court ruled that the federal courts had the discretion to include busing as a desegregation tool to achieve racial balance. While the *Swann* decision addressed *de jure* segregation in the South, it failed to address *de facto* segregation which persisted elsewhere in the country. In Georgia, Governor Jimmy Carter saw that *Swann* was "clearly a one-sided decision; the Court is still talking about the South,

the North is still going free". In the 1974 *Milliken v. Bradley* decision,
the U.S. Supreme Court placed an important limitation on *Swann* when
they ruled that students could be bused across district lines only when
evidence of *de jure* segregation across multiple school districts existed.
The impact of *Swann* and *Milliken* was, thus, limited mainly to the
South, while *de facto* segregation was prevalent in many areas of the
North.

The extent of the trend for white voter abandonment of the
Democratic Party became crystal clear in the 1972 election. Nixon won
the election in a landslide, carrying 49 states with 60.7% of the popular
vote, the widest popular vote margin of any US presidential election.
More importantly, for the discussion we are engaged in here, he was the
first Republican to sweep the South. My enthusiastic vote was included
in that 60.7%. I was a graduate student at Brigham Young University at
the time. Amazingly, however, less than two years later, on August 9,
1974, Richard Nixon achieved another historic first. He became the first
US President to resign from office. He resigned to avoid almost certain
impeachment and removal from office due to his personal involvement
in the cover-up of the Watergate scandal. I was among the last 10% of
his loyal supporters to accept the necessity for his resignation.

The stage having been set by the events of the 1960's and 1970's
and the resultant conversion of the white voters of the South to the
Republican Party, the Republican Party recognized the grand opportunity
presented to it and moved to consolidate its grip on the newly gained
electorate, and all those electoral votes. The Republican Party of
Lincoln, the liberal party of "united we stand and divided we fall," was
poised to become the party of "states' rights," "social conservatism," and

"strict construction" of the Constitution. I can remember the mantra that I was very enamored with, "We don't need big brother from Washington telling us what to do."

While I don't ever remember being a segregationist at heart, I was a devout Republican from the beginning of my attention to politics. I can remember my first perceptions, in the 1960's, of the excesses and gross misdirection of the Democratic Party. The escalation of the disastrous Vietnam War during the Kennedy and Johnson administrations, which got dumped in the lap of President Nixon, surely sullied the social achievements of the Democrats in the Civil Rights Act, the Voting Rights Act, and Medicare. The Tax and Spend and Pork Barrel politics of the Democratic Party, that so enraged me as my wife and I worked hard to try to achieve some level of economic stability for our family, continued from 1933, the time of the Great Depression, till 1995, except for two short years (1947-1949) following the end of World War II and two short years following the Korean War (1953-1955).

As a devoted Republican, I was so sure that once the Republicans took control of Congress, sound financial management would be the order of the day. Those delusions have long since faded into reality. The parties seem to compete on who can spin the Deficit Meter the fastest and who can fund the most Pork Barrel projects. Don't you just love career politicians. Americans are strongly in favor of term limits for Congress. Unfortunately, the goats are guarding the cabbage patch.

If, together, we are going to accomplish the monumental tasks which this book is about, resolution of the abortion and gun rights issues in America, we will have to do so in spite of the kicking and screaming of the career politicians who are determined to perpetually divide us for their political interest.

BOOK I - BABIES

CHAPTER 1

DEVELOPMENT OF THE ABORTION ISSUE

The controversy and debate over the issue of abortion has been overtly raging in the United States and much of the rest of the world for more than 50 years.   Since 1970 there have been approximately 62 million legal induced abortions performed in the US. It is no wonder that it is such a virulent issue. Abortion statistics and trends are discussed in detail in a subsequent chapter.

However, it is important to understand, at the outset, that abortion is not a new issue. Abortion was common in North America during the period from 1600 to the late 1800's. In the thirteen British colonies that became the original thirteen states of the United States, as well as the other British colonies of North America, abortions were legal if they were performed prior to quickening (first movement felt by mother). From American Independence in 1776 until the mid-1800's, abortion was legal in most states even though it was generally considered to be morally and socially unacceptable. Of course, slave owners prohibited their women slaves from having abortions. The slave owners wanted their slaves to produce as many children as possible since these children belonged to the slave owners.

We must also remember that the original Americans, those who we refer to as Native Americans, or, from a more scientific standpoint, indigenous Americans, had their own beliefs and practices regarding abortion. In traditional Native American societies, we understand that there is no word for abortion. Native Americans instead referred to a woman using herbs and methods "to make her period come." They used a variety of methods including the use of black root and cedar root as abortifacient agents. Traditionally, this was viewed as a woman exercising control over her body. Women often relied on other women in their tribe for assistance who were knowledgeable about the herbs and methods, and were keepers of the herbs.

The first Anti-abortion laws were enacted in the United States by some states in the 1860's. These first laws were largely unenforced. However, stricter laws followed within a few years and they were more vigorously enforced. This resulted in the development and widespread utilization of illegal abortions. That problem continued to worsen until it reached a crescendo in the latter half of the 1900's.

The landmark decision of the United States Supreme Court in the case of *Roe v. Wade* in 1973, while seemingly settling some of the abortion issues, at least so long as the decision stands, has served to substantially fan the fires of the controversy. Before the *Roe v. Wade* decision, abortion upon request was available in only four states, Alaska, Hawaii, New York and Washington. However, the trend in the late 1960's and early 1970's was toward increasing availability in other states. By 1973, in addition to the four states where abortion was available upon request, abortion was allowed in certain circumstances in fourteen other states. Most of the remaining thirty-two states prohibited abortions in most cases.

The summary of the Court's decision in *Roe v. Wade*, as stated by the Court itself, is as follows:

> 1. A state criminal abortion statute of the current Texas type, that excepts from criminality only a lifesaving procedure on behalf of the mother, without regard to pregnancy stage and

without recognition of the other interests involved, is violative of the Due Process Clause of the Fourteenth Amendment.

(a) For the stage prior to approximately the end of the first trimester, the abortion decision and its effectuation must be left to the medical judgment of the pregnant woman's attending physician.

(b) For the stage subsequent to approximately the end of the first trimester, the State, in promoting its interest in the health of the mother, may, if it chooses, regulate the abortion procedure in ways that are reasonably related to maternal health.

(c) For the stage subsequent to viability, the State in promoting its interest in the potentiality of human life may, if it chooses, regulate, and even proscribe, abortion except where it is necessary, in appropriate medical judgment, for the preservation of the life or health of the mother.

Roe v. Wade, 410 U.S. 113, 164 (1973)

The effect of the Roe v. Wade decision was that states could not prohibit or even regulate abortions during the first three months of a woman's pregnancy, and they could regulate during the time period between the end of the first three months and the attainment of viability by the fetus only to promote the health of the mother. Only after the attainment of viability, i.e. ability to live outside the womb of the mother, could a state, in the interest of the potentiality of human life, prohibit abortion. The power to prohibit an abortion after viability would be subject only to an exception where necessary for the preservation of the life or health of the mother.

In rendering its decision, the Court stated that "We, therefore, conclude that the right of personal privacy includes the abortion decision, but that this right is not unqualified, and must be considered against important state interests in regulation." *Roe v. Wade* at 154. The Court recognized that the woman's right to privacy was preeminent during the first trimester and thereafter until attainment of viability of the fetus. However, her right to privacy yielded to the interest of the State in protecting a fetus that had attained viability.

In virtually every presidential election since the *Roe v. Wade* decision was handed down, abortion has been a defining issue. Proponents of both sides of the issue have forced candidates to take a position and candidates have used their position on the abortion issue as a major tool for energizing support and getting the vote out. The reason of course is that sitting presidents select and nominate judges to fill vacancies on the Supreme Court and the Federal Appellate Courts. The election of a president who would be expected to nominate conservative judges to the Supreme Court who presumably would be more likely to vote to overturn, or at least substantially modify *Roe v. Wade,* became a principal objective of much of the conservative electorate. Similarly, the election of a president who would be expected to appoint liberal judges who presumably would be more respectful of a woman's right to privacy and hence more likely to vote to uphold the right of a woman to have an abortion, became a permanent plank in the platform of the liberal electorate.

I believe that the fact that this controversy continues to rage and that Americans continue to be extremely perplexed and deeply divided by this seemingly unresolvable conflict over issues involving life, liberty and moral conscience, demonstrates the great worth and undying character of the American people and American society. The fact that

Americans do not slip easily into a state of complacency over such a profound issue is a tribute to the moral fiber of this great nation.

I first remember an awareness of the abortion dilemma during my high school years in the 1960's. There were occasional rumors of girls from our high school going "north" from our rural Mississippi town to a state where abortion was legal. I also remember some discussion of the dangers of back alley abortions. However, because the state I resided in prohibited abortions, I do not recall much discussion or concern by the average citizen in the area where I lived, about the moral dilemma posed by the abortion issue. Abortion was wrong and illegal and that was the end of the question. *Roe v. Wade* altered the landscape of the abortion issue in that corner of the world.

When the *Roe v. Wade* decision was handed down and abortion became legal in all fifty states, this issue immediately became a serious social, political, moral and religious issue throughout the United States and has remained such. My wife, our two children at the time, and I were living in a small, mostly Mormon town in Idaho. The perspective on abortion of the people in that area of the nation was not much different than that of the residents of my hometown in rural Mississippi.

Since the time of the *Roe v. Wade* decision, I have been tormented by this issue, which is probably the most provocative, disturbing and divisive long-term issue in American society. My own philosophical struggle with this question has been a primary motivating force driving me to write this book. Despite the fact that we Americans may never agree on some of the underlying questions relating to this issue, I do believe that an overall consideration of the conflicting principles compels us to reach an agreement on and a resolution of the political and legal aspects of this issue.

CHAPTER 2

LIFE

When does life begin? When does an unborn fetus become a "person"? Is or should the answers to these questions be the same? Various answers have been offered for each of these questions which include:

1. Conception
2. First heartbeat
3. Commencement of brain wave activity
4. Sustained brain wave activity
5. Movement
6. Varying periods of gestation
7. Medically assisted viability
8. Unassisted viability
9. Sentience
10. Live birth
11. Self-awareness

The most conservative view is that human life begins and that a person exists from the moment of conception, that is, at the moment that a sperm cell and an egg cell unite. Under this view, a fertilized egg is a person even before it attaches (implantation) to the uterine wall. Hence even the use of a "morning after pill" which prevents the attachment of a fertilized egg to the uterine wall, results in the end of a human life and is, therefore, unacceptable. At the other end of the spectrum, are those who advocate that until a child is born alive, has taken its first breath, and has begun life separate from its mother, it is not a person.

A step from the most conservative position are those who advocate that once a fetus has a beating heart or its first brain activity, it is biologically a human being and therefore should be treated as a person. Somewhat further into the spectrum are those that advocate that once the fetus begins to move ("quickening") it is surely then a living person and should be protected.   Still further into the spectrum are those who advocate that once a fetus has progressed to the stage that it could survive outside the womb of the mother, typically referred to as "viability", whether on its own or through medical intervention, it is a person. Advances in medical science have resulted in the substantial widening of the gap between natural viability and medically assisted viability. Even further into the spectrum, perhaps one step removed from live birth, are those who advocate that until the brain of the fetus has progressed to the point that it is a sentient being, it is not a person.

To adequately ponder the issue of when an embryo or a fetus becomes a person, we must thoroughly review both the scientific evidence and the religious considerations.

CHAPTER 3

SCIENCE

In the purest sense, the beginning of life is before fertilization of an egg cell by a sperm cell. The egg cell and the sperm cell are living cells before they are joined in fertilization. If a living and viable egg cell were not produced in an ovary of a woman, there could be no fertilization. Likewise, if a living and viable sperm cell were not produced in a testicle of a man, there could be no fertilization. Those who advocate for life beginning at conception, generally assert three things. First, they assert that fertilization of an egg cell is the beginning of a biological process involving cell production and division directed by genetic codes that will result in the formation of a fetus and finally a baby. Second, they assert that ensoulment occurs at conception and that conception and ensoulment come from a divine source. Finally, they assert that no woman or man is entitled to interfere with this divine process once it is commenced at conception. Accordingly, they attribute the status of personhood to the biologically developing entity from the moment of conception.

We will endeavor at this point to consider the science which relates to the question of whether a fertilized egg, an embryo, or a fetus should be afforded the same status as that of a newborn baby or a human at any stage of life. The implications of determining the minimum requirements for recognition of the beginning, as well as the ending, of "personhood" and legal protections attributed to that status, relate not only to abortion but also to in-vitro fertilization, biomedical cloning, stem cell research, and brain death.

It must be noted, as we begin the discussion about the science of when an embryo or a fetus becomes a person, that the spin imposed on the basic scientific facts by those advocating for personhood at conception, those advocating for personhood at various times between conception and birth, those advocating for personhood at biological viability, and those advocating for personhood at live birth is confusing and very diverting from any attempt to answer the personhood question based upon scientific fact alone. As an example, we will discuss below the matter of first embryonic 'heartbeat'.

Within the first day following fertilization, the fertilized egg (blastocyte) begins rapid cell division. The rapid cell division experienced by a blastocyte continues during the three days it takes for the blastocyte to pass through the fallopian tube into the uterus and attach (implantation) to the wall of the uterus.

Within approximately three weeks following implantation, 3-1/2 weeks after fertilization, an embryo begins to form, which includes some of the first nerve cells. Within four weeks following fertilization, development of the placenta begins. Although the embryo is only about 5 mm (1/5 inch) long, about the size of a grain of rice, a microscopic examination of the embryo will reveal that a primitive face has begun to develop with dark circles for eyes and the beginning appearance of the mouth, lower jaw, and throat.

This is probably the point at which, for our discussion of the development of the embryo and the fetus, it is important that we clarify the methodology and the terminology that we will be using for the age of the embryo and the fetus. The American College of Obstetrics and Gynecology in 1965 attempted to redefine "conception" to mean implantation rather than fertilization. However, medical dictionaries and general English language dictionaries, both before and after 1966 defined "conception" as fertilization. Because it is impossible, at least with present technology, to determine the moment of conception, the tendency has been to base the age of the embryo and the fetus on the date of the first day of the woman's last menstrual period. This is referred to as the "gestational age." Although there is a potential for inaccuracies using this method as well, due to variations in ovulation dates, other methods employed to determine gestational age, such as a growth stage determination from measurements of the head and abdomen using an ultrasound, also have inaccuracies. Obviously, every fetus will not have the same size head or abdomen at the same gestational age. Even with an accurate determination of gestational age, growth and development at each week of gestation will vary from fetus to fetus. Accordingly, gestational age is the time measurement used most frequently in referencing the stage of the embryo, including particularly abortion statutes in various states and in court decisions, including *Roe v. Wade*. If an age is stated for a stage of an embryo or a fetus below, without clarification, the author will be referring to a gestational age. It should be remembered that time since conception is approximately 2 weeks less than gestational age.

What is referred to, by abortion critics and by the anti-abortion state legislatures in the new abortion statutes intended to test the Supreme Court's present resolve regarding *Roe v. Wade*, as 'fetal heartbeat', may first be detected by a vaginal ultrasound as early as 5 1/2 to 6 weeks gestational age. At that time, a fetal pole, the first visible sign of a developing embryo, may sometimes be seen on the vaginal ultrasound. The question arises, what is the phenomenon that is detected

and characterized as fetal heartbeat? It is perhaps more correctly

described as a flutter detectable by the vaginal ultrasound in the area that

will become the heart of the baby. The flutter is from a group of cells

generating electrical signals that will become the future "pacemaker" of

the heart. The embryo (not technically a fetus until 8th week of gestation)

does not have a formed heart nor a cardiovascular system. It seems that

to refer to this phenomenon as the first fetal heartbeat is incorrect and

misleading, if it is intended to suggest that the embryo has a formed and

functional heart which is circulating fetal blood through a fetal

circulatory system. To make sure we keep this in proper perspective, we

must remember that the embryo is 1/5 of an inch long, the size of a grain

of rice, and weighs 1/25 (0.04) of an ounce.

The embryo at 6 weeks gestation produces nerve cells that will be

incorporated in areas of the brain of the fetus and the first electrical

nerve activity occurs about that time. However, that initial electrical

nerve activity is not to be confused with the continuous and complex

activity of a developed human brain. The neuron activity in the embryo

is very limited, not arising even to the level of the neural activity in

persons determined to be brain-dead or to the level of very primitive

animals.

At 8 weeks gestation, the embryo is deemed to have developed

into a fetus. During weeks 8 to 10, rapid development of the cerebrum

occurs. By the end of the third month, the fetus has well-formed arms,

hands, fingers, feet, and toes. All the organs are present but further

development is necessary for the organs to become fully functional. The

circulatory and urinary systems begin functioning and the liver produces bile. At the end of the third month, the fetus is about four inches long and weighs about one ounce. During weeks 12 to 16, the development of the frontal and temporal poles of the brain is noted. By 17 weeks, the sulci or indentations of the cortex, which later become the folds of the cerebrum, develop.

Movement of the fetus will usually begin within 15 weeks. Although the development of the brain of the fetus continues rapidly at this point, the brain function of the fetus at 15 weeks is still very primitive, functioning on the order of complexity as the brain of very primitive animal organisms capable of responding only in a reflexive fashion to stimuli. The fetus is not close to being a sentient being at this point.

In considering and analyzing the status of the fetus in regard to the state of brain development at the various stages of gestation, it would seem necessary to remember that it is the brain which, upon maturity, enables a human being to live as a conscious, self-aware being. It is not until week 19 that synapses, the points where neurons come together to interact and communicate, begin to develop. Despite the fact that a fetus may survive (approximately 50% chance of survival), with medical support, at a gestational age of 24 weeks, it is not until 30 weeks gestational age that synaptic growth reaches its peak rate. During the period between week 24 and week 30, folding (larger surface area) of the cortex and myelination (insulation) of neurons occur. It is at a gestational age of 30 weeks that the earliest information processing in the cerebral cortex of the fetus can be referred to as constituting a capacity for sentience, that is a capacity for perceiving and feeling. By week 34, the fetal brain is capable of controlling breathing and body temperature independent of the woman.

At the time of a full-term birth, usually 39 to 41 weeks gestational age, although the brain of the child largely resembles that of an adult, it is far from fully developed. Rapid synaptic growth continues until the third or fourth month after birth and the complexity of the cortex continues to increase for many years after birth. Synapse development continues into old age, even until death. It is interesting to note that the earliest a child is believed to be self-aware is approximately 15 months after full term birth.

It seems to the author that, from a purely scientific viewpoint, there are two preeminent facts that bear on the question of when the biological status of the fetus should influence the abortion decision. First, no sustainable or complex nervous system is in place and the fetal brain is not viable until approximately 24 weeks gestational age, and only then with the aid of modern intensive medical support. The survival rate for the fetus if birth occurs at 23 weeks is less than 5%. The survival rate at 24 weeks is approximately 50%. Even though survival of the fetus may occur at twenty-four weeks with intensive medical support, the brain of the fetus is only capable of enabling possible survival, not of enabling even a sentient condition, much less a self-aware condition, of the fetus. However, even though the fetus is not a sentient being, and certainly not a self-conscious and self-aware being, at 24 weeks, since the life of the fetus is sustainable independent of the woman, albeit with modern and intensive medical support, the fact that the fetus can survive independently of the woman and thereafter independently develop into a sentient, thinking, self-aware, and self-conscious human being with a normal brain, is a preeminent fact.

While viability was found by the Supreme Court in 1973 in *Roe v. Wade* to be at the end of the second trimester, which is a gestational age of 28 weeks, modern medical science has improved since 1973. Even in *Roe v. Wade*, the Court acknowledged that "Viability is usually placed at about seven months (28 weeks) but may occur earlier, even at 24 weeks." If medically assisted viability is to be the standard by which Roe v. Wade is to be applied, then a gestational age of 24 weeks (22 weeks since conception) would be the appropriate applicable time period.

Among those who do not advocate for the prohibition of abortion from the moment of conception, there are many who do advocate for a much earlier cut-off date than 24 weeks. If the decision is to be based upon science, we must consider the question of whether it would be appropriate to attribute personhood rights to a fetus at a gestational stage where the nature of the brain activity and capability of the fetus is no more than that of an adult who has suffered severe brain damage and is considered brain dead and accordingly a legally appropriate candidate for organ donation. The proponents of early term restrictions on abortion argue that the latter has no conscious future while the former, if allowed, will likely grow into a fully functioning human being in a few months.

A fertilized egg cell is microscopic. A four-week blastocyte is the size of a small grain of sand. A six-week embryo is the size of a grain of rice. At about 6 weeks, a signal referred to by some as a "heartbeat" can usually be detected with a vaginal ultrasound, but even at 8 weeks, the fetus is only about 1 inch in length and weighs less than 1/8 of an ounce.   At 15 weeks, the fetus' nervous system begins its earliest functions and has grown to about four inches in length but still weighs only 2 ounces. At approximately 18 weeks, the quickening, the first movement felt by the woman, usually occurs. At that time, the fetus is approximately six inches long and weigh about one-half pound. If born prematurely at 24 weeks gestational age, the fetus has approximately a 50% chance of surviving with intensive medical care from neonatal intensive care units. While the Supreme Court acknowledged in *Roe v. Wade* that survival of the fetus at 24 weeks was a possibility, the probability of survival has increased to approximately 50% with medical advances. However, the incidence of major disabilities for the child as a result of such a premature birth is high. Also, despite attaining biological viability, at 24 weeks the fetus has not achieved the brain development stage of a sentient being, and certainly is not a self-aware, self-conscious being. At the 28 weeks gestational age (end of second trimester) viability stage established by the Court in *Roe v. Wade*, the fetus will have grown to about twelve inches in length, will weigh approximately two pounds, and will have a probability of survival, with neonatal intensive care, of greater than 90%.

The policies and practices regarding the resuscitation of extremely premature newborns vary considerably from state to state and may vary even between cities and counties of the same state. The decision will typically involve the consideration of gestational age, weight, the medical presentation of the premature baby, the opinions of medical practitioners, the desires of the parents, and other factors. The decision making process is fraught with inherent conflict due to the high risk of mortality or severe disability of very premature babies, the probability of futile and very expensive medical care, and the moral and ethical dilemma between religious convictions regarding the sanctity of life and the other factors. Left to their own medical evaluation, most neo-natologists would not provide intensive care at 23 weeks, but would from 26 weeks.

Notwithstanding the foregoing biological facts, many advocate that because a fertilized egg will likely develop into a human being, the fertilized egg and all embryonic and fetal stages that follow, deserve the legal status and rights of personhood, because it is at the moment of conception that each human being's life begins. They argue that anyone who truly values the sanctity of human life could not believe otherwise. As discussed in detail elsewhere in this book, this is the present official position of the Catholic Church and most Evangelical Christian Churches. However, there is a substantial divergence of opinion even among Catholics and Evangelical Christians on this issue.

In consideration of the question of the extent that science should influence public policy and court decisions regarding abortion, the author believes that it is extremely important that reliable science is taken into consideration. If the only science a person contemplating the question knows is that a "heartbeat" is usually detectable with a vaginal ultrasound at 6 weeks gestational age, the first electrical "brainwave" activity is also usually detectable at 6 weeks gestational age, and a fetus physically reacts to stimuli at 15 weeks, then that person's opinion is likely to be based upon misleading information. We must keep in mind that at 6 weeks the embryo is the size of a grain of rice, and even at 15 weeks it is only 4 inches long, weighs only 2 ounces and its brain is only at a very primitive stage of development. The author does not suggest that any of the science diminishes the right of a person to believe that life and personhood begins at conception. However, when an attempt is made to impose that religious belief on a woman who may not share that religious belief, in reliance upon "heartbeat" starting at 6 weeks which surely means the embryo is then a person, we must be willing to acknowledge the scientific facts. It is the author's observation that the persons, groups and publications which advocate for the "heartbeat"- 6 weeks abortion deadline, do not acknowledge that the embryo is only the size of a grain of rice and has no real developed heart or circulatory system at 6 weeks.

As discussed above, even at the 24-week gestational age threshold of medically assisted viability, a fetus is not close to being a sentient being and is far from being a self-aware, self-conscious person. The question is are we willing to accept or are we inclined to reject the premise that, despite the very diverse personal, religious and ethical viewpoints of the people of America, it is appropriate for the religious convictions of a particular group to be thrust on the rest of Americans by force of law. The question then becomes whether or not we are prepared to base the public policy, legal, and ethical standards on science. If we are, then we must be prepared to consider the real, complete and complex scientific facts which the author has attempted to describe above and to summarize in the following table.

Gestational Age	Time Since Conception	Stage of Fetus	Physical Characteristics of Fetus
6 weeks	4 weeks	Flutter detectable by vaginal ultrasound in the area that will become the heart of the baby. The flutter is from a group of cells generating electrical signals that will become the future "pacemaker" of the heart. The embryo (not technically a fetus until 8th week of gestation) does not have a heart nor a cardiovascular system. Erroneously referred to as first fetal heartbeat.	Embryo is approximately 5 mm (1/5 of an inch) long and weighs 1/25 (0.04) of an ounce (about the size of a grain of rice)
6 weeks	4 weeks	First nerve electrical activity. Erroneously referred to as first brain wave activity. The nerve electrical activity is not to the level of a very primitive animal or a person deemed to be brain dead.	Embryo is approximately 5 mm (1/5 of an inch) long and weighs 1/25 (0.04) of an ounce (about the size of a grain of rice)
12 weeks	10 weeks	All organs formed but not developed. Heartbeat detectable with external ultrasound	Fetus is approximately 2 inches long and weighs 1/2 ounce
15 weeks	13 weeks	The circulatory and urinary systems begin functioning and the liver produces bile. Fetal brain development is rapid, but brain function is still very primitive, functioning on the order of complexity as the brain of very primitive animal organisms capable of responding only in a reflexive fashion to stimuli.	Fetus is approximately 4 inches long and weighs 2 ounces

18 weeks	16 weeks	First movement felt by mother (quickening)	Average 5.6 inches long and weighs 6.7 ounces
23 weeks	21 weeks	0-5% chance of survival if born	Average 11.5 inches long and weighs 1.1 pounds Fetus is non-sentient - not capable of thinking or self-awareness. Sensory and motor functions of cerebral cortex only partially developed. Partial Lung development.
24 weeks	22 weeks	40-70% chance of survival if born	Average 11.8 inches long and weighs 1.3 pounds. Fetus is non-sentient - not capable of thinking or self-awareness. Sensory and motor functions of cerebral cortex only partially developed. Partial lung development.
28 weeks	26 weeks	Legal viability under *Roe v. Wade* >90% chance of survival if born	Average 14.8 inches long and weighs 2.2 pounds. Lungs are mostly developed.
30 weeks	28 weeks	Earliest information processing in cerebral cortex that could be referred to as sentience	Average 16 inches long and weighs 3 pounds. Earliest possible stage that fetus is sentient.
39-41 weeks	37-39 weeks	Full term	Cerebral cortex, though primitive, begins to function and lungs are fully developed

Thus, looking at the questions of when does life begin and when does the unborn become a person from a purely biological standpoint, one can make a number of basic observations. First, from the moment of conception the fertilized egg contains all the DNA for a person that will be if that fertilized egg successfully attaches to the uterine wall and successfully progresses through the period of gestation to birth. Further, from the moment of conception, the fertilized egg is living in the sense that, given proper nourishment, cell reproduction follows the pattern defined by the DNA and hence from the moment of conception a fertilized egg is biologically "living" tissue. However, it is difficult to make a credible argument, from a purely scientific standpoint, that a fetus is a "person" until the fetus progresses to the point that it possesses a brain that is at least functioning to the level that it can direct the functioning of organs for the preservation of the life of the fetus outside the womb of the woman. It must be remembered that, even then, the premature baby will not reach the level of development to be a sentient being, capable of the most basic consciousness, such as remembering the smell of embryonic fluid or the voice of its mother, for 6 more weeks, at 30 weeks gestational age.

There are many anti-abortion publications that purport to rely upon scientific and medical facts relating to fetal development as a basis for their anti-abortion advocacy. As an example, the following are excerpts from "Is a Baby Human from the Beginning?", by Human Life International, July 23, 2013.

> After fertilization, there are 46 chromosomes (or 47 in the case of Down syndrome), the combination of one set of 23 chromosomes from the mother and another set from the father. The resulting being is genetically human and alive, and therefore, by standard biological definition, a human being. From fertilization to natural death, there exists an unbroken continuum of human development during which the person needs only oxygen, water, and nutrients to live and develop physically.
>
> . . . . .
>
> **Fertilization:** The father's sperm and the mother's egg unite. Genetic instructions from each of the two individuals combine to form a unique individual, barely visible to the human eye. *Taber's Cyclopedic Medical Dictionary* describes what happens next: "Following fertilization, cells multiply, which results in formation of a morula, which in turn develops into a blastocyst consisting of a trophoblast and inner cell mass."[1]
>
> . . . . .
>
> **20 Days:** The heart of the baby human is in the advanced stages of formation. Her eyes begin to form. Her brain, spinal column, and nervous system are virtually complete.
> **24 Days:** The preborn baby's heart begins to beat.

28 Days: The baby's muscles are developing. Her arm and leg buds are visible, and her first neocortical cells appear. The neocortex is the seat of complex thinking and reasoning, and it is present in no other mammal. The preborn child has grown in size by a factor of 10,000 since fertilization. Blood flows in the baby's own veins, separate from her mother's blood.

. . . . .

42 Days: The baby's heart energy output is an incredible 20% of an adult's already. The cartilage skeleton is completely formed and ossification into bone begins. The baby's brain coordinates voluntary movement of muscles and the involuntary movement of organs. Reflex responses are present. The baby's mother misses her second menstrual period.

43 Days: The preborn baby's brain waves can be recorded.

45 Days: The baby begins spontaneous and voluntary body movements, and her milk teeth buds are present.

7 Weeks: The lips of the baby human are sensitive to touch, and her ears resemble her family's pattern. The first fully developed neurons (nerve cells) appear on the top of her spinal cord, beginning construction of the brain stem. This portion of the brain regulates vital functions such as breathing, heartbeat, and blood pressure.

8 Weeks: The preborn baby is about 1-1/2 inches long and 1/30 of an ounce in weight. All organs are present, complete, and functioning except the lungs. Her stomach produces digestive juices, her liver makes blood cells, and her kidneys are functioning. Her taste buds are forming and her unique fingerprints are being engraved. Her eyelids and the palms of her hands are sensitive to touch. Of the 45 total generations of cell replication that will take place by mature adulthood, fully two-thirds have already taken place.

9 Weeks: The preborn baby can bend her fingers around an object placed in her palm. Her fingernails are forming and she sucks her thumbs.

10 Weeks: All sections of the preborn baby's body are sensitive to touch. She swallows, squints, frowns, and puckers up her brow. If her palm is stroked, she will make a tight fist.

11 Weeks: The preborn child makes all facial expressions, including a smile. She is now breathing amniotic fluid steadily and will continue to do so until birth. Her fingernails and toenails are present. Her taste buds are working; she will drink more amniotic fluid if it is artificially sweetened, and less if it is given a bitter taste.

12 Weeks: Vigorous activity shows the distinct personality of the baby human. Some babies hiccup constantly, others may cry. The baby can kick, turn over, curl and fan her toes, make a fist, and open her mouth and press her lips tightly together.

13 Weeks: The preborn child's facial expressions resemble those of her parents. Her movements are vigorous and graceful. Her vocal chords are present, and, in rare cases when air enters the uterus temporarily, babies have been heard crying. The sex of the baby can be determined. She can now hear.

4 Months: The preborn baby can grasp with hands, swim, and turn somersaults. Her mother may feel her movements for the first time. Her eyelashes are now present. Rapid eye movement (REM), indicative of dreaming, can now be recorded. A very bright light shined on the mother's abdomen will cause the baby to slowly move her arms and cover her eyes. Loud music will cause the baby to cover her ears.

5 Months: The preborn baby human has formed her own unique sleeping habits by now. She responds to sounds that are of frequencies that exceed adults' audible range. She may be soothed to sleep by gentle music. Fine hair grows on her head and eyebrows.

6 Months: Most babies are viable at this point (24 weeks, or about 60% of full gestation). Eyelashes appear. The baby's weight is about 22 ounces, and her height is about 9 inches.

7 Months: The baby's weight increases to over one kilogram or 2.2 pounds. The baby's eye teeth are now present. Her eyes open and close and she explores her surroundings. Her hands can support her entire weight at this time. She recognizes her mother's voice.

.　.　.　.

Human development begins at fertilization, and that new creature is a baby human.

Notes:

1. "Fetal Development," *Taber's Cyclopedic Medical Dictionary.* Subsequent information on fetal development is also from this source.

The progression of development of the embryo and then the fetus in the womb of the woman is indeed miraculous and beautiful. The reverence for human procreation and for the unborn expressed by those who are against abortion, perhaps at any stage after conception, is admirable and inspiring. The foregoing excerpts from the Human Life International article are a worthy example. The problem with a description of fetal development such as this one, are the many misleading statements.   Let us consider a few examples:

> *After fertilization, there are 46 chromosomes (or 47 in the case of Down syndrome), the combination of one set of 23 chromosomes from the mother and another set from the father. The resulting being is genetically human and alive, and therefore, by standard biological definition, a human being.*

> *The father's sperm and the mother's egg unite. Genetic instructions from each of the two individuals combine to form a unique individual, barely visible to the human eye.*

The suggestion that a fertilized egg cell is a "human being" when, as is acknowledged, it is "barely visible to the human eye," simply because it contains all the genetic code for a new person, appears to be a gross misstatement.

> *From fertilization to natural death, there exists an unbroken continuum of human development during which the person needs only oxygen, water, and nutrients to live and develop physically.*

This statement ignores the fact that from fertilization until at least 24 weeks gestational age, the oxygen, water, and nutrients, as well as the other numerous, essential biological substances provided to the fetus through the placenta, can only be supplied by the woman.

20 Days: *The heart of the baby human is in the advanced stages of formation. Her eyes begin to form. Her brain, spinal column, and nervous system are virtually complete.*
24 Days: *The preborn baby's heart begins to beat.*
28 Days: *. . . her first neocortical cells appear. The neocortex is the seat of complex thinking and reasoning, and it is present in no other mammal.*

The statement that at 20 days the "brain, spinal column and nervous system are virtually complete" is another gross misstatement. As the article itself states, at 28 days (8 days later), "her first neocortical cells appear." If the first cells of the thinking and reasoning part of the brain has just begun to develop, the brain could not have been "virtually complete" 8 days earlier. As we have already discussed, the brain will not have progressed to the point that it can support life outside the womb, even with neonatal intensive care, until 24 weeks gestational age, and the brain will not have progressed to the point of support of the most basic level of sentience, until 30 weeks gestational age.

28 Days: *. . . Blood flows in the baby's own veins, separate from her mother's blood.*

The embryo is approximately 5 mm (1/5 of an inch) long and weighs 1/25 (0.04) of an ounce. It is about the size of grain of rice.

.　.　.　.　.

42 Days: *The baby's heart energy output is an incredible 20% of an adult's already.*

The embryo becomes a fetus at 8 weeks gestation and is about 5/8 of an inch (0.63 inch) long. It is about the size of a blueberry. The claim that the energy output of the fetus' heart is 20% of that of an adult is obviously a gross overstatement.

The baby's brain coordinates voluntary movement of muscles and the involuntary movement of organs. Reflex responses are present.

The fetus' brain will not progress to the very earliest stage of sentience until 30 weeks gestation. Voluntary muscles are the muscles that are under conscious control and can be controlled at will or the organism can choose when to use them. A reflex response to a stimulus is not the same as a voluntary movement of muscles.

43 Days: The preborn baby's brain waves can be recorded.

Electrical signals generated by developing brain cells do not constitute brain waves indicative of a thinking organism.

45 Days: The baby begins spontaneous and voluntary body movements . . .

As stated, the fetus' brain will not progress to the very earliest stage of sentience until 30 weeks gestation. Voluntary movement implies conscious movement controlled at the will of the fetus. The fetus is not near that stage of development. A reflex response to a stimulus is not the same as a voluntary movement. The fetus is only about 2/3 of an inch long and weighs only a small fraction of an ounce.

7 Weeks: The lips of the baby human are sensitive to touch . . .

An earthworm is sensitive to touch and is capable of a reflex response to a number of stimuli. Earthworms have a brain connected to nerves from their skin and muscles. Their nerves can detect light, vibrations, and even some tastes, and their muscles make movements in response. The earthworm has five hearts.

The first fully developed neurons (nerve cells) appear on the top of her spinal cord, beginning construction of the brain stem. This portion of the brain regulates vital functions such as breathing, heartbeat, and blood pressure.

The fact that the first fully developed neurons of the brain stem are first appearing at 9 weeks gestation is indicative of the primitive state of development of the fetus.

8 Weeks: The preborn baby is about 1-1/2 inches long and 1/30 of an ounce in weight. All organs are present, complete, and functioning except the lungs.

The assertion that all of the organs of the fetus, except the lungs, are "complete and functioning," is very misleading. As noted, the fetus is only 1-1/2 inches long, and weighs only 1/30 of an ounce.

9 Weeks: The preborn baby can bend her fingers around an object placed in her palm. Her fingernails are forming and she sucks her thumbs.
10 Weeks: All sections of the preborn baby's body are sensitive to touch. She swallows, squints, frowns, and puckers up her brow. If her palm is stroked, she will make a tight fist.

An ant will grab a crumb of bread or a seed and carry it back into the ant colony. Nightcrawlers can pull leaves into their burrows using their strong mouths. A crab or lobster will grasp your finger if given an opportunity. A fetus of 10 weeks gestational age is not capable of any conscious act.

11 Weeks: The preborn child makes all facial expressions, including a smile.

12 Weeks: . . . The baby can kick, turn over, curl and fan her toes, make a fist, and open her mouth and press her lips tightly together.
13 Weeks: . . . She can now hear.

These statements suggest that fetus voluntarily and knowingly makes facial expressions, smiles, kicks, turns over, and moves its toes, fingers, mouth and lips. These are clearly not voluntarily actions and movements. Similarly, the fetus response to sound is only reflexive in nature. Fetal brain development at 15 weeks gestation is rapid, but brain function is still very primitive, functioning on the order of complexity as the brain of very primitive animal organisms capable of responding only in a reflexive fashion to stimuli.

4 Months: The preborn baby can grasp with hands, swim, and turn somersaults. . . . A very bright light shined on the mother's abdomen will cause the baby to slowly move her arms and cover her eyes. Loud music will cause the baby to cover her ears.
5 Months: . . . She may be soothed to sleep by gentle music. . .

Again, brain development of the fetus continues and the movements and responses to stimuli are more intricate, but they are still not close to being voluntary movements and responses. The fetus is still approximately 4 weeks away from viability and approximately 10 weeks away from earliest sentience.

6 Months: Most babies are viable at this point (24 weeks, or about 60% of full gestation). . . . The baby's weight is about 22 ounces, and her height is about 9 inches.
7 Months: . . . Her eyes open and close and she explores her surroundings. . . She recognizes her mother's voice.

The beauty and complexity of the development of the human embryo and fetus from a fertilized egg are astonishing. It is easy to understand how the amazing and astonishing grandeur of the developing fetus, coupled with religious convictions about when the organism that will develop from the fertilized egg becomes a person, compel some to oppose abortion from the moment of conception or at some early period of gestation. Those who have such a reverence and respect for the developing fetus deserve our respect and admiration. However, beliefs regarding personhood at conception, at six weeks gestation, at twelve weeks gestation, or at any gestational age prior to viability, must be recognized for what they are - beliefs. Those who are determined to impose those beliefs on others, forfeit our respect and admiration. While they could use that reverence and respect to influence the beliefs and voluntary actions of others, they choose instead to try to control the lives of others with an imposition of their beliefs regarding a most personal and private matter.

CHAPTER 4

RELIGIOUS CONSIDERATIONS

It would be impossible to appreciate and understand the fervor and intractability of the positions of many American citizens on this issue without examining the religious and philosophical underpinnings of their various points of view.

Summary of Hindu View on Abortion.

Although plagued by the challenges of violence and war like the rest of humanity, Hindus tend to be very life affirming. Peace and non-violence are major tenets of Hinduism. "Ahimsa," which means "non-harm," is central to Hindu life.

The basic spiritual objective in the practice of Hinduism is attainment of the state of "moksha". Moksha is described in the Vedas, the earliest sacred Hindu scriptures, as liberation from the cycle of birth and death through self-knowledge and the eternal connection of Atman (soul, self) and metaphysical Brahman. Moksha means liberation, freedom, emancipation of the soul. This ultimate state of the soul is also identified as "Brahma-nirvana" in verses 2.72 and 5.24-26 of the Bhagavad Gita, a later Hindu scripture. Brahma-nirvana is described as the state of release or liberation, a union with the metaphysical Brahman, and an experience of egoless bliss. The progress of the soul, Atman, of a person to a state of moksha or Brahman-nirvana requires the soul to cycle, repeatedly, through birth and death, i.e. reincarnation. It has been suggested that the scribes for the Bhagavad Gita borrowed the term Brahma-nirvana from Buddhism which had an earlier use of the term "nirvana".

The Garbha Upanishad (one of 108 Upanishads) attributed to the ancient guru Rishi Pippalaada in approximately 2000 B.C., states "In the seventh month, life or the Jivan enters the body shaped so far". However, it is generally accepted in most Hindu sects that ensoulment occurs at conception. The concept stated in the Garbha Upanishad that Jivan, the soul, does not enter the body until the 7th month, is not cited by advocates of the life at conception view, and they refer to abortion at any state of gestation as the death of a "human person". Other more general references in the Hindu scriptures are relied upon for that position. Those Hindu scriptures refer to abortion as garbha batta (womb killing) and bhrunaghna (killing the undeveloped soul or embryo slayer). The Caraka Samhita, a Hindu medical text, states that the soul is joined with matter in the act of conception. The later smrti texts also contain prohibitions against abortion, as well as heightened protections for pregnant women. Killing either a fetus or a mother is equated to the worst crime possible in Hindu society, killing a Brahman (a priest):

> *"If the fetus is alive, one should attempt to remove it from the womb of the mother alive…" (sutra 5). If it is dead, it may be removed. In case the fetus is alive but cannot be safely delivered, surgical removal is forbidden for "one would harm both mother and offspring. In an irredeemable situation, it is best to cause the miscarriage of the fetus, for no means must be neglected which can prevent the loss of the mother" (sutras 10-11).*
> *A slayer of an embryo is like the slayer of a priest.*

Krishna Yajur Veda 6.5.10

Hence, it appears that Hindu tradition from the earliest times has condemned the practice of abortion, except when the life of the mother is at risk. It is said that though abortion is wrong, it is worse for a child to kill his mother.

As stated above, the purpose of each cycle of life as a human being for a Hindu is to progress toward liberation from the cycle of rebirth and death. For each soul, the realization of its karmic destiny toward this goal is the purpose of human life. Although those who advocate for the concept of ensoulment at conception understand that the soul of the aborted fetus will be born anew in another body, abortion is viewed as an obstruction to the normal process of re-birth, and therefore it is to be condemned. Some argue that reincarnation supports at least a tolerance of abortion. Under the doctrine of reincarnation, abortion only deprives the soul of one of many births that it will have. Obviously, the consequences of abortion are not as bad in the framework of reincarnation as in those religions where a soul gets only one chance to be born and where abortion deprives the soul of its one and only possibility of life. Notwithstanding this obvious difference, because of the law of karma, each baby has a role to play in this world. To kill a fetus before it has the chance to experience and work on its karma is a disruption of the purpose of life. Hindus commonly believe that souls wait for very long periods of time to experience re-birth. No wonder then that they would commonly view abortion with disfavor. It is considered an act against rita (universal order) and ahimsa (noninjury). Swami Omkarananda stated, "Imagine, through millions of abortions around the world, day in and day out, how many wonderful scientific and spiritual geniuses - doctors, men of excellence of every kind, sages, saints, benefactors of mankind, builders of a better culture and civilization - are destroyed even before they can take a breath of fresh air here on Earth!"

It must be remembered, though, that Hinduism is thousands of years older than Christianity and includes sects and schools with a large range of beliefs and practices. As with Christians and other religious groups, individual Hindu sects and schools may follow and teach very different beliefs, depending upon the tradition and the guru who is followed by the sect or school. Regardless of the sect, one of the great beauties of Hinduism is that it is never too late. Maybe it was a mistake for a woman to have an abortion. Regardless, her baby will find another embodiment eventually and she will work through whatever karmic consequences there may be to her decision.

The question arises as to what extent does and to what extent should, the religious beliefs of the Hindus dictate or affect the law regarding abortion in Hindu societies, particularly the Republic of India. To see how the religious concepts of Hinduism which relate to abortion manifest themselves in the law of the nation of India, we need to look primarily at the Medical Termination of Pregnancy Act, enacted in 1971. The Medical Termination of Pregnancy (MTP) Act establishes the situations and conditions in which abortion can legally be performed in the nation of India. Abortion is permitted for a broad range of conditions and circumstances up to 20 weeks of gestation:

- When continuation of pregnancy is a risk to the life of a pregnant woman or could cause grave injury to her physical or mental health;

- When there is substantial risk that the child, if born, would be seriously handicapped due to physical or mental abnormalities;

- When pregnancy is caused due to rape (presumed to cause grave injury to the mental health of the woman);

- When pregnancy is caused due to failure of contraceptives used by a married woman or her husband (presumed to constitute grave injury to mental health of the woman).

Under the India MTP Act, only the consent of woman whose pregnancy is being terminated is required, except in the case of a minor i.e. below the age of 18 years, or a mentally ill woman, in which case the consent of a guardian is required.

It must be noted that the broad range of circumstances under which abortion is permitted in India under the MTP Act, are routinely relied upon by a married woman to obtain an abortion when the real objective of the woman and her husband is to abort a fetus which has been determined to be female. The cultural, societal and economic preferences for a male child over a female child provoke many married couples to resort to early testing to determine the sex of the fetus and to terminate the pregnancy if the child will not be male. Hence, familial concerns and societal biases may take precedence over religious considerations in such situations. After all, the soul will be returning anyway, just at a later date.

A very graphic example of the tragic result that may arise out of a conflict between different religions, and the imposition at law of one over the other, occurred in Ireland. A young Indian mother died in an Irish Catholic hospital that refused to abort though it would be the only way to save her life and the child was not going to live. In this situation, Hinduism readily permits abortion. Savita Halappanavar was 31 years old and only 17 weeks pregnant when she died. The hospital refused to take her family's religious beliefs into consideration and imposed theirs instead.

Summary of Buddhist View on Abortion:

The Buddhism concept of Nirvana has a meaning similar to the concept of moksha or Brahman-nirvana described above for Hinduism, but it is different in some very significant aspects. Where the state of Brahman-nirvana of Hinduism represents a state wherein the soul unites with Brahman (God), Buddhism suggests that there is no soul and no god. In Buddhism, Nirvana is a transcendent state in which there is neither suffering, desire, nor sense of self, and the subject is released from the effects of karma and the cycle of death and rebirth. It represents the final state of Buddhism. The state of Nirvana is a state wherein there is no longer a sense of self. The attainment of Nirvana is a complete escape from the suffering, worries and passions of mortal life and the external world.

In consideration of the questions posed in Buddhism relating to the issue of abortion, the First Precept of Buddhism is the primary factor.

The Mahayana Brahajala (Brahma Net) Sutra explains the first precept this way:

A disciple of the Buddha shall not himself kill, encourage others to kill, kill by expedient means, praise killing, rejoice at witnessing killing, or kill through incantation or deviant mantras. He must not create the causes, conditions, methods, or karma of killing, and shall not intentionally kill any living creature.

From the traditional Buddhist viewpoint, abortion is considered to be a violation of the first precept of Buddhism because it involves the deliberate destroying of a life. Accordingly, it is presumed to generate bad karma for the mother and the abortionist. Because it results in a disruption of the cycle of birth, death and rebirth, it is argued that it also generates bad karma for the fetus. The fetus suffers bad karma because it is deprived of the opportunities that an earthly existence would have given it to earn good karma, and instead is returned immediately to the cycle of birth, death and rebirth. Thus, abortion hinders its spiritual progress.

While traditional Buddhists regard life as starting at conception, there are some sects that advocate otherwise, and, accordingly, believe that an abortion in the first trimester does not involve the taking of life. In considering these alternative points of view, it must be remembered that there is no Buddhist central authority, and that the foundational principle of Buddhism is that each person is solely responsible for her or his own progression toward Nirvana.

It must also be considered that there are cases where not having an abortion may result in the birth of a child with medical conditions that cause it to suffer. Traditional Buddhist thinking does not deal with these cases, but it has been argued by some Buddhists that if the child would be so severely handicapped that it would undergo great suffering, abortion is permissible.

The Dalai Lama has said:

Of course, abortion, from a Buddhist viewpoint, is an act of killing and is negative, generally speaking. But it depends on the circumstances.

If the unborn child will be retarded or if the birth will create serious problems for the parent, these are cases where there can be an exception. I think abortion should be approved or disapproved according to each circumstance. Dalai Lama, New York Times, 28/11/1993.

Buddhists that believe that abortion is acceptable in certain circumstances suggest that an abortion may be a compassionate outcome because the present embodiment is not the right time and circumstance for the person to begin a new cycle of rebirth. Since life is a continual change which really has no beginning and no ending, those Buddhists advocate that altering the cycle of death and rebirth with an abortion will not ultimately have a unalterable negative effect. Similar to the quote of the Dalai Lama in the New York Times article mentioned above, when asked about abortion at a conference, the Dalai Lama spoke of it as a violation of the first precept, but he added that sometimes circumstances are such that abortion can result from a compassionate decision, and that compassion can be cultivated as a way of being, and not as an attitude conditioned by personal judgment.

Since traditional Buddhists advocate for the fetus becoming a living sentient being at conception, traditionalists do not recognize a distinction between early term and late term abortions. They advocate that just to attain a human birth at all is considered a cause for celebration, since only in human form can a sentient being understand the true nature of its opportunity to journey toward enlightenment. However, in practice in Buddhist countries, there are recognized distinctions. For instance, in Sri Lanka and Thailand the "moral stigma" associated with an abortion increases with the development of the fetus. Further, abortion laws in many Buddhist countries recognize a threat to the life or physical health of the mother as an acceptable justification for abortion, even though it may be perceived as an event with negative karmic consequences. Tibetan Buddhists believe that a woman who has had an abortion should be treated compassionately, and guided to atone for the negative act through appropriate good deeds and religious practices, aimed at improving the karmic outcome for both the mother and the aborted fetus. While abortion is negatively viewed in Myanmar, it is employed frequently to prevent out-of-wedlock births. Buddhists in Japan and Taiwan are viewed as being more tolerant of abortion, and that is reflected in the laws of Japan and Taiwan. However, women in Japan and Taiwan who resort to abortion, frequently participate in rituals intended to placate the spirit of the aborted fetus and to reduce the feelings of guilt of the mother.

In the end, the analysis of abortion under Buddhism, is not a question of the right to life of the fetus in contrast to the right to choose of the mother. It is a question of harm versus benefit. The question is what approach will result in the minimization of human suffering. Will abortion in a particular situation result in reducing human suffering in comparison to allowing the pregnancy to progress to birth.

Considering the foregoing discussion of abortion under Buddhism, it seems that Buddhism argues away from voting for or against abortion or passing laws regulating or restricting abortions. Buddhists assert that the abortion debate in Western cultures and countries reflects only a Western obsession with control, not consciousness. Even the traditional Buddhist will likely acknowledge that the belief in the "right to life" merely reflects the Western impulse to control and shape reality. In contrast, it seems that Buddhism suggests an emphasis on reducing the circumstances that lead women to conclude that they need to have an abortion, rather than suggesting intervention and control of such situations by enacting laws.

Summary of the Islamic View on Abortion:

Analysis of the position of Islam on abortion arguably begins from a more definite starting point than the other major world religions. That is because the Quran, the holy scripture of Islam, contains rather detailed descriptions of the various development stages of embryonic and fetal development, and a principal spiritual implication of one particular stage.

Quran 22:5 states as follows:

5   O people! If you are in doubt about the Resurrection, We created you from dust, then from a small drop, then from a clinging clot, then from a lump of flesh, partly developed and partly undeveloped. In order to clarify things for you. And We settle in the wombs whatever We will for a designated term, and then We bring you out as infants, until you reach your full strength. And some of you will pass away, and some of you will be returned to the vilest age, so that he may not know, after having known. And you see the earth still; but when We send down water on it, it vibrates, and swells, and grows all kinds of lovely pairs.

Quran (23:12-14) further describes the stages of development as follows:

12   We created man from an extract of clay.
13   Then We made him a seed, in a secure repository.
14   Then We developed the seed into a clot. Then We developed the clot into a lump. Then We developed the lump into bones. Then We clothed the bones with flesh. Then We produced it into another creature. Most Blessed is God, the Best of Creators.

The foregoing passages from the Quran have been interpreted as meaning that the soul enters the fetus when the bones are "clothed" with flesh. The foregoing passages and the following Hadith of Muhammed have been widely accepted by Muslim scholars as establishing the time of ensoulment as 120 days (4 months) following conception.

> Allah's Apostle, the true and truly inspired said, "(as regards your creation), every one of you is collected in the womb of his mother for the first forty days, and then he becomes a clot for another forty days, and then a piece of flesh for another forty days. Then Allah sends an angel to write four words: He writes his deeds, time of his death, means of livelihood, and whether he will be wretched or blessed (in religion). **Then the soul is breathed into his body ...**"

(emphasis added)

It should be noted that while the most widely accepted view is that ensoulment occurs at four months following conception, a minority of Muslim scholars advocate that ensoulment occurs at 40 days following conception, and, perhaps a smaller minority advocate that ensoulment occurs at conception.

The adherents of Islam belong largely to two main denominations, Sunni and Shia Islam. Although there are presently many ethnic groups who have joined the adherents of Islam, historically the root of the Sunni branch of Islam is Arabic and the root of the Shia branch of Islam is Persian. The blood feud and the theological division between Sunnis and Shiites has persisted since the death of the prophet Muhammad in 632 AD. A dispute over succession to the prophet Muhammad led to warfare, which included initially the Battle of Jamal and Battle of Siffin. In the following Battle of Karbala, Hussein ibn Ali and his household were killed by the ruling Umayyad Caliph Yazid I. A desire for revenge for the murder of Hussein ibn Ali divided and continues to divide the Islamic community. Presently, worldwide approximately 85% of Muslims are Sunni and 15% are Shia. The conflict between Sunni and Shia seems to be ever increasing. Extreme violence such as mosque and market place bombings is widespread in the region. Larger scale conflicts such as the Saudi Arabia-Iran proxy war in Yemen and the Syrian Civil War are evidence that the sectarian conflict between Sunni and Shia is raging. That division has contributed to the current doctrinal differences, including differences in the position on abortion.

In addition to the Quran, hadith are the record of the words, actions, and silent approvals, traditionally attributed to the prophet Muhammad, which include a narrative record of the sayings or customs of Muhammad and his companions. Within Islam the authority of hadith ranks second only to that of the Quran. This is based upon content of the Quran which commands Muslims to obey the prophet Muhammad and to follow his example.

> *24:54 Say, "Obey God and obey the Messenger." But if they turn away, then he is responsible for his obligations, and you are responsible for your obligations. And if you obey him, you will be guided. It is only incumbent on the Messenger to deliver the Clarifying Message.*

> *33:21 You have an excellent example in the Messenger of God; for anyone who seeks God and the Last Day, and remembers God frequently.*

Because the number of verses of the Quran which pertain to law is relatively small, hadiths are heavily relied upon for direction on the details of everyday life for Muslims. What is referred to as Sharia law, is derived largely from hadith and not directly from the Quran.

However, not all Muslims believe all hadith accounts are divine revelation. As a matter of fact, a small minority of Muslims called Quranists rely entirely on the Quran and reject all hadith.   The primary reason for the variation in the acceptance of hadith is that hadith were not written down by Muhammad's followers as the sayings or events occurred or even immediately after the death of Muhammad. It was generally not until several generations later that they were gathered and compiled. The questionable and even contradictory statements of purported hadith led to research and authentication of hadith becoming a major field of study in Islam. The differing collections of hadith that are accepted by the respective branches of Islam is the primary source of doctrinal differences between them.

For most Muslim communities, views on abortion are shaped by accepted hadith as well as by the opinions of legal and religious scholars and commentators. The Quran does not directly address intentional abortion, allowing greater discretion for the laws of individual Muslim majority countries. As stated above, according to the majority view, the fetus is believed to become a living soul four months after conception, and abortion after that point is generally viewed as impermissible. Many Islamic scholars advocate for exceptions to this rule for certain circumstances.

There are four different Sunni doctrinal groups - Hanafites, Shafites, Hanbalites, and Malikites. Each of these sects have their own and differing views on the stage of gestation and under what circumstances abortions should be permitted. Malikites, for example, do not condone abortion in any of the stages of gestation.

Because a large majority of Muslims agree that ensoulment occurs at four months following conception, they also generally agree that abortion should not be allowed after four months have passed since conception. They consider abortion after four months to be the taking of life, for which the participants will be subject to consequences in the afterlife and should be subject to penalty in this life. Most Sunni scholars generally agree that abortion should be allowed prior to four months, if it is deemed necessary. However, they also generally consider abortion without a reasonable cause to be detestable. Aborting a pregnancy before ensoulment is deemed the same degree of offense as 'Azal' (i.e. measures to hinder conception) and sterilization. The graveness of the sin increases very much after the "soul is breathed into the body" or, as it is also described, "the spirit is blown into the fetus".

Muslims seem to universally agree that the life of the woman takes precedence over the life of the fetus. The woman is considered the "original source of life", while the fetus is only "potential" life. Muslim scholars and jurists seem to agree that abortion is allowed at any gestation stage to save the life of the woman, because the greater evil, the death of the woman, should be prevented by the lesser evil, the abortion of the fetus. Scholars and jurists acknowledge that they must defer to the woman's physician to determine whether abortion is necessary to save the life of the woman.

The Shia, unlike the Sunni, have a number of Ayatollahs who are jurists qualified and empowered to render rulings on matters of Islam law. The rulings are presumably binding on the Shia. Presently there are approximately 45 living Ayatollahs. The Ayatollahs seem to be in general agreement that abortion is allowed up to four months, if the life of the woman is in danger. However, other than to save the life of the woman during the first four months, abortion is generally forbidden, no matter the stage of gestation or the circumstances. Although a few of the Ayatollahs have issued rulings providing for some very limited exceptions for severe fetal deformities or for a fetal or maternal condition that will likely result in extreme difficulties for the mother or the family, the vast majority of the Ayatollahs have not issued rulings allowing any such exceptions. The mental condition of the woman or economic hardships for the family have been generally rejected by the Ayatollahs as suitable reasons for abortion. Despite the seemingly intransigent position of the Ayatollahs, some Shiite Muslim scholars have stated that abortion should be permitted if the woman's physician concludes the child will likely be handicapped in some substantial way, such as mental handicaps or physical deformities, that would make care exceptionally difficult for the parents.

Some Muslims scholars have stated that a child resulting from a rape is a legitimate child and thus that it would be just as sinful to abort that child as any other. Those scholars would permit the abortion of a fetus resulting from rape only if the fetus is less than four months from conception, or if it endangers the life of its mother. However, other scholars have stated that when the pregnancy is unplanned and therefore unwanted, particularly in the case of rape, the parents should have the choice to abort the fetus and thus prevent the disgrace that awaits both mother and child. A child born as a result of rape, like one born as a result of adultery, in most, if not all, Muslim communities, is very likely to be treated as a lowly, shunned member of the community and is likely to suffer all his or her life from a deprivation of rights and opportunities for advancement. His or her family is similarly likely to suffer a social stigma with lost rights and opportunities. For the foregoing reasons, Muslim scholars were urged to make exceptions in the 1990's following rapes of Kuwaiti women by Iraqi soldiers, and the rape of Bosnian and Albanian women by Serbian soldiers.

Notwithstanding the foregoing discussions, in practice, access to abortion varies greatly between respective Muslim majority countries as there is a great variation among those Muslim majority countries regarding legally acceptable bases for abortion. The Organisation of Islamic Cooperation, an international organization founded in 1969, consists of 57 member states with a collective population of over 1.8 billion. Of the 57 members, 53 are Muslim majority countries. The remaining 4 countries have a Muslim plurality. Twelve members of the Organization of Islamic Conference allow unrestricted access to abortion. With the exception of Turkey and Tunisia, those 12 countries are mainly former Soviet Bloc states. Bahrain, a politically and socially conservative Muslim state, is the 12th among these countries to permit unrestricted access to abortion. In nearly one-half of the 53 Muslim majority countries, including Iraq, Egypt, and Indonesia, abortion is only legally permitted if the life of the woman is threatened by the pregnancy. Seven other socially conservative members, Kuwait, Qatar and Iran in the Middle East, and Benin, Burkina Faso, Chad, and Guinea in Africa, permit abortion in the first 4 months of gestation for fetal deformities. No Muslim majority country bans abortion when the woman's life is at risk. Other reasons that are permitted by certain Muslim majority countries include preserving a woman's physical or mental health, fetal impairment, incest, rape, or economic or social reasons.

The Islamic Republic of Iran has the largest Shia majority of the Muslim majority countries, having a population of nearly 70 million, 90% of which are Shia. It is also the most influential Shia majority country. Iran is the only Islamic Republic whose legal system is founded solely on Shia Islamic law, while it also allows democratic representation. The seminaries of the holy city of Qom attract students of Islamic theology and theologians from around the world. Iran seems to set the religious and social trends for the other Shia majority countries, Iraq and Bahrain, as well as the Shia communities of Shia minority countries, such as Kuwait, Yemen, Lebanon, Qatar, Syria, Saudi Arabia, Afghanistan and the United Arab Emirates.

The Iranian Parliament, in 2004, enacted laws allowing therapeutic as well as non-therapeutic abortions during the first 4 months of gestation, under certain circumstances. Therapeutic abortions are those recommended by the healthcare provider to protect the mother's physical or mental health. Therapeutic abortion may be performed under 51 medical conditions. As mentioned above, Iran is the first Islamic country in contemporary times that has attempted to combine principles of theocracy and religious law with representative, parliamentary democracy. People vote for representatives to the Parliament. The Parliament debates and passes laws independent of the executive and judiciary branches. The laws passed must, however, go before a special body, the Guardian Council. This Council, comprising six jurists, chosen by the supreme religious leader, and six lawyers, chosen by the parliament, examines laws for conformity to contemporary religious rulings, according to Articles 71 and 96 of the Iranian Constitution. If a part of the bill violates any of the standing Islamic rulings, it is sent back for amendment before ratification. If the impasse still cannot be resolved, it may be sent to the Expediency Council, a mediating body, for further deliberations before final approval or rejection.

The Iranian Parliament, in 2004, also enacted a law requiring the approval of three specialists for a therapeutic abortion. This was apparently intended to prevent misuse of abortion for unjustified purposes, and to reduce the risk to physicians performing abortions.

> *Therapeutic abortions may be performed under the following conditions. First, the fetus must be less than four months of age, that is, before the spirit is breathed into it. Second, the fetus must be suffering from profound developmental delay or profound deformations or malformations. Third, these fetal problems must be causing extreme suffering or hardship for the mother or the fetus. Fourth, the life of the mother should be in danger. Fifth, both the mother and the father give their consent to the procedure. The physician performing the abortion shall not be penalized for the performance of these services.*

It seems that a number of Shia and Sunni scholars have been motivated to allow abortions for limited social and medical reasons because of the expanding populations and limited health budgets. The introduction of a theocracy in the Islamic Republic of Iran imposed a heightened role of responsibility on the Ayatollahs and other religious leaders and scholars for social planning and public health issues. It has been estimated that approximately 80,000 abortions are performed in Iran each year for married women of reproductive age. It has also been estimated that in excess of $15,000,000.00 U.S. is expended for those abortions, which are mostly illegal and unsafe. Despite the substantially greater restrictions on abortion in Iran as compared to Turkey, the rate of abortion in Iran is approximately one half of the rate in Turkey. The authorities having responsibility to deal with health crises may be largely responsible for "istislah", i.e. public interest in situations where there is no clear basis in the Quran or hadith, and "istihsan" , i.e. when a decision on a certain case differs from that of prior similar cases because the case is stronger for abortion.

Accordingly, the Ayatollahs, in their ongoing rulings on medical and health affairs, rather than considering abortion related questions from an isolated doctrinal perspective as they tended to do in the past, appear to be increasingly inclined to consider the social and medical implications. The Ayatollahs are not immune, after all, to the public health crisis of the reality of the more than 80,000 illegal, unsafe abortions performed in Iran every year, which seriously endanger the life of the women. Abortion for medical reasons to save the life of the mother has always been permitted. Now technological advancement in genetic testing and imaging has provided for earlier detection of serious or terminal congenital conditions of the fetus. Public health considerations of serious or terminal fetal deformities and the financial hardships to be borne by the family, insurance or public assistance programs, have become more pre-eminent for the Ayatollahs who are no longer responsible just for the theoretical, theological issues. As discussed above, in Iran both legal and theological considerations must be and have been addressed before the new laws could be enacted. New laws will also be the subject of continuous scrutiny to verify that the implementation is consistent with Sharia Law.

Regardless of the status of the law in the various Sunni and Shia majority nations, every Muslim has the duty to remember that life is truly sacred and always to be respected. Every birth should the source of true joy to the mother and her family. However, Muslims also believe that the Quran is protective of and uplifting to the status of women in Muslim society. Many Muslims believe then that women should have control on matters of reproductive choice and other matters concerning their bodies, particularly prior to the time that the soul is breathed into the fetus, which, as stated above, is widely accepted to be 4 months after conception.

<u>Summary of Judaism View on Abortion:</u>

Judaism relies principally on the teachings of the Tanakh and the Talmud, for doctrinal matters. The Tanakh, referred to frequently as the Hebrew Bible, is comprised of the Torah, the five books attributed to Moses – Genesis, Exodus, Leviticus, Numbers and Deuteronomy, and nineteen other books, which are divided into two groups, the Prophets and the Writings. These 24 books of the Tanakh also comprise what is identified in the Christian Bible as the Old Testament. However, the Old Testament of the Christian Bible is divided differently, into 39 books.

The Talmud is comprised of the Mishnah and the Gemara. The Mishnah is the first major written collection of Jewish oral traditions, often referred to as the Oral Torah, and is the first major written work classified as Rabbinic literature.   The Gemara is a collection of written Rabbinical analyses and commentaries on the Mishnah.

Neither the Torah nor the other books of the Tanakh, contains any direct reference to intentional pregnancy termination, only to a birth or miscarriage following a violent altercation. A principal passage of the Torah referred to in analyses and commentary on abortion is Exodus 21:22-25, which concerns a man who inadvertently strikes a pregnant woman, causing her to have a miscarriage. The passage reads:

> *22   When men have a fight and hurt a pregnant woman, so that she suffers a miscarriage, but no further injury, the guilty one shall be fined as much as the woman's husband demands of him, and he shall pay in the presence of the judges.*
> *23   But if injury ensues, you shall give life for life,*
> *24   eye for eye, tooth for tooth, hand for hand, foot for foot,*
> *25   burn for burn, wound for wound, stripe for stripe.*

The foregoing modern translation of this passage, which appears in the American Bible, is clear that the "injury" referred to is to the woman. However, in relying on an alternative earlier translation:

> *And if men strive together, and hurt a woman with child, so that her fruit depart, and yet no harm follow, he shall be surely fined ... But if any harm follow, then thou shalt give life for life...,*

the first century Jewish-Greek philosopher and historian Philo Judaeus asserted that the term "harm" in this early translation referred exclusively to the child, and whether only a fine was imposed or the life of the perpetrator was forfeited depended on the gestational stage of the fetus. However, later Talmudic commentators seem to have agreed that the term "harm" in this earlier translation refers only to the woman, which appears to be the more logical interpretation of this translation. Accordingly, historically unless the woman was harmed in the altercation as well, only a fine was imposed for causing a miscarriage.

Under the Talmud, a fetus is not deemed a fully viable person, but rather a being of "doubtful viability". This distinction is manifested in the handling of matters relating to the death of a fetus. For example,

Jewish mourning rites do not apply to an unborn child. The fetus is referred to as "an appendage of its mother".

In a modern translation, Genesis 9:6 reads:

Anyone who sheds the blood of a human being, by a human being shall that one's blood be shed; For in the image of God have human beings been made.

An alternative direct translation of Genesis 9:6 from the Hebrew, referred to in the Talmud, reads:

He who spills the blood of man in man shall have his blood spilt.

An interpretation contained in the Talmud (Sanhedrin 57b) of this translation of Genesis 9:6, is that the spilling of "the blood of man in man" refers to the killing of a fetus. The word translated as "man" in the verse is deemed to be gender neutral.

In Judaism, the fetus, while considered to be alive to a limited extent and to be a potential person which is worthy of protection, is not considered to be a person and alive to the extent that if it endangered the woman's life, it's life would have priority over or even be considered equal in priority to the life of the woman. If a pregnancy risks the life of the woman, the Rabbis uniformly agree that the woman's life takes precedence and that the fetus should be aborted to save the woman's life. This would clearly not be the case if the fetus were considered to be a living person.

The Talmud contains other examples which elucidate the status of the fetus in Judaism. One involves the sale of a cow, which is found, after the sale, to have been pregnant prior to the sale. The Talmud teaches that the seller is not entitled to an additional payment for the fetus from the buyer and that the fetus belongs to the buyer, the fetus being part of the body of the sold cow. In another example, a woman is pregnant at the time she converts to Judaism. The Talmud confirms that the conversion of the pregnant woman will result in the child being born Jewish despite the fact that the child was conceived prior to her conversion.

A belief relied upon by many opponents of abortion is that life begins at conception. As stated above, this belief is not supported by Jewish law. Furthermore, a fetus is not considered to be a person, and is, therefore, not entitled to the protections afforded to persons under Jewish law. Under Jewish law, a fetus attains the status of a full person only at birth. The Talmud (Yevamot 69b) indicates that prior to forty days of gestation the fetus is "mere water." The Talmud further states that the ancient rabbis regarded a fetus as part of the woman until the birth of the child.   This concept supports the broadly held belief among Jewish scholars and adherents, including Orthodox, Conservative, and Reform Jews, that, regardless of the theological and ethical viewpoint held on abortion, women should be solely empowered and solely responsible to make decisions concerning their own bodies, including particularly decisions regarding obtaining an abortion. Some Jewish scholars even advocate for a child not obtaining status as a person, entitled to all the protections afforded to persons, until the child has been proven to be viable by living for 30 days outside the womb of the mother.

Even from the viewpoint of examining abortion on a purely theological and ethical basis, Jewish law views abortion as necessary in certain cases. If the fetus threatens the life of the woman, and the choice is between the health of the two of them, the woman must always be chosen. This is because the fetus is a "potential human life" and not a person until birth, and, therefore, has none of the rights and privileges of a human being.

Notwithstanding the lack of personhood of the fetus, aborting a fetus without appropriate reason, namely a sufficiently strong physical or psychiatric reason, is not condoned under Jewish law. As stated above, a small minority of Jewish scholars even go so far as advocating for the ancient analysis of Philo Judaeus that Genesis 9:6 prohibits shedding the "blood of man within man", a phrase understood to be a fetus, and provides that the perpetrator "shall have his blood spilt". Further, under Jewish tradition, the body of a person is merely on loan to the person, as it is created by God and thus is the property of God. Accordingly, intentional self-injury, including a range of actions from suicide to getting a tattoo, are prohibited under Jewish law, which leads to the conclusion that a person's right to make choices regarding her or his body is limited.

While the legal status of a fetus is important with respect to the level of legal protection afforded a fetus, with regard to the ultimate question of the morality of abortion under Jewish law, the issue of ensoulment would arguably be preeminent. However, Rabbis have expressed a wide variety of opinions regarding the moment of ensoulment, varying from as early as the moment of conception to as late as the time the child learns to speak. The moment of ensoulment has been the subject of much disagreement and remains unclear in Jewish law and tradition. As a result, the issue of ensoulment plays virtually no role in Jewish considerations of the morality of abortion.

Rabbinic authorities generally approve of abortion, not only if the woman's life is in danger, but even if the continuation of the pregnancy may cause significant injury to her health. However, as stated above, aborting a fetus without a sufficiently strong physical or psychiatric reason is condemned in the Jewish faith. The prevention of severe mental illness would clearly be generally accepted as a sufficiently strong psychiatric reason. For example, the prevention of very serious post-natal depression would generally be sufficient grounds for abortion, as would anticipated development of suicidal tendencies in the woman. However, a Rabbinic authority would likely take into account the gestational stage of the pregnancy at the time abortion is being considered, the anticipated severity of the potential psychological illness, the nature and quality of the medical advice relied upon, and the potential for treating the depression or other psychological condition.

In case of a pregnancy conceived from rape, modern Rabbinic authorities would be in general agreement that the pregnant woman should be spared of the great mental anguish that would derive from delivering a child resulting from rape. In cases involving pregnancy resulting from adultery however, there is a division of opinion among Rabbinic authorities. Some would say that the shame to be borne by the woman will be a deterrent against the sin of adultery by others. Others would seek to save the pregnant woman from the mental pain and anguish that will be derived from the shame.

While the majority of Rabbinic authorities would find that abortion is permissible at any stage of the pregnancy if the well-being of the pregnant woman is jeopardized. In contrast, however, if the issue is only the well-being of the future child, abortion would generally not be condoned. Abortion will generally not be condoned out of fear or concern over what the child might have to endure during its life. However, there is a split of authority if the pregnant woman expresses anguish about her own mental, emotional, or psychological condition resulting from an impending birth of a child that will likely suffer from deformity or other serious challenges. Some Rabbinic authorities would condone an abortion based upon the woman's mental anguish, while others would not.

In cases of non-therapeutic abortion, then, the major consideration is the pain of the woman, and not the fate or condition of the fetus, which becomes the determining factor in a non-therapeutic abortion being condoned or not condoned by Rabbinic authorities. There is much diversity of opinion on whether such abortions should be condoned, and, if so, under what conditions.

However, whatever their theological opinions on abortion in any given situation, a vast majority of Jewish scholars and Rabbis agree that decision making with respect to abortion must be left in the hands of the woman, who may consult her husband, her physician, and her rabbi as she deems appropriate. Regardless of the morality or immorality of an abortion in a particular circumstance, as perceived by Rabbis and Jewish scholars, they generally agree that the moral responsibility for the decision must be borne by the woman and that she alone has the right to decide how to apply her personal standards.

A number of recent surveys have all confirmed that most American Jews strongly support legalized abortion. A 2011 report of Polls of Jews in America found that 88% of American Jews were pro-choice. In July 2012, Tablet Magazine, an online Jewish publication, quoted the Public Religion Research Institute's 2012 Jewish Values Report: "American Jews are overwhelmingly in favor of abortion in all (49%) or most (44%) cases. There is little denominational or demographic variation on this level of overall support." The author went on to summarize:

> "That's 93%, folks. The report goes to explain that while opinions are more varied by political affiliation among Jews, over 75% of Jewish Republicans believe that abortion should be legal in all or most cases. From the data, it seems that Wasserman Schultz isn't saying anything that isn't reflective of the vast majority of Jewish opinion. In fact, it seems that access to abortion is the issue upon which the most Jews agree."

A 2015 Pew Research Forum survey found that 83 percent of American Jews, more than any other religious group, were of the opinion that abortion "should be legal in all/most cases."

Due to long-standing Jewish support for separation of religion and government in American life, all four non-Orthodox Jewish movements - Reform, Reconstructionist, Conservative and Humanist - are on record opposing any governmental regulation of abortion. Moreover, many Orthodox authorities take the same position. As stated above, regardless of their opinions on abortion in any given situation, a vast majority of Jewish scholars agree that decision making with respect to abortion must be left in the hands of the woman involved, in consultation as she deems appropriate, with her husband, her physician, and her rabbi. In the US, within the context of her Jewish heritage, she can make a decision as she is permitted to do under US law.

Some Orthodox Rabbis, in the US and elsewhere, strongly oppose abortion, some even considering it a form of murder at any time after conception. However, there are many Orthodox rabbinic sources that support abortion when a mother's health is in danger even if her life is not at risk. That includes a situation when a fetus is conclusively determined to suffer from severe abnormalities, when a mother's mental health is in danger, or when the pregnancy is the result of a forbidden sexual union, including rape. However, these rulings are not universally accepted and differ between sources, and thus many Orthodox rabbis are cautious about laying down firm standards, insisting instead that cases be considered under individual circumstances.

The Rabbinical Assembly Committee on Jewish Law and Standards, the primary authority of Conservative Judaism, takes the view that an abortion is justifiable if a continuation of pregnancy might cause the woman severe physical or psychological harm, or when the fetus is judged by competent medical opinion as severely defective. The fetus is a life in the process of development, and the decision to abort should never be taken lightly. Before reaching her final decision, Conservative Judaism holds that the woman should consult with the biological father, other members of her family, her physician, her Rabbi and any other person who can help her in assessing the many grave legal and moral issues involved.

Reform Judaism permits abortion, not only when the woman's life is at stake, but also when a pregnancy is "a result of rape or incest; when through genetic testing, it is determined that the child to be born will have a disease that will cause death or severe disability, and the parents believe that the impending birth will be an impossible situation for them," and for several other reasons. More generally, the "Reform perspective on abortion can be described as follows: Abortion is an extremely difficult choice faced by a woman. In all circumstances, it should be her decision whether or not to terminate a pregnancy, backed up by those whom she trusts (physician, therapist, partner, etc.). This decision should not be taken lightly (abortion should never be used for birth control purposes) and can have life-long ramifications. However, any decision should be left up to the woman within whose body the fetus is growing."

The Reform Movement has acted to oppose legislation that would restrict the right of women to choose to abort a fetus, especially in situations in which the health of the woman is endangered by continued pregnancy. This pro-choice position has been linked by some Reform authorities to the value that Reform Judaism places upon autonomy—the right of individuals to act as moral agents on their own behalf. In writing against a legal ban on so-called "partial birth abortion," Rabbi David Ellenson, president of the Reform Movement's Hebrew Union College, has written, "This law as it has been enacted unquestionably diminishes the inviolable status and worth that ought to be granted women as moral agents created in the image of God."

In the United States, Conservative Judaism, Reconstructionist Judaism and Reform Judaism are usually aligned with the interfaith Religious Coalition for Reproductive Choice. Orthodox organizations such as the Orthodox Union and Agudas Yisrael have occasionally partnered with pro-choice organizations when necessary to ensure that abortions will be available to women whose lives are endangered by the fetus.

Before 2014, in Israel, abortion was allowed, under a 1977 law, with the approval of a termination committee, if the woman was unmarried, if the woman was under the age of 17 (the legal marriage age in Israel) or over the age of 40, if the pregnancy was conceived under illegal circumstances (rape, statutory rape, etc.) or an incestuous relationship, if birth defects were likely, or if there was a risk to the health or life of the woman. According to the Israel Central Bureau of Statistics report from 2004, in 2003 most abortion requests were granted, with 19,500 legal abortions performed and 200 requests for abortion denied. Reasons for termination went as follows: the woman was unmarried (42%), because of illegal circumstances (11%), health risks to the woman (about 20%), age of the woman (11%) and fetal birth defects (about 17%).

The Israeli Cabinet revised the 1977 law in 2014 to allow abortion on demand for nearly every woman in the country seeking an abortion. The law of the only Hebrew nation in the world is thus consistent with the prevailing philosophy in Judaism shared, regardless of their theological opinions on abortion in any given situation, by a vast majority of Jewish scholars as well as a vast majority of the adherents of Judaism. That is that decision-making with respect to abortion must be left in the hands of the woman involved, in consultation, as she deems appropriate, with her husband, her physician, and her rabbi.

Summary of Native American View on Abortion:

The present view of Native Americans on abortion is varied. Some Native Americans who have adopted a Christian tradition, particularly those who have adopted a Catholic tradition, are generally opposed to abortion. Indians for Life is an example of pro-life Native

American organization which is affiliated with Catholic pro-life groups and with the National Right to Life Committee.

Traditionally, in Native American communities, matters pertaining to women have been the province of women. All decisions regarding a woman's reproductive health were her decisions and her decisions alone. Her right to make those decisions was respected and her decisions were not subject to scrutiny or criticism. We mentioned above that in traditional Native American societies there was no word for abortion. Native Americans instead referred to a woman using herbs and methods "to make her period come." The women used a variety of methods for inducing an abortion, including the use of black root and cedar root. Traditionally, this was viewed as a woman exercising control over her body. Women often relied on other women in their tribe for advice, mentoring, and assistance concerning reproductive health. This included reliance on other women of the tribe who were knowledgeable about the herbs and methods "to make her period come."

Today, however, many Native American women lament their perception that they are no longer free to make decisions concerning their reproductive health. Instead, these decisions are *de facto* regulated by federal legislation and regulations that limit the reproductive health services provided by the Indian Health Service (IHS). This problem is amplified by the Indian Health Service failing even to comply with its own abortion policy at many of its clinics. Because of income inequality, poverty and discrimination, and since abortions are not performed on reservations, Federal statutes and policies have a disproportionate impact on Native American women's ability to obtain an abortion and to obtain other reproductive healthcare services. The result is that it is even harder for Native American women to get the care they need than for poor Caucasian women.

Native American women experience a higher rate of unintended pregnancy than their Caucasian counterparts. Teenage pregnancy and unintended pregnancy rates continue to increase among the Native American community. These disproportionately high unintended pregnancy rates undoubtedly lead to more abortions. Since Native American populations were targeted during the appalling eugenics movement beginning in the early 1900's, it is understandable that the Native American community is suspicious of any purported reproductive justice plans originating with the Federal Government.

Summary of the Christian View on Abortion:

Because my personal history and my faith tradition is that of a Christian, my life experiences allow me to relate more intimately to the issue as it is approached from the perspective of the Christian faith. However, as will be apparent from a reading of the following, the view of the issue among Christians is highly divergent. Some of the principal reasons for the divergence are explored below.

Christians of profound religious and moral conviction disagree on the question of when life begins and when the unborn becomes a person. For instance, some Christians point to the passage from Genesis wherein God created Adam from the dust of the earth and breathed into him the breath of life and he became a living soul. The following verse from the King James translation of the Bible will be familiar to many Christians:

> *The LORD God formed man of the dust of the ground, and*
> *breathed into his nostrils the breath of life; and man became a*
> *living soul* <u>King James Bible</u>, *Genesis 2:7*

The translation of this verse which appears in the New American Bible is as follows:

> *The LORD God formed man out of the clay of the ground and*
> *blew into his nostrils the breath of life, and so man became a*
> *living being.* <u>New American Bible</u>, *Genesis 2:7*

The New American Bible, believed by most Bible scholars to be a more accurate translation, describes God as a potter who formed man out of clay. The word "being" in the New American Bible translation more literally means "soul" as stated in the King James Bible. Devout Christians who hold a liberal view on the issue of abortion, refer to the foregoing verse from the Hebrew scriptures, which is sacred to Jews and Christians.

The author was unable to find any reference to any verses of the Hebrew scriptures or the Christian scriptures, that state that life begins at conception or that the unborn becomes a person at conception. Further, as discussed previously, neither the Torah nor the other books of the Tanakh, commonly referred to by Christians as the Old Testament or the Hebrew Bible, contain any direct reference to intentional pregnancy termination, only to a birth or miscarriage following a violent altercation. Likewise, there is no direct reference to intentional pregnancy termination in the New Testament. Accordingly, for Christians, an analysis of the abortion issue from a theological or scriptural viewpoint, must depend on an indirect analysis of certain passages of the books of the New Testament.

Christians generally believe that the New Testament is the fulfillment of the covenant of God with human kind and the related prophesies expressed in the Old Testament. Christians further generally believe that the New Testament expresses and interprets the new covenant of God with Christians manifested by the life, death, resurrection, and ascension of Jesus to heaven, as well as his teachings relating to charity, love, sin, repentance, forgiveness, and eternal life.

The New Testament is comprised of twenty-seven books, which include the four Gospels, the Acts of the Apostles, twenty-two Epistles, and the Book of Revelation. The four Gospels present a history of the earthly life of Jesus and Jesus' teachings on theological and spiritual matters. The Gospels of Matthew and John respectively, are traditionally attributed to two of the original twelve Apostles of Jesus, though scholarly analysis has cast doubt on that traditional belief. The Gospel of Mark is generally believed by scholars to be written by Mark, a follower or disciple of the Apostle Peter and the Gospel of Luke is believed to be written by Luke, a follower or disciple of Paul, a former persecutor of Christians who never met Jesus before his crucifixion but who was converted due a purported spiritual encounter with Jesus a few years after the ascension of Jesus to heaven. Excepting only Matthias, who was chosen by the eleven Apostles to replace Judas Iscariot, Paul is the only follower of Jesus to be attributed the title of Apostle other than the original twelve selected by Jesus.

The Acts of the Apostles, generally ascribed to Luke the purported author of the third Gospel, presents a history of the early years of the Christian Church.

The Epistles, which are generally written in the form of letters to congregations of Christians or to individual evangelists identified in the respective Epistles, present instructions and admonitions to the recipients, and ultimately to all Christians. Fourteen of the Epistles are traditionally attributed to Paul, but at least one of those, the Epistle to the Hebrews, is believed by most scholars to be written by an unidentified author. Of the other seven Epistles, commonly referred to as the General Epistles, two are traditionally attributed to the Apostle Peter, three to the Apostle John, one to the Apostle James, and one to the Apostle Jude. However, the reliability of the identification of the authors of the General Epistles is subject to dispute among biblical scholars.

The Book of Revelation, positioned at the end of the New Testament because of its prophetic and apocalyptic content, is traditionally attributed to the Apostle John. However, there is scholarly skepticism regarding whether this book, any of the three Epistles traditionally attributed to John, or the Gospel of John were actually written by the Apostle John.

The difficulty faced by Christians in addressing the issue of abortion, is that despite being quoted extensively in the Gospels regarding paramount issues dealing with the matters of the heart and soul and regarding the eternal life of mankind, Jesus is not quoted as saying anything directly relating to intentional termination of a pregnancy. He is also not quoted as saying anything directly relating to the moment of ensoulment of a fetus. The foregoing is also true regarding the instructions and exhortations contained in the Epistles, whether correctly attributed to the Apostles or not. Again, despite instructions and exhortations regarding issues of preeminent importance, there is nothing directly relating to intentional pregnancy termination or to the time of ensoulment of a fetus presented in any of the Epistles.

For Christians, perhaps the most illuminating passage of scripture relating to abortion is the following passage in the first chapter of the Gospel of Luke (Revised New American Bible):

> ***Announcement of the Birth of Jesus.***
> *26 In the sixth month, the angel Gabriel was sent from God to a town of Galilee called Nazareth,*
> *27 to a virgin betrothed to a man named Joseph, of the house of David, and the virgin's name was Mary.*
> *28 And coming to her, he said, "Hail, favored one! The Lord is with you."*
> *29 But she was greatly troubled at what was said and pondered what sort of greeting this might be.*
> *30 Then the angel said to her, "Do not be afraid, Mary, for you have found favor with God.*
> *31 Behold, you will conceive in your womb and bear a son, and you shall name him Jesus.*
> *32 He will be great and will be called Son of the Most High, and the Lord God will give him the throne of David his father,*
> *33 and he will rule over the house of Jacob forever, and of his kingdom there will be no end."*
> *34 But Mary said to the angel, "How can this be, since I have no relations with a man?"*
> *35 And the angel said to her in reply, "The holy Spirit will come upon you, and the power of the Most High will overshadow you. Therefore the child to be born will be called holy, the Son of God.*
> *36 And behold, Elizabeth, your relative, has also conceived a son in her old age, and this is the **sixth month** for her who was called barren;*
> *37 for nothing will be impossible for God."*

*38 Mary said, "Behold, I am the handmaid of the Lord. May it be
done to me according to your word." Then the angel departed
from her.*

Mary Visits Elizabeth.
*39 During those days Mary set out and traveled to the hill
country in haste to a town of Judah,
40 where she entered the house of Zechariah and greeted
Elizabeth.
41 When Elizabeth heard Mary's greeting,* **the infant leaped in
her womb**, *and Elizabeth, filled with the holy Spirit,
42 cried out in a loud voice and said, "Most blessed are you
among women, and blessed is the fruit of your womb.
43 And how does this happen to me, that the mother of my
Lord should come to me?
44 For at the moment the sound of your greeting reached my
ears, the infant in my womb leaped for joy.*

When Mary visited her cousin Elizabeth, the soon to be mother of John
the Baptist, Elizabeth reported that upon hearing the greeting of Mary
"the infant in my womb leaped for joy." The angel Gabriel had informed
Mary at the time of her conception that her cousin Elizabeth was in her
sixth month of pregnancy. *Luke 1: 36.* Mary set out "in haste" "in those
days" from Nazareth to the home of her cousin Elizabeth in a town of the
"hill country" of Judah. *Luke 1:39.* Although the town is not specifically
identified, the distance from Nazareth to the hill country of Judah would
have been about 90 miles. Even walking, it would have likely taken
Mary less than a week to make the journey from Nazareth to the home of
Elizabeth.

The unborn John the Baptist is "the infant" referred to in this
passage, and Elizabeth was approximately 6 months pregnant when
Mary visited her.   This event is considered by most Christians as strong

evidence that the ensoulment of John the Baptist had occurred by 6 months in the womb.

The history of the practice of the Christian faith, of course, begins with the Catholic Church. Other than the Assyrian Church which diverged from the Catholic Church at the Council of Ephesus in 431 A.D., and the Oriental Orthodox Church which diverged from the Catholic Church at the Council of Chalcedon in 451 A.D., the Catholic Church was essentially the Christian Church until the great schism between the Roman Catholic Church and the Eastern Orthodox Church was formalized in 1054 A.D. The Eastern Orthodox Church has two major divisions, the Greek Orthodox Church and the Russian Orthodox Church. The Roman Catholic Church experienced the Protestant Reformation which purportedly began with Martin Luther nailing his ninety-five theses to the church door in Wittenberg, Germany on October 31, 1517. The Catholic Church presently has approximately twenty-two other sects which have differences in rites from the Roman Church and which differ in the extent of their communion with the Roman Church and in the extent of their consent to the authority of the Pope, the Bishop of Rome.

Since the Protestant Reformation was initiated by Martin Luther in 1517, many Protestant denominations have formed. The Center for Global Christianity at Gordon-Conwell Theological Seminary, an evangelical Protestant organization, estimates that there are currently approximately 47,000 Protestant denominations. Although there may some criticism of the methodology used in arriving at such a large number, there seems to be general agreement that there are thousands of Protestant denominations. Further, the Association of Religion Data

Archives estimates the total number of non-denominational Christian Churches at more than 35,000. Some of the Protestant denominations claim to be "sola scriptura," which is Latin for "scripture alone." They adhere to the theological doctrine that the Christian scriptures are the sole infallible source of faith and practice. Other Protestant denominations include faith traditions and some rely on early church councils, such as the First Council of Nicea in which writings were selected for inclusion in the Bible and the Nicene Creed was adopted as a summary statement of the Christian faith.

Considering the extent of the fragmentation of the Christian faith, it is not surprising that there would be considerable divergence on theological and doctrinal issues. This is particularly true on the issue of abortion, since, as discussed previously, there is very little in either the Old Testament or the New Testament to elucidate this matter.

It is interesting and informative to consider the history of the abortion issue as it relates to ancient cultures which had an influence on the development of the Christian perspective. For example, the Assyrians, whose ferocious, skilled and weaponized army dominated the middle east from about 900 BC to 600 BC, prohibited abortion, apparently not because of any moral or ethical concern, but because of the constant demand for warriors.

The Greek Empire began to develop in about 800 BC and dominated the region around the Mediterranean until about 300 BC. The Greek Septuagint translation of Exodus 21:22-23 clarified the distinction between an unformed and a formed fetus. Only after the fetus was developed was it was treated as an individual person by the Greeks. The renowned Greek philosopher Aristotle stated his opinion that ensoulment of males occurred at 40 days after conception and ensoulment of females occurred at 90 days after conception. This distinction between the early fetus and the more developed fetus was common in the ancient world.

Plato, on the other hand, the teacher of Aristotle and the student of Socrates, believed that ensoulment did not take place until birth. The influence of Plato, who is hailed as one of the founders of western religion and spirituality, contributed to the prevailing practice in the developing western civilization that abortion was not to be treated as the killing of a person.

Finally, the Greek philosopher and scientist Pythagoras believed that ensoulment occurred at conception. As early as the third century, Christianity seems to have adopted the Pythagorean view that ensoulment occurred at conception, but that concept seems to have been short lived. The position was supported by St. Gregory of Nyssa and St. Maximus the Confessor in the fourth century, but it appears to have been soon rejected based on the concept discussed above derived from the Septuagint translation of Exodus 21:22-23 that only a formed fetus possessed a human soul. St. Augustine of Hippo wondered whether ensoulment might occur prior to formation, but he took the position that abortion could not be characterized as the killing of a person until formation had occurred. So, while St. Gregory and St. Maximus held that human life began at conception, St. Augustine affirmed Aristotle's concepts of ensoulment occurring at some point after conception, after which point abortion was to be considered homicide. This position of St. Augustine and others, apparently a clear majority of the Christian leaders of the time, is not to be confused, however, with the position of St. Augustine and the others regarding the sin associated with the act of abortion. Abortion was condemned by St. Augustine as a serious sin from the moment of conception.

The prevalent, though not uniformly accepted, belief of early Christians, which was also the prevalent belief of the Greeks, was that a fetus does not have a soul until quickening, and therefore early abortion was not murder. "Quickening" was generally defined as the moment the woman first felt movement of the fetus in her womb. There was even some disagreement among early Christians about whether early abortion was even a sin, but most early Christians considered abortion a sin even before ensoulment. The magnitude of the sin was, for some early Christians, on a level with general sexual immorality. Others viewed the severity as on the level with oppression of the poor and needy. It must be remembered that the historical setting in which Christianity grew was one in which abortion, infanticide and exposition (discussed below) were commonly used to limit the number of children, especially females, that a family had to support, or to avoid the social impact of a pregnancy or birth resulting from adultery, rape, incest, or prostitution.

The prevailing belief among Christians was that ensoulment occurred at some point after conception and most likely at quickening, i.e. when the fetus began to move in the womb of the woman. Pope Innocent III, Pope from January 8, 1198 until 1216; St. Thomas Aquinas, Italian Dominican friar, Catholic priest, and Doctor of the Church, who lived from 1225 to March 7, 1274; and Pope Gregory XIV, Pope from December 5, 1590 until his death in 1591, believed that a fetus does not have a soul until quickening, and therefore early abortion was not murder, though later abortion was. St. Thomas Aquinas taught that abortion was still wrong, even when not murder, regardless of when the soul entered the body.

Pope Stephen V, Pope from September 885 to his death in 891, a predecessor of St. Thomas Aquinas, opposed abortion at any stage of pregnancy. Likewise, Pope Sixtus V, Pope from 24 April 1585 to his death in 1590 approximately 300 years after St. Thomas Aquinas, opposed abortion at any stage of pregnancy.

At the time of Constantine, the first Christian Roman Emperor, in the 4th Century, there was a relaxation of attitudes toward abortion and "exposure" of children. At this time, many Christians were very poor and had a very difficult time providing for their families. The practice of "exposing" children involved parents leaving a child they felt they could not care for, in the wilds exposed to the elements and predators. Other persons, who may not have been able to have children, were entitled to take the exposed child as their own. From that time until the 16th Century, there was an ongoing debate among Christian writers and philosophers on whether and at what stage of pregnancy an abortion was murder. The extreme poverty of many Christians caused Christian leaders to take a more tolerant attitude toward poor people who exposed their children or to a woman who had an abortion. While most early confessors imposed equal penances for abortion whether it was an early or pre-formation abortion, or was a late or post-formation abortion, confessors during the Middle Ages acknowledged a distinction, imposing heavier penances for late or post-formation abortions and a less severe penance for early or pre-formation abortions.

The position of St. Thomas Aquinas, that ensoulment occurred at quickening - the beginning of movement of the fetus in the womb of the woman - remained the Catholic Church's position until 1869, when automatic excommunication for abortion was no longer limited to abortion of a *formed* fetus. Pope Pius IX declared in 1869 that excommunication would be the penalty for abortion at any stage of pregnancy. This change has been interpreted as a declaration by Pope Pius IX that ensoulment occurs at conception. This view is based upon the belief that the infusion of the soul into the body is a divine act and that the soul comes from a divine source.

Despite the Catholic view of abortion from 1869 on, the development of English common law was influenced by Aristotle's view that ensoulment occurred at quickening, which was understood to be about four months following conception.

CURRENT VIEW OF VARIOUS CHRISTIAN CHURCHES

<u>Roman Catholic Church</u>:

In summary, the Roman Catholic Church, currently holds the position that life comes from a divine source and begins at conception, and, accordingly, abortion at any stage amounts to the killing of a person, i.e. murder. The doctrine of the Catholic Church does not allow selective abortion even if the woman is at risk of serious injury or death.

The current position of the Catholic Church, as of 1970, is stated in Canon 2350 of the Code of Canon Law, issued in 1917 by Pope Benedict XV, and on the encyclical *Casti Connubi* issued by Pope Pius XI in 1930. In *Casti Connubi* Pope Pius XI stated:

> 63. But another very grave crime is to be noted, Venerable Brethren, which regards the taking of the life of the offspring hidden in the mother's womb. Some wish it to be allowed and

left to the will of the father or the mother; others say it is unlawful unless there are weighty reasons which they call by the name of medical, social, or eugenic "indication." Because this matter falls under the penal laws of the state by which the destruction of the offspring begotten but unborn is forbidden, these people demand that the "indication," which in one form or another they defend, be recognized as such by the public law and in no way penalized. There are those, moreover, who ask that the public authorities provide aid for these death-dealing operations, a thing, which, sad to say, everyone knows is of very frequent occurrence in some places.

64. As to the "medical and therapeutic indication" to which, using their own words, we have made reference, Venerable Brethren, however much we may pity the mother whose health and even life is gravely imperiled in the performance of the duty allotted to her by nature, nevertheless what could ever be a sufficient reason for excusing in any way the direct murder of the innocent? This is precisely what we are dealing with here. Whether inflicted upon the mother or upon the child, it is against the precept of God and the law of nature: "Thou shalt not kill:" The life of each is equally sacred, and no one has the power, not even the public authority, to destroy it. It is of no use to appeal to the right of taking away life for here it is a question of the innocent, whereas that right has regard only to the guilty; nor is there here question of defense by bloodshed against an unjust aggressor (for who would call an innocent child an unjust aggressor?); again there is not question here of what is called the "law of extreme necessity" which could even extend to the direct killing of the innocent. Upright and skillful doctors strive most praiseworthily to guard and preserve the lives of both mother and child; on the contrary, those show themselves most unworthy of the noble medical profession who encompass the death of one or the other, through a pretense at practicing medicine or through motives of misguided pity.

65. All of which agrees with the stern words of the Bishop of Hippo in denouncing those wicked parents who seek to remain childless, and failing in this, are not ashamed to put their offspring to death: "Sometimes this lustful cruelty or cruel lust

goes so far as to seek to procure a baneful sterility, and if this fails the fetus conceived in the womb is in one way or another smothered or evacuated, in the desire to destroy the offspring before it has life, or if it already lives in the womb, to kill it before it is born. If both man and woman are party to such practices they are not spouses at all; and if from the first they have carried on thus they have come together not for honest wedlock, but for impure gratification; if both are not party to these deeds, I make bold to say that either the one makes herself a mistress of the husband, or the other simply the paramour of his wife."

66. What is asserted in favor of the social and eugenic "indication" may and must be accepted, provided lawful and upright methods are employed within the proper limits; but to wish to put forward reasons based upon them for the killing of the innocent is unthinkable and contrary to the divine precept promulgated in the words of the Apostle: Evil is not to be done that good may come of it.

67. Those who hold the reins of government should not forget that it is the duty of public authority by appropriate laws and sanctions to defend the lives of the innocent, and this all the more so since those whose lives are endangered and assailed cannot defend themselves. Among whom we must mention in the first place infants hidden in the mother's womb. And if the public magistrates not only do not defend them, but by their laws and ordinances betray them to death at the hands of doctors or of others, let them remember that God is the Judge and Avenger of innocent blood which cried from earth to Heaven.

It is clear from the foregoing encyclical of Pope Pius XI that the Catholic Church does not even allow deference to saving the life of the woman when the fetus is endangering the life and health of the woman.

The Canon Law of the Roman Catholic Church is often cited by both sides in the abortion debate, usually to point out or to criticize the Church's moral stance. However, it must be remembered that Catholic

Church Canon Law is not a moral code, it is the procedural and penal law of the Catholic Church.

The Catechism of the Catholic Church, a comprehensive statement of the dogma and doctrine of the Catholic Church, includes the following:

2270 Human life must be respected and protected absolutely from the moment of conception. From the first moment of his existence, a human being must be recognized as having the rights of a person - among which is the inviolable right of every innocent being to life.
Before I formed you in the womb I knew you, and before you were born I consecrated you.
My frame was not hidden from you, when I was being made in secret, intricately wrought in the depths of the earth.

2271 Since the first century the Church has affirmed the moral evil of every procured abortion. This teaching has not changed and remains unchangeable.
Direct abortion, that is to say, abortion willed either as an end or a means, is gravely contrary to the moral law:
You shall not kill the embryo by abortion and shall not cause the newborn to perish.74
God, the Lord of life, has entrusted to men the noble mission of safeguarding life, and men must carry it out in a manner worthy of themselves. Life must be protected with the utmost care from the moment of conception: abortion and infanticide are abominable crimes.

2272 Formal cooperation in an abortion constitutes a grave offense.
The Church attaches the canonical penalty of excommunication to this crime against human life.
"A person who procures a completed abortion incurs excommunication latae sententiae," "by the very commission of the offense," and subject to the conditions provided by Canon Law.
The Church does not thereby intend to restrict the scope of

mercy.
Rather, she makes clear the gravity of the crime committed, the irreparable harm done to the innocent who is put to death, as well as to the parents and the whole of society.

2273 The inalienable right to life of every innocent human individual is a constitutive element of a civil society and its legislation:
"The inalienable rights of the person must be recognized and respected by civil society and the political authority.
These human rights depend neither on single individuals nor on parents; nor do they represent a concession made by society and the state; they belong to human nature and are inherent in the person by virtue of the creative act from which the person took his origin.
Among such fundamental rights one should mention in this regard every human being's right to life and physical integrity from the moment of conception until death."
 "The moment a positive law deprives a category of human beings of the protection which civil legislation ought to accord them, the state is denying the equality of all before the law. When the state does not place its power at the service of the rights of each citizen, and in particular of the more vulnerable, the very foundations of a state based on law are undermined.... As a consequence of the respect and protection which must be ensured for the unborn child from the moment of conception, the law must provide appropriate penal sanctions for every deliberate violation of the child's rights."

2274 Since it must be treated from conception as a person, the embryo must be defended in its integrity, cared for, and healed, as far as possible, like any other human being.
Prenatal diagnosis is morally licit, "if it respects the life and integrity of the embryo and the human fetus and is directed toward its safe guarding or healing as an individual....
It is gravely opposed to the moral law when this is done with the thought of possibly inducing an abortion, depending upon the results: a diagnosis must not be the equivalent of a death sentence."

2275 "One must hold as licit procedures carried out on the human embryo which respect the life and integrity of the embryo and do not involve disproportionate risks for it, but are directed toward its healing the improvement of its condition of health, or its individual survival."
"It is immoral to produce human embryos intended for exploitation as disposable biological material."
"Certain attempts to influence chromosomic or genetic inheritance are not therapeutic but are aimed at producing human beings selected according to sex or other predetermined qualities. Such manipulations are contrary to the personal dignity of the human being and his integrity and identity" which are unique and unrepeatable.

(Emphasis added to the foregoing by underlining)

The foregoing excerpts from the Catechism of the Catholic Church state the present, unequivocal and unwavering position of the Catholic Church that life begins at conception, that from the moment of conception the unborn is a person with a soul, and that abortion is murder and can never be tolerated. Further, because the unborn, regardless of the gestational stage, is believed to be a person with the same right to a continued life as a previously born person, in the event of a conflict between the life of the unborn and the life and health of the woman, there can be no deference to the life or health of the woman. This is a position which is singularly strict and singularly disengaged from the life and health of the woman, in comparison even to other religious organizations who are strongly opposed to abortion. The position of the Catholic Church is also clearly unequivocal on the issue of public policy and law regarding abortion. The Catholic Church is simply unwavering on its position that public policy and law must prohibit abortion in any form or under any circumstances.

One retreat from the very strict position of the Catholic Church is provided by Canon Law which provides an exception to automatic excommunication for a woman who aborts because of a direct threat to her life or if there is grave fear or grave inconvenience leading to the abortion decision. The Catholic Church also offers the possibility of forgiveness for women who have had an abortion without any such justification. In that regard, Pope John Paul II wrote:

> I would now like to say a special word to women who have had an abortion. The Church is aware of the many factors which may have influenced your decision, and she does not doubt that in many cases it was a painful and even shattering decision. The wound in your heart may not yet have healed. Certainly what happened was and remains terribly wrong. But do not give in to discouragement and do not lose hope. Try rather to understand what happened and face it honestly. If you have not already done so, give yourselves over with humility and trust to repentance. The Father of mercies is ready to give you his forgiveness and his peace in Sacrament of Reconciliation.

As mentioned previously, many Catholics do not accept the position of the Church described in the foregoing provisions of the Catechism. In some Catholic countries, a majority of Catholics reject the Church's position. For example, the Constitution of the Republic of Ireland was amended in 2018 by a public referendum strenuously opposed by the Catholic Church, and abortion is now available on demand during the first twelve weeks, and thereafter if there is a serious risk to the life or health of the woman.

In a 1995 survey, 64% of U.S. Catholics said they disapproved of the statement that "abortion is morally wrong in every case". On the other hand, a 2013 survey by the Pew Research Center found that, whatever views they held on whether abortion should be legal, 53% of white Catholics in the United States considered abortion morally wrong, as did 64% of Hispanic Catholics. Among Hispanic Catholics, this percentage did not vary significantly between those who went to Mass at least once a week and those who did not, but there was a considerable difference in the case of white Catholics, with 74% of those who went to Mass at least once a week declaring having an abortion to be immoral, as compared with 40% of those whose religious practice was laxer. A 2008 survey found that 65% of American Catholics identified themselves as "pro-choice", but also found that 76% of these "pro-choice" Catholics believed that abortion should be significantly restricted. In the same year some 58% of American Catholic women felt that they did not have to follow the abortion teaching of their bishop. Only 22% of U.S. Catholics held that abortion should be illegal in all cases.

A 1996 survey found that 72% of Australian Catholics say that the decision to have an abortion "should be left to individual women and their doctors."

<u>Eastern Orthodox Church</u>:

Like the Roman Catholic Church, the position of the Eastern Orthodox Church is that life begins at conception, and that abortion, including the use of abortifacient drugs, is the taking of a human life. The *Basis of the Social Concept of the Russian Orthodox Church* states that, if it is because of a direct threat to her life that a woman interrupts her pregnancy, especially if she already has other children, she is not to be excommunicated from the church because of this sin, which however she must confess to a priest and fulfill the penance that he assigns. In case of a direct threat to the life of a mother if her pregnancy continues, especially if she has other children, it is recommended to be lenient in the pastoral practice. The woman who interrupted pregnancy in this situation shall not be excluded from the Eucharistic communion with the Church provided that she has fulfilled the canon of Penance assigned by the priest who takes her confession. The document also acknowledges that abortions often are a result of poverty and helplessness and that the Church and society should "work out effective measures to protect motherhood."

Protestants

As discussed previously, since the Protestant Reformation was initiated by Martin Luther in 1517, many Protestant denominations have formed. The Center for Global Christianity at Gordon-Conwell Theological Seminary, an evangelical Protestant organization, estimates that there are currently approximately 47,000 Protestant denominations. Although there may some criticism of the methodology used in arriving at such a large number, there seems to be general agreement that there are thousands of Protestant denominations. Further, the Association of Religion Data Archives estimates the total number of non-denominational Christian Churches at more than 35,000.

With such denominational and non-denominational diversity among Protestants, it is no surprise that official Protestant denomination views and official non-denominational congregation views on abortion vary considerably. Protestant denominations that are conservative on other issues tend to be conservative on the issue of abortion as well. Similarly, denominations that are liberal on other issues tend to be liberal on the issue of abortion. African-American Protestants are much more strongly anti-abortion than white Protestants.

Even among Protestants who believe that abortion should be a legal option, there are those who believe that it should nonetheless be morally unacceptable in most instances. Former presidents Jimmy Carter and Bill Clinton, both Protestants, addressed this position. President Carter stated that he was philosophically against abortion but he recognized that the legal right to an abortion was the law of the land under *Roe v. Wade*. President Clinton stated that abortion should be "safe, legal and rare." Evangelical Protestants have sought to sharply restrict the conditions under which abortion is legally available.

At the other extreme, some Protestants support freedom of choice and assert that abortion should not only be legal but even morally acceptable in certain circumstances. For example, Protestant supporters of abortion rights include the United Church of Christ, the Evangelical Lutheran Church in America, the Episcopal Church, the Presbyterian Church (USA), and the Lutheran Women's Caucus. The American Baptist Churches USA, Evangelical Lutheran Church of America, the Presbyterian Church (USA) and The United Church of Christ consider abortion permissible under certain restricted circumstances.

According to a 2002 survey conducted by the Roper Center for Public Opinion Research, fundamentalist Christians are more likely to be pro-life than all other respondents, including mainline Protestants. Twenty-eight percent of fundamentalists thought abortion should be illegal even if there was a strong chance of birth defects whereas only nine percent of mainline Protestants held the same opinion. Seventy percent of fundamentalists felt that the desire not to have more children was not a sufficient justification for having an abortion while mainline Protestants were almost evenly divided on this question. However, an overwhelming majority of both fundamentalists and mainline Protestants indicated that they would support abortion in cases where the pregnancy endangered the mother's life.

A 2013 Pew Research survey found that, regardless of their views on the legality of abortion, 75% of white evangelical Protestants, 58% of black Protestants and 38% of mainline Protestants said it was morally wrong to have an abortion. Even the 38% figure for mainline Protestants was higher than the 25% figure for religiously unaffiliated adults. Among the religiously unaffiliated, 28% said that having an abortion was morally acceptable, a view held by only 15% of the population as a whole, while 23% said it was not a moral issue.

It is informative to consider the official positions on abortion taken by various Protestant denominations in the United States.

LUTHERAN CHURCHES

There are three main denominations of Lutherans in the United States. The largest is the Evangelical Lutheran Church in America with about 5 million members. The Lutheran Church- Missouri Synod has about 2.5 million members, and the Wisconsin Evangelical Lutheran Synod has about a half million members.

Evangelical Lutheran Church in America

The official position of the Evangelical Lutheran Church in America (ECLA), as stated in the "ECLA Social Statement on Abortion", is that "abortion prior to viability [of a fetus] should not be prohibited by law or by lack of public funding" but that abortion after the point of fetal viability should be prohibited except when the life of a mother is threatened or when fetal abnormalities pose a fatal threat to a newborn. The ELCA Statement says abortion should be an option of last resort, that the ELCA community should work to reduce the need for elective abortions, and that as a community, "the number of induced abortions is a source of deep concern to this church. We mourn the loss of life that God has created." The ELCA Social Statement on Abortion adds: "The church recognizes that there can be sound reasons for ending a pregnancy through induced abortion. These are the threat to a woman's physical life; when pregnancy has resulted from rape, incest or sexual violence; and fetal abnormalities incompatible with life. The church opposes legal restrictions on abortion and provides health-care benefits to its employees that cover elective abortions. Some hospitals affiliated with the church perform elective abortions.

The Lutheran Church–Missouri Synod

The Lutheran Church-Missouri Synod (LSMS) views abortion as contrary to the will of God. The church has stated that abortion "is not a moral option, except as a tragically unavoidable byproduct of medical procedures necessary to prevent the death of another human being, viz., the mother." The LCMS believes that whether abortion is legal or not, it does not change the fact that abortion is sin. On the topic of whether abortion is allowed in the case of rape or incest, the LCMS has stated that though there are many "emotional arguments for abortion... the fact of the matter is that it is wrong to take the life of one innocent victim (the unborn child)...It is indeed a strange logic that would have us kill an innocent unborn baby for the crime of his father."

Wisconsin Evangelical Lutheran Synod

The Wisconsin Evangelical Lutheran Synod (WELS) adopted a

resolution in July 2011 on social issues. Included in this resolution on social issues is a resolution on the issue of abortion. It confirms the commitment of WELS to the Holy Scriptures which it says "clearly testify to a reverence for the life of the mother and the life of her unborn child as both being equal in value." The resolution further states that because the unborn is a life, the intentional termination of the fetus is a serious sin, considering the commandment against murder in the Bible. The resolution further states in the event of endangerment to the life of the mother and the child, that effort must be made to save both the mother's and baby's life, but if that is not possible, then there should be effort to save at least one life. There is no deference to the life of the mother.

ANGLICAN COMMUNITY

The positions taken by the various denominations of the Anglican Community vary considerably and is the source of ongoing conflict within the community.

Episcopal Church

The Episcopal Church has adopted a number of resolutions relating to abortion. The church recognizes that the decision regarding termination of a pregnancy must be left to the woman and that it is her legal right to make the decision. However, as a matter of doctrine, the Church has reaffirmed that all human life is sacred from its inception until death and that all abortion is regarded as having a tragic dimension. Accordingly, the church believes that the right should be exercised only in extreme situations. The church condones abortion only in cases of rape or incest, cases in which a mother's physical or mental health is at risk, or cases involving fetal abnormalities. The church strongly opposes "abortion as a means of birth control, family planning, sex selection or any reason of mere convenience." At the same time, the church also condemns violence against abortion clinics and it has officially supported public events and other efforts promoting the protection of the reproductive rights of women.

It is interesting to note, however, the effect of the dichotomy between doctrinal belief and recognition of individual rights and free will among the Episcopal Church membership. Anglicans for Life, previously known as National Organization of Episcopalians for Life (N.O.E.L.), which claims to have more than 2 million members, is an independent organization working for pro-life issues.

Anglican Church in North America

The Anglican Church in North America (ACNA) was founded in 2009 by former members of the Episcopal Church in the United States and the Anglican Church of Canada who disagreed with the liberal doctrinal and social trends and positions of their former churches. They considered the current liberal positions and trends to be contradictory to the foundational and traditional doctrine of the Anglican community. The ACNA now also includes ten congregations in Mexico and a missionary diocese in Cuba. In 2017, the ACNA reported having a membership of 134,593 in 1,037 congregations and 30 dioceses.

The ACNA is decidedly pro-life, stating that "all members and clergy are called to promote and respect the sanctity of every human life from conception to natural death".

The Church of England

The Church of England officially stated in 1980 that: "In the light of our conviction that the fetus has the right to live and develop as a member of the human family, we see abortion, the termination of that life by the act of man, as a great moral evil. We do not believe that the right to life, as a right pertaining to persons, admits of no exceptions whatever; but the right of the innocent to life admits surely of few exceptions indeed." However, the church also recognizes that in some instances abortion is "morally preferable to any available alternative." It does not appear that the official position of the Church of England on abortion has changed since 1980.

The Anglican Church of Australia

In December 2007, the Melbourne diocese recommended that abortion be decriminalized, on the basis that "the moral significance [of the embryo] increases with the age and development of the foetus". It is interesting to note that the committee representing the Melbourne diocese was comprised of women. The Anglican Church of Australia, however, has not taken an official position on the abortion issue to date.

QUAKERS

The Quakers, as with other contentious issues, has not taken an official stance on the issue of abortion. It is worth noting, however, that the American Friends Service Committee voiced support for abortion rights in the 1970's.

CHRISTIAN CHURCH (DISCIPLES OF CHRIST)

The Christian Church known as the Disciples of Christ has officially confirmed support for a woman's right to reproductive freedom, for freedom and responsibility of conscience of each individual, and for the sacredness of life of all persons. The Church has consistently opposed legislation seeking to impose on all Americans any specific religious belief regarding abortion.

COMMUNITY OF CHRIST

The Community of Christ states that they recognize that there is inadequacy in any simplistic answer that defines all abortion as murder or as a simple medical procedure, and recognize a woman's right in deciding the continuation or termination of pregnancy.

CHURCH OF GOD IN CHRIST

The Church of God in Christ (COGIC) is a traditionally pro-life Pentecostal Christian denomination, both male and female leaders and clergy of COGIC have always ardently voiced and actively taken opposition to all types of abortions, "except only in the absolutely necessary case of saving the life of the mother."

PRESBYTERIAN CHURCHES

Presbyterian Church (U.S.A.)

In 2006, the General Assembly, the governing body of the Presbyterian Church (U.S.A.), confirmed its position that the termination of a pregnancy is a personal decision. The Presbyterian Church (U.S.A.) remains pro-choice. While the church disapproves of abortion as a means of birth control or as a method of convenience, it seeks "to maintain within its fellowship those who, on the basis of a study of Scripture and prayerful decision, come to diverse conclusions and actions" on the issue. The church believes that the choice to receive an elective abortion can be "morally acceptable," however, the denomination does not condone late abortions where the fetus is viable and the mother's life is not in danger.

Other Presbyterian Denominations

The Orthodox Presbyterian Church, the Presbyterian Church in America, the Reformed Church in America, and the Christian Reformed Church in North America are all pro-life.

United Church of Christ

The United Church of Christ has strongly supported abortion rights since 1971 and remains a strong advocate of a woman's reproductive rights, including the right to a medically safe abortion. The church is an organizational member of the National Abortion and Reproductive Rights Action League.

METHODIST CHURCHES

United Methodist Church

The United Methodist Church was a founding member of the Religious Coalition for Reproductive Choice in 1973, the year the *Roe v. Wade* decision was issued by the U.S. Supreme Court. The website of the Coalition contained the following statement: "Subsequently, if sex serves purposes beyond reproduction, then a woman has the legal right to both prevent and interrupt a pregnancy". Interestingly, the Taskforce of United Methodists on Abortion and Sexuality was formed in 1987 to further the pro-life ministry in The United Methodist Church. In 2008 the United Methodist General Conference went on record as continuing to support the work of the Religious Coalition for Reproductive Choice. Since that time, however, there has been a growing conservative movement on social issues, including abortion, among the United Methodist Church membership. The result was that, on May 19, 2016, the General Conference voted to withdraw support of the Religious Coalition for Reproductive Choice. The vote of delegates attending the

General Conference was 425-268, manifesting a very decided change in the attitude of United Methodists regarding the issue of abortion.

While the United Methodist Church now opposes abortion, it affirms that it is "equally bound to respect the sacredness of the life and well-being of the mother and the unborn child." The church sanctions "the legal option of abortion under proper medical procedures" but rejects abortion as a method of gender selection or birth control and stresses that those considering abortions should prayerfully seek guidance from their doctors, families and ministers.

The Methodist Church of Great Britain

The Methodist Church of Great Britain (MCGB) believes its congregants should work toward the elimination of the need for abortion by advocating for social support for mothers. The MCGB further states that "Abortion must not be regarded as an alternative to contraception, nor is it to be justified merely as a method of birth control. The termination of any form of human life cannot be regarded superficially and abortion should not be available on demand, but should remain subject to a legal framework, to responsible counselling and to medical judgement."

AMERICAN BAPTIST CHURCH IN THE U.S.A.

The American Baptist Church in the U.S.A. recognizes the different views on abortion among its members. Accordingly, the American Baptist Churches' General Board encourages women and couples considering the procedure "to seek spiritual counsel as they prayerfully and conscientiously consider their decision." Though the board opposes abortion "as a means of avoiding responsibility for conception, as a primary means of birth control, and without regard for the far-reaching consequences of the act," it does not condemn abortion outright. The church has no official policy on when personhood begins, on whether there are situations in which abortion is acceptable, on whether there should be laws to protect the unborn, or whether there should be laws protecting women's reproductive rights, including the right to choose an abortion.

SOUTHERN BAPTISTS

Former Southern Baptist Convention President W.A. Criswell (1969-1970) welcomed *Roe v. Wade*, saying that "I have always felt that it was only after a child was born and had a life separate from its mother that it became an individual person." He further stated, "and it has always, therefore, seemed to me that what is best for the mother and for the future should be allowed." This was a common attitude among evangelicals at the time. Unsurprisingly, Criswell would later reverse himself on his earlier position.

During the 1971 Southern Baptist Convention, the delegates passed a resolution recognizing that "Christians in the American society today are faced with difficult decisions about abortion", stating that laws should recognize the "sanctity of human life, including fetal life", and calling upon Southern Baptists to work for laws allowing abortion in extreme cases such as rape, severe fetal deformity, and the health of the mother. The stance was described in the media as "hedging" on abortion and a resolution opposing all abortions was defeated. W. Barry Garrett wrote in the *Baptist Press*, "Religious liberty, human equality and justice are advanced by the [Roe v. Wade] Supreme Court Decision." In 1980, the SBC revised their 1971 position by only making exceptions for the life of the mother.

Today, the Southern Baptist Convention, the largest Protestant denomination in the United States, opposes elective abortion except to save the life of the mother. The Southern Baptist Convention calls on Southern Baptists to work to change the laws in order to make abortion illegal in most cases. Richard Land, president of the Southern Baptist Convention's Ethics and Religious Liberty Commission from 1988 to 2013, said that he believes abortion is more damaging than anything else, even poverty.

In a 1996 resolution on partial-birth abortion, the Southern Baptist Convention reaffirmed its opposition to abortion, stating that "all human life is a sacred gift from our sovereign God and therefore … all abortions, except in those very rare cases where the life of the mother is clearly in danger, are wrong."

NATIONAL ASSOCIATION OF EVANGELICALS

The National Association of Evangelicals has passed a number of resolutions, most recently in 2010, stating its opposition to abortion. However, the organization recognizes that there might be situations in which terminating a pregnancy is warranted – such as protecting the life of a mother or in cases of rape or incest.

National Council of Churches

Because of the diverse theological teachings of its member churches, the National Council of Churches does not have an official position on abortion. The NCC instead seeks to provide a space where members can come together and exchange views.

Church of Jesus Christ of Latter Day Saints

Although the Church of Jesus Christ of Latter-day Saints (LDS Church) is not a Protestant faith, its founder, Joseph Smith, as well as all of the early leaders of the church, came from a Protestant background. The church teaches that "elective abortion for personal or social convenience is contrary to the will and the commandments of God." Therefore, the church says, any facilitation of or support for this kind of abortion warrants excommunication from the church. However, the church believes that certain circumstances can justify abortion, such as a pregnancy that threatens the life of the mother or that has come about as the result of rape or incest.

Although not a matter of overt doctrine, it appears that the church takes the position that ensoulment may occur at conception, but if the child is not born alive, the soul returns to a pre-existence and is later granted another opportunity to be born to mortality.

Unitarian Universalist Association

The Unitarian Universalist Association (UUA) is a liberal religious association of Unitarian Universalist congregations. It was formed in 1961 by the consolidation of the American Unitarian Association and the Universalist Church of America. Both of these predecessor organizations began as Christian denominations of the Unitarian and Universalist varieties respectively. Although some of the congregations of the UUA regard themselves as having a Protestant Christian identity, and Unitarian Universalists state that from these traditions comes a deep regard for intellectual freedom and inclusive love, modern Unitarian Universalists see themselves as a separate religion with its own beliefs and affinities.

UUA is devoted to a "free and responsible search for truth and meaning." Unitarian Universalists assert no creed, but instead are unified by their shared search for spiritual growth. As a result, their congregations are welcoming of and include many atheists, agnostics, and theists within their membership. The UUA members and congregations draw wisdom from various religions and philosophies, including humanism, pantheism, Christianity, Hinduism, Buddhism, Taoism, Judaism, Islam, and Earth-centered spirituality. The UUA reportedly has approximately 600,000 members at present in the United States.

Beginning in 1963, the Unitarian Universalist Association of Congregations (UUA) passed a series of resolutions to support "the right to choose contraception and abortion as a legitimate expression of our constitutional rights."

SUMMARY OF RELIGIOUS CONSIDERATIONS

Although the author had some sense of the varying religious beliefs relating to abortion before commencing the research that led to the above presentation, the research was interesting and enlightening. Particularly interesting were the varying positions on when "ensoulment" occurs. The positions range from conception to first breath at live birth.

The most widely held belief among Muslim scholars and adherents is that ensoulment occurs at 4 months following conception. Iran, the dominant Shiite Muslim country, seems to rely heavily on the 4-month ensoulment period as a foundation for its laws allowing therapeutic and non-therapeutic abortions before ensoulment occurs at 4 months. Sunni scholars seem to generally agree that abortion should be allowed up to 4 months, "if necessary", and the prevailing view is that abortion prior to ensoulment is not a serious sin.

The prevailing view in Hinduism seems to be that ensoulment occurs at conception. However, despite that prevailing belief, the laws of the Republic of India generally allow abortion up to 20 weeks of gestation.

The traditional view in Buddhism also seems to be that life begins at conception, and that abortion is a disruption of the progress of the person through the cycle of rebirth and death as the person progresses toward Nirvana. However, the analysis of abortion under Buddhism, is not a question of the right to life of the fetus in contrast to the right to choose of the mother. It is a question of harm versus benefit. The question is what approach will result in the minimization of human suffering. Buddhists generally do not advocate for laws interfering with the decision-making process by the woman.

In Judaism, there is no definitive belief about when ensoulment occurs. However, it is clear that under Jewish law, a fetus is not considered to be a person, and is, therefore, not entitled to the protections afforded to persons. A fetus attains the status of a full person only at birth. The Talmud states that the ancient rabbis regarded a fetus as part of the woman until the birth of the child.   This concept supports the broadly held belief among Jewish scholars and adherents, including Orthodox, Conservative, and Reform Jews, that, regardless of the theological and ethical viewpoint held on abortion, women should be solely empowered and solely responsible to make decisions concerning their own bodies, including particularly decisions regarding obtaining an abortion.

The many Christian denominations have widely divergent views regarding when ensoulment occurs, and accordingly, on the issue of whether and when abortion is permissible. Even the position of the Roman Catholic Church, which presently strongly advocates for ensoulment occurring at conception and for abortion being prohibited at any time after conception, has been subject to variability over the centuries. Although the Catholic Church presently claims to have always opposed abortion at any stage, that position seems to be controverted by the teachings of the highly revered St. Thomas Aquinas (1225-1274), Doctor of the Church, who taught that ensoulment occurred at quickening, when the woman first felt movement of the fetus.

As will be obvious from the discussion presented above, the multitude of Christian Protestant Denominations have widely divergent views on ensoulment and on whether and when abortion should be permitted. The same is true for denominations claiming a Christian foundation that is neither Catholic nor Protestant. The LDS Church, for instance, apparently adheres to the belief that although a soul may be affiliated with a fetus, if the child is not borne alive, whether by miscarriage or abortion, the soul returns to God and then is later afforded another opportunity for birth.

Where does the consideration of the religious implications lead us? The author suggests that, as hard as it may be for those of us with deeply held religious beliefs that tend to define our beliefs relating to abortion, we must admit that what drives our convictions are our religious beliefs. Further, the author suggests that those of us with deeply held religious beliefs must admit to ourselves that it is inappropriate and un-American for the beliefs of a particular religious denomination or group of denominations to impose those religious beliefs upon others who do not share those beliefs. Further, we must make those admissions even if the majority of us share the beliefs. Regardless of whether the belief is shared by a majority of us, it is still a religious belief. This is America, not a theocracy. We must allow others to accept the moral responsibility for their actions in accordance with their faith or beliefs, not ours. That is the advanced citizenship that is America.

RELIGION CONSIDERATIONS OF COURT IN *ROE V. WADE*.

The author found it interesting, after researching the position of the various religions on abortion as described above, that the U.S. Supreme Court in deciding *Roe v. Wade*, had gone through some of the same kind of analysis and summarized a historical review of the treatment of the abortion question by the principal religions of the United States. Following is an excerpt from *Roe v. Wade*.

> Texas urges that, apart from the Fourteenth Amendment, life begins at conception and is present throughout pregnancy, and that, therefore, the State has a compelling interest in protecting that life from and after conception. We need not resolve the difficult question of when life begins. When those trained in the respective disciplines of medicine, philosophy, and theology are unable to arrive at any consensus, the judiciary, at this point in the development of man's knowledge, is not in a position to speculate as to the answer.
>
> It should be sufficient to note briefly the wide divergence of thinking on this most sensitive and difficult question. There has always been strong support for the view that life does not begin until live birth. This was the belief of the Stoics. [Footnote

56] It appears to be the predominant, though not the unanimous, attitude of the Jewish faith. [Footnote 57] It may be taken to represent also the position of a large segment of the Protestant community, insofar as that can be ascertained; organized groups that have taken a formal position on the abortion issue have generally regarded abortion as a matter for the conscience of the individual and her family. [Footnote 58] As we have noted, the common law found greater significance in quickening. Physicians and their scientific colleagues have regarded that event with less interest and have tended to focus either upon conception, upon live birth, or upon the interim point at which the fetus becomes "viable," that is, potentially able to live outside the mother's womb, albeit with artificial aid. [Footnote 59] Viability is usually placed at about seven months (28 weeks) but may occur earlier, even at 24 weeks. [Footnote 60] The Aristotelian theory of "mediate animation," that held sway throughout the Middle Ages and the Renaissance in Europe, continued to be official Roman Catholic dogma until the 19th century, despite opposition to this "ensoulment" theory from those in the Church who would recognize the existence of life from the moment of conception. [Footnote 61] The latter is now, of course, the official belief of the Catholic Church. As one brief *amicus* discloses, this is a view strongly held by many non-Catholics as well, and by many physicians. Substantial problems for precise definition of this view are posed, however, by new embryological data that purport to indicate that conception is a "process" over time, rather than an event, and by new medical techniques such as menstrual extraction, the "morning-after" pill, implantation of embryos, artificial insemination, and even artificial wombs. [Footnote 62]

In areas other than criminal abortion, the law has been reluctant to endorse any theory that life, as we recognize it, begins before live birth, or to accord legal rights to the unborn except in narrowly defined situations and except when the rights are contingent upon live birth. For example, the traditional rule of tort law denied recovery for prenatal injuries even though the child was born alive. [Footnote 63] That rule has been changed in almost every jurisdiction. In most States, recovery is said to be permitted only if the fetus was viable, or at least quick, when the injuries were sustained, though few courts have squarely so held. [Footnote 64] In a recent development, generally opposed by the commentators, some States permit the parents of a stillborn child to maintain an action for wrongful death because of prenatal injuries. [Footnote 65] Such an action, however, would appear to be one to vindicate the parents' interest and is thus consistent with the view that the fetus, at most, represents only the potentiality of life. Similarly, unborn children have been recognized as acquiring rights or interests by way of inheritance or other devolution of property, and have been represented by guardians *ad litem.* [Footnote 66] Perfection of the interests involved, again, has generally been contingent upon live birth. In short, the unborn have never been recognized in the law as persons in the whole sense.

In view of all this, we do not agree that, by adopting one theory of life, Texas may override the rights of the pregnant woman that are at stake.

CHAPTER 5

ROE V. WADE

In considering the profound questions presented to it in the case of *Roe v. Wade*, the U.S. Supreme Court seemed to focus on two preeminent factors. The first was a woman's right to privacy and the second was the stage of viability of a fetus. The court found that a woman had a fundamental right to privacy which substantially limited the right of government to interfere with the reproductive process. That right to privacy was deemed by the Court to be a competing interest against the interest of a state in protecting an unborn.

In summary, the court ruled that:

1.   During the first trimester (12 weeks gestation) a state could not regulate abortion.

2.   During the second trimester (week 13 through week 28 gestation), a state had a limited power to regulate abortion, that being limited to protect the health and safety of the woman.

3.   During the third trimester (week 29 until birth), a state could prohibit abortion.

A principal factor upon which the foregoing was based was a decision by the court, based upon scientific evidence presented to it, that the earliest stage of viability for a fetus was at the end of the second trimester (28 weeks gestational age). The court having decided that a fetus was viable at the end of the second trimester, the state could then intervene, notwithstanding a woman's right to privacy, to protect the unborn.

At this point a widespread misunderstanding regarding *Roe v. Wade* must be cleared up. Many of us average citizens, and, alas, many of the politicians and public figures, who have criticized the *Roe v. Wade* decision and have supported efforts to have *Roe v. Wade* overturned, believe that if *Roe v. Wade* were overturned, then abortion would be illegal in the United States. Even in the most extreme retraction of the *Roe v. Wade* decision, the Supreme Court would simply rule that the question of abortion is a matter of state's rights, i.e., within the realm of the state to regulate health and welfare, and then abortion would become, as it was before *Roe v. Wade*, a matter of state law. The result would be that some states would undoubtedly proceed to make all abortions illegal or would impose very strict limitations on abortion. Other states would likely permit abortions and some states would likely continue to have liberal abortion laws. While the increased difficulty in obtaining an abortion would undoubtedly result in some reduction in the total number of abortions, at least initially, it is unlikely that it would ultimately make a significant difference. If, on the other hand, the right of privacy were more severely limited by a decision reversing or modifying *Roe v. Wade*, such as substantially lowering the stage of viability or imposing a different gestational stage standard, the U.S. Congress could seek to enact a national law imposing uniform and substantially stricter abortion standards for the entire United States.

The English law and American law history of abortion stated by the Supreme Court in *Roe v. Wade* is interesting, and it mirrors some of our previous discussion.

> 3. *The common law.* It is undisputed that, at common law, abortion performed before "quickening" -- the first recognizable movement of the fetus *in utero*, appearing usually from the 16th to the 18th week of pregnancy [Footnote 20] -- was not an indictable offense. [Footnote 21] The absence of a common law

crime for pre-quickening abortion appears to have developed from a confluence of earlier philosophical, theological, and civil and canon law concepts of when life begins. These disciplines variously approached the question in terms of the point at which the embryo or fetus became "formed" or recognizably human, or in terms of when a "person" came into being, that is, infused with a "soul" or "animated." A loose consensus evolved in early English law that these events occurred at some point between conception and live birth. [Footnote 22] This was "mediate animation." Although Christian theology and the canon law came to fix the point of animation at 40 days for a male and 80 days for a female, a view that persisted until the 19th century, there was otherwise little agreement about the precise time of formation or animation. There was agreement, however, that, prior to this point, the fetus was to be regarded as part of the mother, and its destruction, therefore, was not homicide. Due to continued uncertainty about the precise time when animation occurred, to the lack of any empirical basis for the 40-80-day view, and perhaps to Aquinas' definition of movement as one of the two first principles of life, Bracton focused upon quickening as the critical point. The significance of quickening was echoed by later common law scholars, and found its way into the received common law in this country.

Whether abortion of a quick fetus was a felony at common law, or even a lesser crime, is still disputed. Bracton, writing early in the 13th century, thought it homicide. [Footnote 23] But the later and predominant view, following the great common law scholars, has been that it was, at most, a lesser offense. In a frequently cited passage, Coke took the position that abortion of a woman "quick with childe" is "a great misprision, and no murder." [Footnote 24] Blackstone followed, saying that, while abortion after quickening had once been considered manslaughter (though not murder), "modern law" took a less severe view. [Footnote 25] A recent review of the common law precedents argues, however, that those precedents contradict Coke, and that even post-quickening abortion was never established as a common law crime. [Footnote 26] This is of some importance, because, while most American courts ruled, in holding or dictum, that abortion of an unquickened fetus was not criminal under their received common law, [Footnote 27] others followed Coke in stating that abortion of a quick fetus was a "misprision," a term they translated to mean "misdemeanor." [Footnote 28] That their reliance on Coke on this aspect of the law was uncritical and, apparently in all the reported cases, dictum (due probably to the paucity of common law prosecutions for post-quickening abortion), makes it now appear doubtful that abortion was ever firmly established as a common law crime even with respect to the destruction of a quick fetus.

4. *The English statutory law.* England's first criminal abortion statute, Lord Ellenborough's Act, 43 Geo. 3, c. 58, came in 1803. It made abortion of a quick fetus, § 1, a capital crime, but, in § 2, it provided lesser penalties for the felony of abortion before quickening, and thus preserved the "quickening" distinction. This contrast was continued in the general revision of 1828, 9 Geo. 4, c. 31, § 13. It disappeared, however, together with the death penalty, in 1837, 7 Will. 4 & 1 Vict., c. 85. § 6, and did not reappear in the Offenses Against the Person Act of 1861, 24 & 25 Vict., c. 100, § 59, that formed the core of English anti-abortion law until the liberalizing reforms of 1967. In 1929, the Infant Life (Preservation) Act, 19 & 20 Geo. 5, c. 34, came into being. Its emphasis was upon the destruction of "the life of a child capable of being born alive." It made a willful act performed with the necessary intent a felony. It contained a proviso that one was not to be found guilty of the offense "unless it is proved that the act which caused the death of the child was not done in good faith for the purpose only of preserving the life of the mother."

A seemingly notable development in the English law was the case of *Rex v. Bourne*, [1939] 1 K.B. 687. This case apparently answered in the affirmative the question whether an abortion necessary to preserve the life of the pregnant woman was excepted from the criminal penalties of the 1861 Act. In his instructions to the jury, Judge Macnaghten referred to the 1929 Act, and observed that that Act related to "the case where a child is killed by a willful act at the time when it is being delivered in the ordinary course of nature." *Id.* at 691. He concluded that the 1861 Act's use of the word "unlawfully," imported the same meaning expressed by the specific proviso in the 1929 Act, even though there was no mention of preserving the mother's life in the 1861 Act. He then construed the phrase "preserving the life of the mother" broadly, that is, "in a reasonable sense," to include a serious and permanent threat to the mother's health, and instructed the jury to acquit Dr. Bourne if it found he had acted in a good faith belief that the abortion was necessary for this purpose. *Id.* at 693-694. The jury did acquit.

Recently, Parliament enacted a new abortion law. This is the Abortion Act of 1967, 15 & 16 Eliz. 2, c. 87. The Act permits a licensed physician to perform an abortion where two other licensed physicians agree (a) "that the continuance of the pregnancy would involve risk to the life of the pregnant woman, or of injury to the physical or mental health of the pregnant woman or any existing children of her family, greater than if the pregnancy were terminated,"
or (b) "that there is a substantial risk that, if the child were born it would suffer from such physical or mental abnormalities as to be seriously handicapped." The Act also provides that, in making this determination, "account may be taken of the pregnant woman's actual or reasonably foreseeable environment." It also permits a physician, without the concurrence of others, to terminate a pregnancy where he is of the good faith opinion that the abortion "is immediately necessary to save the life or to prevent grave permanent injury to the physical or mental health of the pregnant woman."

5. *The American law.* In this country, the law in effect in all but a few States until mid-19th century was the preexisting English common law. Connecticut, the first State to enact abortion legislation, adopted in 1821 that part of Lord Ellenborough's Act that related to a woman "quick with child." [Footnote 29] The death penalty was not imposed. Abortion before quickening was made a crime in that State only in 1860. [Footnote 30] In 1828, New York enacted legislation [Footnote 31] that, in two respects, was to serve as a model for early anti-abortion statutes. First, while barring destruction of an unquickened fetus as well as a quick fetus, it made the former only a misdemeanor, but the latter second-degree manslaughter. Second, it incorporated a concept of therapeutic abortion by providing that an abortion was excused if it "shall have been necessary to preserve the life of such mother, or shall have been advised by two physicians to be necessary for such purpose."

By 1840, when Texas had received the common law, [Footnote 32] only eight American States had statutes dealing with abortion. [Footnote 33] It was not until after the War Between the States that legislation began generally to replace the common law. Most of these initial statutes dealt severely with abortion after quickening, but were lenient with it before quickening. Most punished attempts equally with completed abortions. While many statutes included the exception for an abortion thought by one or more physicians to be necessary to save the mother's life, that provision soon disappeared, and the typical law required that the procedure actually be necessary for that purpose. Gradually, in the middle and late 19th century, the quickening distinction disappeared from the statutory law of most States and the degree of the offense and the penalties were increased. By the end of the 1950's, a large majority of the jurisdictions banned abortion, however and whenever performed, unless done to save or preserve the life of the mother. [Footnote 34] The exceptions, Alabama and the District of Columbia, permitted abortion to preserve the mother's health. [Footnote 35] Three States permitted abortions that were not "unlawfully" performed or that were not "without lawful justification," leaving interpretation of those standards to the courts. [Footnote 36] In the past several years, however, a trend toward liberalization of abortion statutes has resulted in adoption, by about one-third of the States, of less stringent laws, most of them patterned after the ALI Model Penal Code, § 230.3, [Footnote 37] set forth as Appendix B to the opinion in *Doe v. Bolton, post*, p. 205.

It is thus apparent that, at common law, at the time of the adoption of our Constitution, and throughout the major portion of the 19th century, abortion was viewed with less disfavor than under most American statutes currently in effect. Phrasing it another way, a woman enjoyed a substantially broader right to terminate a pregnancy than she does in most States today. At least with respect to the early stage of pregnancy, and very possibly without such a limitation, the opportunity to make this choice was present in this country well into the 19th century. Even later, the law continued for some time to treat less punitively an abortion procured in early pregnancy.

The Court recognized, in *Roe v. Wade*, the long standing religious, ethical, philosophical, legal and scientific concerns over the abortion issue. Many of us with strong religious convictions have, since the time the *Roe v. Wade* decision was handed down, either struggled to view the decision objectively or have rejected it outright. The author was certainly among that group. However, after much agonizing review and reflection on the decision, the author has concluded that the Court carefully considered all the concerns and reached a conclusion that appropriately respects the conflicting positions. Perhaps the decision just needs to be adjusted, preferably by federal statute, or alternatively by a further Supreme Court decision, to reflect current science related to viability.

CHAPTER 6

ABORTION STATISTICS AND TRENDS

Along with the common misconceptions about the basic scientific facts relating to the abortion issue, which we have discussed extensively, there also appears to be a multitude of prevalent misconceptions about the status, practice, statistics and trends relating to abortion.

Initially, it should be noted that the Centers for Disease Control and Prevention ("CDC"), the US Government public health watchdog agency, collects extensive data on abortion and has done so since at least 1969. The CDC began formally collecting data and preparing "surveillance reports" in 1969, documenting the number and characteristics of women obtaining "legal induced abortions". The term "induced abortion," as it is commonly used in publications, means an abortion caused by a physical procedure performed on or a drug taken by or administered to the woman, as opposed to a miscarriage or other unintended abortion.

The CDC compiles the information on legal induced abortions that most states, the District of Columbia and New York City collect, and uses that information to produce national estimates. The annual CDC estimates are derived from actual counts of every abortion reported to state health departments. However, reporting to the CDC is not mandatory, and some states choose not to report abortions to the CDC. If all the states, the District of Columbia and New York City reported, there would be 52 reporting entities. However, at present only 47 states report and so the CDC receives data from only 49 of the 52 potential data sources. Because not all abortions are reported by the abortion service providers, and because not all states report to the CDC, CDC surveillance reports undercount the actual number of abortions in the US.

The other principal source of abortion statistics is the Guttmacher Institute. The Guttmacher Institute uses a different methodology than the CDC. Guttmacher does not rely solely on state, DC, and NYC reports, as does the CDC, but also periodically surveys abortion providers in all the states. Based upon the more reliable and comprehensive database, Guttmacher produces the most reliable estimates of the total number of abortions in the US for each year.

For 2014, the Guttmacher Institute reported 926,200 abortions, an abortion rate of 14.6 abortions per 1,000 women aged 15 to 44 years. For 2014, the CDC reported only 652,639 abortions, which is only 70% of the Guttmacher estimate. For 2015, CDC reported 638,169 abortions. The abortion rate, based upon the CDC collected data was 11.8 abortions per 1,000 women aged 15 to 44 years, and the abortion ratio was 188 abortions per 1,000 live births. Comparison of the CDC data for 2014 and 2015, confirms the decreasing abortion rate that is evident from the Guttmacher data. Between 1970 and 2015, the CDC has reported nearly 45.7 million legal induced abortions. A more accurate estimate of the actual total number of abortions in the US since 1973 through the end of 2019, is 61.6 million, based upon Guttmacher data. **That's 61.6 million!**

The Guttmacher Institute describes its work and its objectives on its website as follows:

> The Guttmacher Institute is a primary source for research and policy analysis on abortion in the United States. In many cases, Guttmacher's data are more comprehensive than state and federal government sources. The Institute's work examines the incidence of abortion, access to care and barriers to obtaining

services, factors underlying women's decisions to terminate a pregnancy, characteristics of women who have abortions and the conditions under which women obtain them. Guttmacher also tracks abortion-related legislation and policies at the federal and state level, promoting access to abortion services and making an evidence-based case against restrictions that limit access.

Although Guttmacher is a decidedly pro-choice organization, the data collection and analysis of that data are generally considered to be reliable by abortion supporters and abortion opposers alike. In fact, Guttmacher is the primary source of data and data analysis generally relied upon and referred to by abortion opposers. This includes, for instance, the abortion counts reported by US Abortion Clock.org, in the *www.abortioncounters.com* webpage.

Some general observations or conclusions reached by Guttmacher based upon the data it has collected, are:

Eighteen percent of pregnancies (excluding miscarriages) in 2017 ended in abortion.[1]

Approximately 862,320 abortions were performed in 2017, down 7% from 926,190 in 2014.

The abortion rate in 2017 was 13.5 abortions per 1,000 women aged 15–44, down 8% from 14.6 per 1,000 in 2014.[1] This is the lowest rate ever observed in the United States; in 1973, the year abortion became legal, the rate was 16.3.[2]

As of September 1, 2019, 29 states were considered hostile toward abortion rights, 14 states were considered supportive and seven states were somewhere in between.[3]

In 2019, 58% of U.S. women of reproductive age (nearly 40 million women) lived in states that were considered hostile to abortion rights. In contrast, 24 million women of reproductive age (35% of the total) lived in states that were supportive of abortion rights.[3]

At 2014 abortion rates, about one in four (24%) women will have an abortion by age 45.[4]

More than half of all U.S. abortion patients in 2014 were in their 20s: Patients aged 20–24 obtained 34% of all abortions, and patients aged 25–29 obtained 27%.[5] Adolescents made up 12% of abortion patients in 2014: Those aged 18–19 accounted for 8% of all abortions, 15–17-year-olds for 3% and those younger than 15 for 0.2%.[5]

White patients accounted for 39% of abortion procedures in 2014, black patients for 28%, Hispanic patients for 25%, and patients of other races and ethnicities for 9%.[5]

Seventeen percent of abortion patients in 2014 identified themselves as mainline Protestant, 13% as evangelical Protestant and 24% as Catholic, while 38% reported no religious affiliation and the remaining 8% reported some other affiliation.[5]

The vast majority (94%) of abortion patients in 2014 identified as heterosexual or straight. Four percent of patients said they were bisexual; 0.3% identified as homosexual, gay or lesbian; and 1% identified as "something else."[5]

Fifty-nine percent of abortions in 2014 were obtained by patients who had had at least one birth.[5]

Some 75% of abortion patients in 2014 were poor (having an income below the federal poverty level of $15,730 for a family of two in 2014) or low-income (having an income of 100–199% of the federal poverty level).[5]

In 2014, 16% of patients who obtained abortions in the United States were born outside the United States, a proportion comparable to their representation in the U.S. population (17% of women aged 15–44).[5]

In 2014, 51% of abortion patients were using a contraceptive method in the month they became pregnant, most commonly condoms (24%) or a short-acting hormonal method (13%).[6]

In 2017, there were 808 clinics providing abortion services, a 2% increase from 2014. However, between 2014 and 2017, regional- and state-level disparities in abortion access grew: The number of clinics increased in the Northeast (by 16%) and the West (by 4%) and decreased in the Midwest (by 6%) and the South (by 9%).[1]

Seventy-two percent (72%) of clinics offered abortions up to 12 weeks' gestation in 2014, 25% up to 20 weeks and 10% up to 24 weeks.[7]

A committee of the National Academies of Sciences, Engineering and Medicine reviewed the available evidence and confirmed in a 2018 report that abortion is safe and effective.[9]
Exhaustive reviews by panels convened by the U.S. and UK governments have concluded that there is no association between abortion and breast cancer. There is also no indication that abortion is a risk factor for other cancers.[10]

In 2014, the average amount paid for an abortion with local anesthesia in a nonhospital setting at 10 weeks' gestation was $508. The average paid for an early medication abortion (up to nine weeks' gestation) was $535.[7]

Most U.S. abortion patients had health insurance in 2014. Thirty-five percent had Medicaid coverage, while 31% had private insurance.[5] However, insurance does not necessarily cover abortion services; even when it does, patients may not use their coverage for a variety of reasons (for example, because they do not know their plan covers it, they are concerned about confidentiality or their provider does not accept their plan).[11]

Overall, 53% of abortion patients paid out of pocket for their procedure in 2014.[5]

The Hyde Amendment currently bans the use of federal dollars for abortion coverage for people enrolled in Medicaid, the nation's main public health insurance program for low-income individuals. Similar restrictions apply to other federal programs and operate to deny abortion care or coverage to people with disabilities, Native Americans, prison inmates, poor and low-income individuals in the District of Columbia, military personnel and federal employees.[12]

Although the Hyde Amendment bars federal funds from being used to provide Medicaid coverage of abortion, states may use their own, nonfederal funds. Fifteen states have a policy requiring the state to provide abortion coverage under Medicaid.[13]

In 2014, Medicaid was the second-most-common method of payment and was reported by 24% of abortion patients. The overwhelming majority of these patients lived in the 15 states that allowed state funds to be used to pay for abortion.[5] Fifteen percent of patients used private insurance to pay for the procedure. Most patients with private insurance (61%) paid out of pocket.[5]

In 2014, 65% of abortion patients traveled less than 25 miles one way to obtain care, 17% traveled 25–49 miles, 10% traveled 50–100 miles and 8% traveled more than 100 miles.[14]
Greater distances to abortion facilities are associated with increased burden on patients, including higher out-of-pocket costs for associated services such as food, lodging and child care; lost wages;[15] increased difficulty getting to the clinic;[16] delayed care;[17] and decreased use of abortion services.[18]

Abortion patients who lived in states with waiting period requirements and adolescents who lived in parental notification states traveled farther than those in states without such laws.[14]

The proportion of abortion patients who traveled more than 100 miles for services was twice as high among those at or beyond 16 weeks of gestation as among those who were at 12 weeks' gestation or less (14% vs. 7%).[14]

If *Roe v. Wade* were overturned or weakened, increases in travel distances would likely prevent 93,500 to 143,500 individuals each year from accessing abortion care.[19]

If *Roe v. Wade* were overturned or weakened, abortion patients' average distance to the nearest facility would increase by 97 miles, from 25 to 122 miles.[19]

Guttmacher cites the following references for the observations and conclusions stated above.

1. Jones RK et al., *Abortion Incidence and Service Availability in the United States, 2017,* New York: Guttmacher Institute, 2019, https://www.guttmacher.org/report/abortion-incidence-service-availability-us-2017.
2. Jones RK and Jerman J, Abortion incidence and service availability in the United States, 2011, *Perspectives on Sexual and Reproductive Health*, 2014, 46(1):3–14, doi:10.1363/46e0414.
3. Guttmacher Institute, *State Abortion Policy Landscape: From Hostile to Supportive,* 2019, https://www.guttmacher.org/article/2018/12/state-abortion-policy-landscape-hostile-supportive.
4. Jones RK and Jerman J, Population group abortion rates and lifetime incidence of abortion: United States, 2008–2014, *American Journal of Public Health*, 2017, doi:10.2105/AJPH.2017.304042.
5. Jerman J, Jones RK and Onda T, *Characteristics of U.S. Abortion Patients in 2014 and Changes Since 2008*, New York: Guttmacher Institute, 2016, https://www.guttmacher.org/report/characteristics-us-abortion-patients-2014.
6. Jones RK, Reported contraceptive use in the month of becoming pregnant among U.S. abortion patients in 2000 and 2014, *Contraception*, 2018, doi:10.1016/j.contraception.2017.12.018.
7. Jones RK, Ingerick M and Jerman J, Differences in abortion service delivery in hostile, middle-ground and supportive states in 2014, *Women's Health Issues*, 2018, doi:10.1016/j.whi.2017.12.003.

8. Jatlaoui TC et al., Abortion surveillance—United States, 2013, *Morbidity and Mortality Weekly Report*, 2016, Vol. 65, No. SS-12, https://www.cdc.gov/mmwr/volumes/65/ss/ss6512a1.htm.
9. National Academies of Sciences, Engineering and Medicine, *The Safety and Quality of Abortion Care in the United States,* 2018, http://www8.nationalacademies.org/onpinews/newsitem.aspx?RecordID=24950.
10. Boonstra HD et al., *Abortion in Women's Lives*, New York: Guttmacher Institute, 2006, https://www.guttmacher.org/report/abortion-womens-lives.
11. Jones RK, Upadhyay UD and Weitz TA, At what cost?: payment for abortion care by U.S. women, *Women's Health Issues,* 2003, 23(3):e173-e178.
12. Donovan M, In real life: federal restrictions on abortion coverage and the women they impact, *Guttmacher Policy Review*, 2017, 20:1-7, https://www.guttmacher.org/gpr/2017/01/real-life-federal-restrictions-abortion-coverage-and-women-they-impact.
13. Guttmacher Institute, State funding of abortion under Medicaid, *State Laws and Policies (as of January 2018)*, 2018, https://www.guttmacher.org/state-policy/explore/state-funding-abortion-under-medicaid.
14. Fuentes L and Jerman J, Distance traveled to obtain clinical abortion care in the United States and reasons for clinic choice, *Journal of Women's Health,* 2019, https://doi.org/10.1089/jwh.2018.7496.
15. Gerdts C et al., Impact of clinic closures on women obtaining abortion services after implementation of a restrictive law in Texas, *American Journal of Public Health,* 2016, 106:857–864.
16. Upadhyay UD et al., Denial of abortion because of provider gestational age limits in the United States, *American Journal of Public Health,* 2014, 104:1687–1694.
17. White K et al., Experiences accessing abortion care in Alabama among women traveling for services, *Women's Health Issues*, 2016, 26:298–304.
18. Joyce T, Tan R and Zhang Y, Abortion before & after *Roe, Journal of Health Economics*, 2013, 32:804–815.
19. Myers C, Jones RK and Upadhyay UD, Predicted changes in abortion access and incidence in a post-*Roe* world,

Contraception, 2019,
https://doi.org/10.1016/j.contraception.2019.07.139.

As the Guttmacher graph below demonstrates, the rate of abortions increased steadily over the eight year period between 1973, the year of the *Roe v. Wade* decision, and 1981. However, from 1981, the abortion rate has gradually but steadily declined. The rate in 2017 was about 20% less than the rate in 1973.

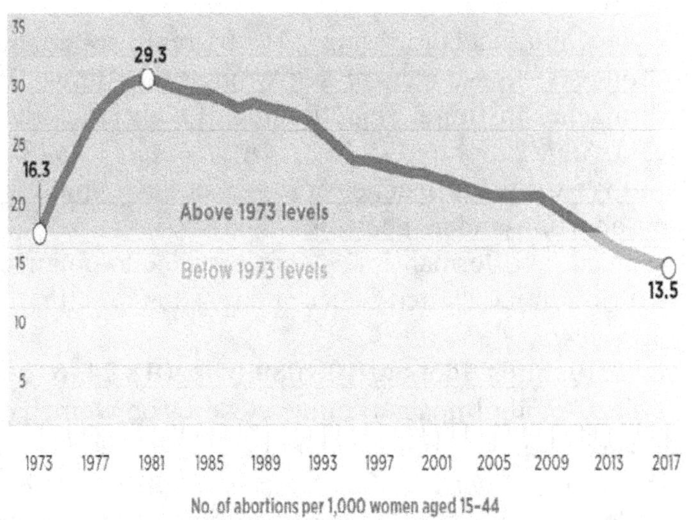

However, to further understand the significance of the abortion rate increase between 1973 and 1981, the CDC data for the time period of 1970-1973 presented in the table below should be considered. It is clear that the abortion rate was already steadily increasing before the *Roe v. Wade* decision.

CDC ABORTION SURVEILLANCE REPORT DATA

Year	Number of abortions reported to CDC	Induced abortions ratio per 1,000 live births
1970	193,491	52
1971	485,816	137
1972	586,760	180
1973	615,831	196

As the following graph from Guttmacher also demonstrates, the gradual but steady decline in the abortion rate between 1981 and 2017

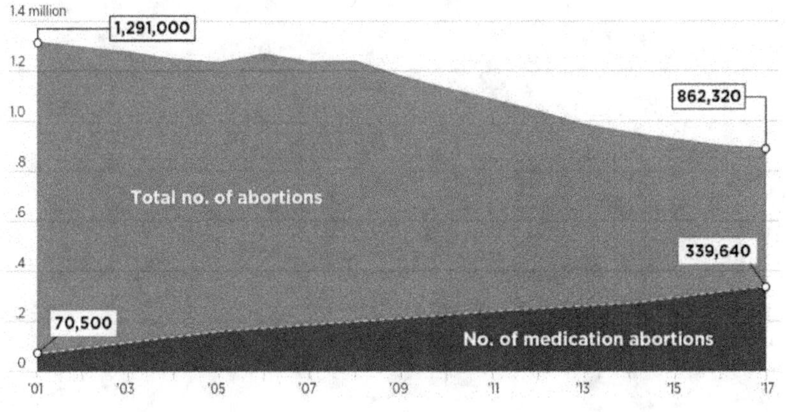

was despite a steady increase, during at least the last half of that time period, in the availability, effectiveness, and use of medication induced abortions.   Medication abortion ameliorated several of the challenges faced by women in electing abortion. In 2017, approximately 40% of abortions were medication induced.

The number of abortions that have occurred in the US is staggering. The total number of legal induced abortions since 1970 in the US is approximately 62 million. Considering that the total population of the US is presently approximately 329 Million, the number of legal induced abortions is equal to approximately 19% of the current total population of the US.

Perhaps the most significant misconception that many of us have regarding the current state of abortion in the US is at what stage abortions are usually performed. As noted in the figure, in 2016, two-

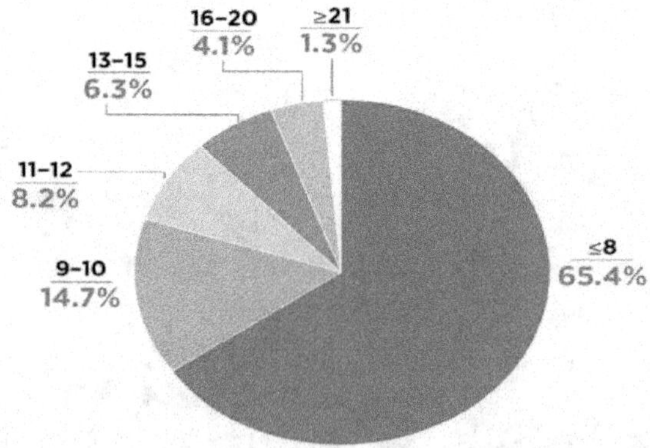

thirds of all abortions occurred at 8 weeks gestation or earlier, 88% occurred at 12 weeks or earlier, and 98.7% occurred at 20 weeks or earlier. These statistics were considered very important by the author in developing the proposal presented in a subsequent chapter for a *Legal Resolution* of the abortion issue.

One last observation that should be noted, based upon the Guttmacher data, follows from the abortion rate table presented below. There does not appear to be any present correlation between the increases in abortion restrictions adopted in certain states during the time period of 2011-2017 and the steady decline in the US abortion rate which began in 1981, continued through the time period of 2011 through 2017, and continues on to the present time.

The astonishing number of abortions performed in the US since 1970 and the ongoing rate of abortions performed each year understandably cause abortion opposers to lose a lot of sleep and to say a lot of prayers. Even though the abortion rate continues to decline, there will likely be approximately 780,000 abortions performed in the US in 2020, the year of publication of this work. It is likely that the percentage of pregnancies that will end in abortion will continue to be approximately 18%, the rate observed for 2017.

However, with these overwhelming statistics in mind, it is very easy to forget that each pregnancy involves an individual woman with a very personal and unique situation to deal with. We have previously addressed the religious issues that have historically influenced public policy decisions and will likely continue to influence private decisions by women regarding abortion.

	Clinics that provide abortions			Abortion rate by state of occurence			Number of abortion restrictions enacted
	2011	2017	Change in no. of clinics 2011–2017	2011	2017	% change in abortion rate 2011–2017	Total enacted 2011–2017
U.S. total	839	808	-31	16.9	13.5	-20.1	394
MIDWEST							
Illinois	26	25	-1	17.0	16.6	-2.3	0
Indiana	10	6	-4	7.3	5.9	-18.5	37
Iowa	17	8	-9	9.7	6.3	-34.6	16
Kansas	3	4	1	12.5	12.2	-2.2	31
Michigan	30	21	-9	15.3	14.2	-7.3	5
Minnesota	7	7	0	10.7	10.1	-5.9	0
Missouri	4	3	-1	5.0	4.0	-19.6	10
Nebraska	3	3	0	7.2	5.5	-24.2	6
North Dakota	1	1	0	9.5	7.9	-16.8	15
Ohio	18	9	-9	12.9	9.4	-27.4	14
South Dakota	1	1	0	3.9	3.1	-19.8	15
Wisconsin	4	3	-1	7.0	5.9	-16.2	7
NORTHEAST							
Connecticut	21	26	5	21.3	17.7	-16.9	0
Maine	5	16	11	9.9	8.8	-11.0	0
Massachusetts	12	19	7	17.8	13.5	-24.4	0
New Hampshire	5	4	-1	12.9	9.2	-29.0	4
New Jersey	24	41	17	27.1	28.0	3.5	0
New York	94	113	19	34.2	26.3	-23.0	0
Pennsylvania	20	18	-2	15.1	13.1	-13.1	2
Rhode Island	2	2	0	19.8	16.7	-15.4	0
Vermont	3	6	3	11.7	11.4	-2.4	0
SOUTH							
Alabama	6	5	-1	10.0	6.4	-35.7	13
Arkansas	3	3	0	7.6	5.5	-27.1	29
Delaware	4	4	0	28.4	10.5	-62.9	0
District of Columbia	5	4	-1	28.5	30.2	5.9	0
Florida	72	65	-7	23.7	18.6	-21.7	9
Georgia	19	15	-4	16.8	16.9	0.7	6
Kentucky	2	1	-1	4.6	3.8	-18.0	4
Louisiana	7	4	-3	13.1	10.6	-19.1	20
Maryland	21	25	4	28.6	25.0	-12.7	0
Mississippi	1	1	0	3.7	4.3	16.7	7
North Carolina	21	14	-7	14.6	14.6	0.2	13
Oklahoma	3	4	1	7.9	6.2	-21.4	23
South Carolina	3	4	1	7.1	5.3	-25.3	10
Tennessee	9	8	-1	13.1	9.2	-29.4	11
Texas	46	21	-25	13.5	9.4	-30.2	22
Virginia	21	16	-5	16.3	9.5	-41.5	7
West Virginia	2	1	-1	7.0	4.4	-36.7	6
WEST							
Alaska	4	4	0	12.4	8.6	-30.6	8
Arizona	15	8	-7	12.7	9.2	-27.4	24
California	160	161	1	23.0	16.4	-28.8	0
Colorado	24	18	-6	14.2	10.9	-23.3	0
Hawaii	6	4	-2	21.1	12.0	-42.9	0
Idaho	2	3	1	5.4	3.9	-27.4	7
Montana	7	5	-2	12.3	8.3	-32.3	3
Nevada	8	7	-1	20.6	16.4	-20.2	0
New Mexico	7	6	-1	13.0	11.7	-10.1	0
Oregon	15	16	1	14.1	11.9	-15.7	0
Utah	4	3	-1	5.4	4.4	-18.1	8
Washington	32	40	8	16.0	12.1	-24.3	0
Wyoming	1	2	1	1.1	1.3	19.8	2

Note: Abortion rate is the number of abortions per 1,000 women aged 15–44. Source: Guttmacher Institute.

We have also addressed the scientific facts that should continue to influence the public policy decisions as well as the private decisions by women relating to abortion. We are now able, using the statistics presented above, to quantify the scope of the collective expression of those individual situations and decisions. As mentioned above, the high percentage (98.7%) of abortions that are completed by gestational week 20 is a very encouraging and enlightening statistic. It appears that a significant reduction in the gestational age for lawful abortions commensurate with updated scientific and medical information regarding fetal viability could be adopted without substantially interfering with a woman's right to privacy or her ability to exercise her personal moral judgment in the decision. This would also further remove the abortion process from the realm of the heinous late term abortions.

CHAPTER 7

PHILOSOPHICAL RESOLUTION

It is the opinion of the author that the reason there has not been a legal resolution of the abortion issue is that there has been no philosophical resolution. Those on one side of the issue include those who believe that until a child is born alive, it is not a person, and that the right to privacy of the woman is preeminent since the unborn is totally dependent upon and derived from the mother. Those believe that she should have the absolute right and authority to terminate the pregnancy and have the unborn removed from her body at any time before viability. Some even believe she should have the right to terminate the pregnancy at any time prior to the time the child is born and breathes its first breath. On the other side there are those with unwavering conviction that life and personhood begin at conception and that to terminate a pregnancy, at any time after conception, is murder. These highly divergent and uncompromising positions, are difficult to reconcile.

The privacy and liberty of a woman and her right not to have government controlling her reproductive process, are powerful considerations. Putting a woman in jail because she refuses to allow a fertilized egg, an egg produced in and by her body, to grow into a person in her body seems un-American. On the other hand, surgically removing a fetus in a late stage of gestation, including particularly procedures that have been referred to as "partial birth" abortions, seem ghastly and barbaric for a civilized society which otherwise places such value on human life.

The question is can we somehow reach a philosophical resolution between these two competing interests and ideologies. The author believes that we can and that we must.

The author suggests that the resolution must begin with an acknowledgment by those who are adamantly opposed to abortion, that their opposition to an early stage abortion, is based entirely upon religious convictions. It seems impossible, other than on religious grounds, to make a credible argument that a fertilized egg or an early stage embryo which has no heart and no brain is a person and entitled to the same protection as a living, breathing child surviving outside the womb of the mother. They likewise must recognize that for government to impose the collective will of any group of citizens upon a woman, particularly in the early stages of pregnancy, thereby forcing her to allow a fertilized egg or early stage embryo to grow into a fully developed human being in her womb, would be a serious infringement on the personal liberties of the woman. The author wonders how many of us who would try to impose our collective will on a woman would be willing to have the unborn transferred to our body and have government force us to allow the unborn to progress to viability.

On the other hand, a resolution would require the recognition of those on the other side of the issue that, no matter how we justify it, abortion, particularly a late term abortion, is a barbaric practice. It results in the destruction, at the very least, of a human being in the making. The suctioning of the brain of a medically viable fetus, thereby killing the fetus so that it does not visibly display the life that is in it at the moment it is removed from the womb seems to defy all notions of who we are as Americans and our respect for human life.

Thus, we all must acknowledge that there are competing, moral, and well-founded interests and ideologies on both sides of this issue and that persons of unquestionable character and conviction, even unwavering religious conviction, differ substantially in their positions on this issue. We must therefore proceed toward a philosophical resolution which recognizes and respects the differences of opinion. A philosophical resolution seemingly must recognize that during the early stages of pregnancy, a woman's right to privacy and liberty must be preeminent. Government should not have the right to impose the collective will of any majority upon a woman to force her to allow a fertilized egg to grow into a human being in her body. However, once the woman has had a reasonable opportunity to exercise her right to privacy and her personal liberty, an abortion, which ultimately becomes a barbaric destruction of a largely developed and viable human being, cannot be condoned. A voluntary election to terminate, at the discretion of and for the convenience of the woman, a late term pregnancy of a viable fetus, once the woman has had a reasonable opportunity to terminate the pregnancy at an earlier stage, should not be permitted at law.

Once a philosophical resolution is reached based upon a mutual respect and recognition of the competing interests and the fact that a philosophical resolution is possible, then the legal resolution which is discussed hereafter becomes a much easier task.

It is interesting to note that many persons or groups who oppose abortion, advocate exceptions to abortion prohibitions for rape, incest, severe deformity, or health of the mother. By advocating these exceptions, such abortion opponents are clearly recognizing that the rights of the woman must be taken into consideration, at least in some circumstances. By acknowledging that the question of the life of the unborn is not preeminent and controlling in all situations, they are tacitly acknowledging that the rights of the woman must be balanced against the potential life of the unborn. They are merely advocating a more limited balance.

The question of whether abortion is right or wrong, justified or unjustified, at any stage in the development of the fetus, is not ultimately the definitive question. We would not ever be able to resolve such a question. The question, instead, is who has the moral responsibility for making the decision. The author suggests, that in the early stage of the pregnancy, the moral responsibility for the decision as to whether a fertilized egg will be allowed to remain in the body of a woman and to mature and grow into an embryo and then a fetus, must be relegated to the woman. It is, after all, her body. Her body does not become the property of the state or federal government just because she has a fertilized egg within her body. Until the fetus has matured to the stage where it could be biologically recognized as a person of its own and capable of living outside the womb of the mother and hence arguably entitled to its own rights and protections, the moral responsibility for the decision as to whether the development process will continue must be relegated to the woman. She must make the decision about when the living organism growing inside her becomes a person, based upon her beliefs and not the beliefs of any other person or group.

Once, however, the development of the fetus has reached a stage where it can be recognized biologically as a person of its own and capable of living independently of the woman, then the question of who must exercise the moral responsibility for the decision becomes substantially more difficult. The U.S. Supreme Court in *Roe v. Wade* ruled that a state could take upon itself the moral, as well as the legal, responsibility for that decision after a fetus reaches viability, which the court found was the end of the second trimester, i.e. 26 weeks from fertilization or a gestational age of 28 weeks. With the advances in medical science that have occurred in the years since the 1973 decision in *Roe v. Wade*, this time period is scientifically out of date. Viability is now arguably as early as a gestational age of 24 weeks, although the medically assisted rate of survival is still only about 50% at that stage. Simply applying the rationale of *Roe v. Wade* to medical advances would result in a state being authorized to elect to exercise that moral responsibility as early as 24 weeks.

Borrowing lines from the movie *The American President*, the President, played by Michael Douglas, states in a press conference:

> America isn't easy. America is advanced citizenship. You've gotta want it bad, 'cause it's gonna put up a fight. It's gonna say, "You want free speech? Let's see you acknowledge a man whose words make your blood boil, who's standing center stage and advocating at the top of his lungs that which you would spend a lifetime opposing at the top of yours."

Isn't America great! Persons who advocate either of the opposing extreme views on abortion, or anything in between, have the absolute right to do so. However, when it comes to trying to reach a resolution, all of us have to recognize that the citizens of America have very divergent, well thought, and heartfelt positions on this issue. The question is not and must not be, what any particular segment of the American public believes, based upon religious or any other convictions.

The question is what should be imposed upon the divergent citizenry of this amazing country, by force of law. Is it right and acceptable to impose the view that life begins at conception, by force of law, upon a woman who does not believe that, based upon her religious or other convictions? On the other hand, should abortion of an unborn that is capable of living outside the womb of the woman be permitted, by force of law, at any time prior to birth, based upon an asserted right of privacy of the woman or for convenience or population issues? The answer to both of those questions should be "no".

We are capable of a philosophical and a legal resolution. We are capable of the "advanced citizenship" of America. Now is the time. It is time to take the abortion issue out of politics.

CHAPTER 8

LEGAL RESOLUTION

The decision of the Supreme Court in *Roe v. Wade*, rather than settling the issue, has resulted in an endless and seemingly boundless controversy. Furthermore, if this decision were overturned, the result would be a continuation of a perpetual controversy. Some states would prohibit abortions completely. Others might allow abortions at any time prior to live birth. The divisive and erosive conflict would continue perpetually. Politics would continue to be polluted and perverted by this issue. The rights of women would be seriously jeopardized in some states while the heinous practice of late term abortions might continue in others. We, as a people, are capable of a philosophical and legal resolution of this issue that will promote both the preservation of the right or privacy and liberty of women and the recognition of the sanctity of life.

The author proposes enactment of a federal statute providing the following:

1.   A woman shall be entitled to have an abortion procedure performed to terminate a pregnancy and remove the aborted fetus from her body, at any time up to a fetal gestational age of 20 weeks. Beginning with a fetal gestational age exceeding 20 weeks, a woman shall not be entitled to have an abortion performed, unless her life or health will be seriously jeopardized by the continuing pregnancy, as determined by her medical doctor.

2.   The fetal gestational age for a woman seeking an abortion procedure shall be determined by a licensed medical doctor licensed in the state where the abortion procedure is sought, and the medical

doctor's determination of the fetal gestational age shall be based upon a physical examination of the woman, the latest blood testing and non-radiation imaging generally accepted in the medical community for determining fetal gestational age, and information provided by the woman relating to the gestational age of the fetus. Any determination that the continuation of a pregnancy will seriously jeopardize the life or health of the woman will be made by her medical doctor. An "abortion procedure" shall be defined to include a medication induced abortion or any other medical procedure deemed appropriate by the woman's medical doctor.

3.	A woman submitting to an abortion and any medical doctor or other person performing an abortion involving a fetus with a gestational age of 21 weeks shall be guilty of an Infraction, unless the abortion is performed to preserve the life or health of the woman, as determined by her medical doctor. *(The penalty for an Infraction is imprisonment for 5 days or less and a fine of $5,000.00 or less.)*

4.	A woman submitting to an abortion and any medical doctor or other person performing an abortion involving a fetus with a gestational age of 22 weeks shall be guilty of a Class B Misdemeanor, unless the abortion is performed to preserve the life or health of the woman, as determined by her medical doctor. *(The penalty for a Class B Misdemeanor is imprisonment for 31 days to 6 months and a fine of $5,000.00 or less.)*

5.	A woman submitting to an abortion and any medical doctor or other person performing an abortion involving a fetus with a gestational age of 23 weeks shall be guilty of a Class A Misdemeanor, unless the abortion is performed to preserve the life or health of the woman, as determined by her medical doctor. *(The penalty for a Class A Misdemeanor is imprisonment for 6 months to 1 year and a fine of $100,000.00 or less.)*

6.   A woman submitting to an abortion and any medical doctor or other person performing an abortion involving a fetus with a gestational age of 24 weeks or greater shall be guilty of a Class E Felony, unless the abortion is performed to preserve the life or health of the woman, as determined by her medical doctor. *(The penalty for a Class E Felony is imprisonment for 1 year to 5 years and a fine of $250,000.00 or less.)*

7.   A woman submitting to an abortion and any medical doctor or other person performing an abortion involving a fetus with a gestational age of 26 weeks or greater shall be guilty of a Class D Felony, unless the abortion is performed to preserve the life or health of the woman, as determined by her medical doctor. *(The penalty for a Class D Felony is imprisonment for 5 years to 10 years and a fine of $250,000.00 or less.)*

8.   The gestational ages for the foregoing sanctions for any pregnancy resulting from rape or incest shall be increased by 2 weeks for each sanction stage.

9.   In the case of a pregnancy involving a minor, the minor shall be deemed to be an adult for purposes of making any and all decisions relating to an abortion, and the gestational ages for the foregoing sanctions shall be increased by 2 weeks for each sanction stage.

10.   In the case of a pregnancy involving a woman found by a court to be mentally incompetent, the court appointed guardian or

guardian ad litem shall be responsible for making decisions relating to an abortion, and the gestational ages for the foregoing sanctions shall be increased by 2 weeks for each sanction stage.

11.   In the case of a pregnancy involving a fetus found to have an abnormality which is likely to result in a significant birth defect, as determined by a medical doctor licensed in the state where the abortion procedure is sought, the gestational ages for the foregoing sanctions shall be increased by 2 weeks for each sanction stage.

12.   The United States government does by this statute preempt the regulation of abortion within the United States and its territories.

The author believes that the foregoing proposed legal resolution provides an appropriate balance between the right of privacy/personal liberty of a woman and proper respect for the sanctity of human life. It would place moral responsibility on a woman for the decision whether to retain or terminate a pregnancy during the earlier stages of that pregnancy, and provides for the exercise by the Federal government of its moral responsibility to protect the life of the unborn who has reached a gestational age wherein it is at or near viability, based upon modern medical science. It would provide for uniformity in regard to this issue throughout the United States and its territories and substantially eliminate abortion as a political issue. Further, it would achieve a philosophical resolution with which a substantial majority of Americans would agree and over which they would breathe a collective sigh of relief. Finally, it would eliminate the heinous and barbaric practice of late term abortions.

The increasing sanctions, beginning with an Infraction at 21 weeks, a Class B Misdemeanor at 22 weeks, a Class A Misdemeanor at 23 weeks, a Class E Felony at 24 weeks, and a Class D Felony at 26 weeks seem to provide an appropriate progression of sanctions correlated with the increasing likelihood of viability of the fetus, and provide an additional period of notice that would inherently protect the woman and her medical doctor from a mistake as to the gestational age of the fetus. Of course, if there is a serious threat to the life or health of the woman, abortion may have to be considered at a later gestational stage, as noted in the proposed statute. Pregnancies involving rape or incest victims, minors, or mentally incompetent women would also require special considerations, as also noted in the proposed statute. Pregnancies involving fetal abnormalities which will lead to probable birth defects would also require special considerations, as further noted in the proposed statute.

CHAPTER 9

CONCLUSION

I am a Catholic. I was formerly a Mormon and before that a Baptist. For approximately 2-1/2 years I was in the Deaconate Formation program of the Salt Lake City Diocese of the Catholic Church. Although I loved the program and my fellow devotees, and I looked forward to the opportunity to serve in the clergy of the Catholic Church, I eventually observed that the long-term effect of my service on my family would not be acceptable, and so I withdrew from the program. Although I remain a devout Catholic, and my communion with 2000 years of Christians is very dear to me, I have a great respect for the rights of others to have different beliefs. Some of the persons that I admire most are agnostic or atheist. Their kindness and concerns come from within and are not distorted by some sense of what they feel obligated to believe.

As discussed in great detail in Chapter 4, the present position of the Catholic Church is that ensoulment occurs at conception and, accordingly, that the unborn is a person, a living soul, from the moment of conception. While, from a religious point of view, it is plausible that there is a spiritual nexus between a fertilized egg and a soul, it is certainly a mystery how a human soul could reside in a fertilized egg. That mystery continues as fetal development occurs, as it remains a mystery how a human soul could reside in a developing fetus before the fetus has developed to the point that it is at least minimally sentient, or even to the point that it is capable of conscious thought. While some of us with strong religious convictions may be inclined to accept these mysteries, others, with or without strong religious convictions are not so inclined.

The proposal for the philosophical and legal resolution of the abortion issue is not about what is right or wrong. It is not about whose religious convictions are correct, if any. It merely recognizes that Americans of profound character and diverse religiosity have widely divergent views on this issue. It asks the conservative Christian to recognize that an absolute ban on abortion would not be based on biology or science, but on religion. It is impossible to support the position that an early term fetus is a person, based upon scientific inquiry. That conclusion can only be reached based upon a religious conviction. A conservative Christian must recognize that it is un-American and unacceptable to impose such religious beliefs on others by force of law. Thoughtful and kind persuasion, not compulsion, should be the order of the day for those of us with such strong convictions.

Similarly, the proposal asks those who consider a woman's right to choose as preeminent, even beyond the time of viability, as defined by *Roe v. Wade*, and perhaps even up to the time of birth, to recognize that this ideology results in the practice of late term abortions, which is considered barbaric and heinous by a vast majority of Americans. They must recognize that in all cases, except where the mother's life becomes at risk due to later pregnancy developments, the exercise of reason and prudence by the woman would have provoked her to exercise the right to terminate the pregnancy at an earlier gestational age. They must recognize that it is reasonable to require a woman to exercise her right prudently and expeditiously. As the Supreme Court has stated, it is not an unlimited right.

It is worth stating again, we are capable of a philosophical and a legal resolution. Now is the time. It is time to take the abortion issue out of politics and away from politicians on both sides who attempt to divert attention from their abject failures on other matters severely affecting the lives of ordinary citizens. It is time to end their use of rhetoric of their professed, whether real or fabricated, ideology on the abortion issue. It is time to take our country back from the demagogues. We can only do that if we vote for politicians who commit to the resolution of the abortion issue.

BOOK II – GUNS

CHAPTER 1

DEVELOPMENT OF THE GUNS ISSUE

King George III was determined to treat the American colonies

just as he treated the other holdings of the vast British empire. He

wanted revenue, and lots of it, and would tolerate no opposition from the

colonists burdened with his demands. They were to consider themselves

very fortunate to be the benefactors of the economic vitality of the

British Empire and to have the protection of Great Britain from

international enemies and their treacherous plundering.

Beginning in 1764, the British parliament enacted a series of Acts

imposing substantial revenue burdens on the American colonies. These

included the Stamp Act, the Sugar Act, and the Townshend Acts. The

Townshend Acts included a number of new taxes, including taxes on tea,

glass, paper, paint, and lead. Unsurprisingly, these Acts were not

received well by the colonists and the British brought in soldiers to keep

order. Because they were colonies, they had no representation in the

British Parliament, and "taxation without representation" became a

mantra of the colonial resistance.

Massachusetts, particularly Boston, became a focal point for the

rebellion. On March 5, 1770 an argument arose between soldiers and

colonists on the streets of Boston and British soldiers opened fire on a

group of the American colonists, killing five of the colonists. This event

was referred to by colonists all over the American colonies as the

"Boston Massacre" and it became a rallying cry for the growing

rebellion. Although the American Revolution would not start for another five years, the event provoked a change in the attitude of many colonists toward King George and British rule.

The Boston Tea Party of 1773, perhaps the most provocative and most remembered event of the resistance preceding the armed conflict of the revolution, marked the defiance of the colonists to British "taxation without representation." The Boston Tea Party provoked King George to increase the military presence in Boston and the British Parliament to pass the punitive Intolerable Acts. The British Navy instituted a blockade of Boston Harbor in June of 1774 until colonists paid for the tea dumped overboard the previous year. This hardline approach resorted to repetitively by King George, the infallible and supreme monarch, in dealing with the American colonies, eventually extinguished the loyalty of most of the colonists to the crown and to Great Britain and vigorously fanned the fires of the rebellion.

The fomenting conflict between the colonies and Great Britain provided the backdrop and the impetus for the First Continental Congress which convened on September 5, 1774 and adjourned on October 26, 1774. The First Continental Congress included delegates from 12 of the 13 British colonies that later became the original 13 states. The initial discussions were about whether they should continue to try to preserve their union with Great Britain, and, if so, how to appropriately express their grievances for the onerous actions of the British government. Ultimately, however, a plan to create a Union of Great Britain and the Colonies was rejected by the delegates. Instead, they agreed to petition King George for a repeal of the Intolerable Acts and for redress of their grievances. The appeal fell on the deaf ears of

King George and the British Parliament. The conditions were ripe for escalating conflict at the end of 1774 and the beginning of 1775.

Guns were at the forefront of the attention of the British military. Without guns and ammunition the colonists could not successfully contend with the British forces. The British military leadership in Boston got word that the rebels had a large stash of guns and ammunition in Concord. On April 18, 1775, revolutionary leaders in Boston were alerted, apparently by a rebel spy, that the British troops were poised to march during the night to Concord, with the intent to search for the guns and ammunition they believed the rebels had stashed there. Paul Revere, William Dawes and Samuel Prescott were dispatched to warn revolutionary leaders Samuel Adams and John Hannock, who were headquartered in Lexington, and the rebel forces of Lexington and Concord.

The 700 British troops completed the 14-mile march from Boston to Lexington by dawn on April 19, 1775. They found 77 militiamen congregated on the town green, who were promptly ordered, "Throw down your arms! Ye villains, ye rebels." Although the vastly outnumbered militiamen were ordered to disburse by their commander, a shot was fired. Whether a redcoat or a militiaman fired the first shot has never been determined. This shot, the "shot heard round the world" in the immortal words of Ralph Waldo Emerson, was the beginning of the American Revolutionary War. It was followed by several volleys fired by the British soldiers at the grossly outnumbered militiamen before the redcoats could be stopped by the British officers. Eight militiamen were killed and nine more were wounded. Only one of the British riflemen was wounded.

The British then marched on to Concord, just 5 miles further, to complete the search for arms for which that they had been dispatched. Most of the arms had been relocated and so very few were found. By the time the British were ready to return to Boston, almost 2,000 militiamen had converged on Concord. Fighting started soon after, with the militiamen engaging in the guerilla tactics for which they became famous, or infamous in the eyes of the British, namely firing at the British from behind trees, buildings and other objects. Before long, the redcoats were in hasty retreat.

Although there was a large contingent of British reinforcements in Lexington by the time the fleeing redcoats reached Lexington, the militiamen from Lexington and Concord and the surrounding area were also soon joined by militiamen from Marblehead and Salem, and before long the militiamen had the redcoats on the run again. The war was on.

Historians point to the lack of marksmanship of the militiamen at the start of the war. They were poorly trained and poorly equipped in comparison to the highly trained and well-armed redcoats. On the day of the Lexington and Concord battle, there were as many as 3,500 militiamen on the heels of the rapidly retreating redcoats and firing at them more or less as rapidly as they could reload their muskets. Yet only approximately 250 Redcoats were killed or wounded. Perhaps considering that only about 90 militiamen were killed or wounded by the fleeing British, the marksmanship does not sound so bad in comparison.

A principal fact to note here is that the militiamen had guns and ammunition. Although a number of other muskets were used by the militiamen, the British made "Brown Bess" muzzle loading musket was commonly used by the American soldiers in the American Revolutionary

War. All of the muskets fired a single shot ball or a shotgun type cluster shot of multiple smaller shots.

One advantage the British soldiers typically had over the militiamen, and later over the infantrymen of the Continental Army, was the bayonet. All of the British soldiers had a bayonet, while a majority of the revolutionary infantrymen did not. This often proved to be a deadly advantage because of the long loading time and limited range of the muskets. When the forces charged each other and converged in hand-to-hand combat, the bayonet was a formidable weapon extending beyond the barrel of the musket.

The possession of muskets and ammunition for its infantry was essential in the war that was rapidly escalating in 1975. However, the rebellion would have been much more difficult, perhaps impossible, without one more weapon, the cannon, and to a lesser extent, the mortar.

The ragtag but highly motivated militiamen having chased the redcoats from Concord and Lexington back to Charleston, just north of Boston across a narrow stretch of Boston harbor, they corralled those forces in Charleston and the remaining British forces in Boston and established a siege line cutting off all access to the city by land. However, because the American forces had no artillery and no navy, they could do nothing about the harbor, and the British used the naval access to Boston harbor to reinforce their troops during the remaining months of 1775 and early 1776. Also, the British heavily fortified the city against invasion by placing cannon at the south land access route to Boston and on several of the hills around the city. They elected, however, not to fortify the Dorchester Heights, a decision that ultimately proved fortuitous for the American Forces.

The colonies convened the Second Continental Congress in May, 1775, shortly after the battles of Lexington and Concord, to organize the defense of the colonies. George Washington, prominent Virginia landowner and politician and former colonel of the Virginia colonial forces during the French and Indian War, upon receiving the news of the events at Lexington and Concord and recognizing the unavoidable onset of war, hastily departed his home on Mount Vernon on May 4, 1775 to join the Continental Congress in Philadelphia. The Continental Congress created the Continental Army on June 14, 1775, and Samuel Adams and John Adams nominated Washington to become its Commander in Chief. He was unanimously elected commander in chief by the Continental Congress the next day, June 15, 1775. Each colony was also urged to establish and train a militia as Massachusetts and several other colonies had already done.

General Washington was immediately distressed by the stalemate at Boston. Without cannon, the Continental forces had no way to rout the British from Boston. He wrote to his brother that "the inactive state we lie in is exceedingly disagreeable." In November 1775, Washington dispatched Henry Knox, a 25 year old bookseller turned militiaman and avid student of military history and artillery, to retrieve to Boston the dozens of cannon and mortar that had been captured from the British at Fort Ticonderoga, New York.

Knox persevered through the onset of the harsh New England winter and made it to Fort Ticonderoga. He disassembled and prepared for transport 58 of the best cannons and mortars, which ranged in size from smaller 3-pounders to massive 24-pounders. Using sleds, oxen and flat bottom boats, Knox and his men succeeded in transporting the artillery over water and sometimes very difficult terrain, including mountains and forests, the 300 miles to General Washington outside Boston, by the end of January 1776.

By March 1776, Washington had the cannons in place on Dorchester Heights, from which the city and the British ships in the harbor were in clear view and in range of the cannons. General Washington did not have to use much gunpowder or many cannon balls over the three days it took for a shocked General Howe to confirm that the British would withdraw from Boston. It did not take Howe that long to conclude that, with cannons in the hands of the Continental Army, Boston was indefensible. The British forces and the remaining loyalists in Boston departed by sea to Nova Scotia within a week, and on March 17, 1776, the Continental Army took Boston. This series of events confirmed the indispensability of cannons for the Patriots to effectively contend with the British forces.

About three months later, on July 4, 1776, the Second Continental Congress adopted the Declaration of Independence, formally disavowing the allegiance of the colonies to and declaring their independence from the British Crown and Great Britain. However, nearly a year and a half of debate was required after adoption of the Declaration of Independence for the delegates of the Second Continental Congress to reach an agreement on the Articles of Confederation and Perpetual Union that became the first constitution of the United States of America. On November 15, 1777, the Articles of Confederation was sent to the states for ratification. The Articles of Confederation was not finally ratified by all 13 states until March 1, 1781, after it became reasonably clear that America would be victorious in its war for independence. A few months later, in October, 1781, Cornwallis surrendered to Washington at Yorktown, Virginia, where the British were hopelessly trapped and their escape by sea was cut off by the French navy.

The Articles of Confederation were intended, as the name suggests, to preserve the independence and sovereignty of the states. The weak central government was to perform only those limited functions which the states agreed could be best performed by a central government. The states were rightly concerned over ceding power to a central government, having been embroiled in a bloody war to establish their independence from a tyrannical central government. It was not until three years after the formal end to the American Revolution with the signing of the Treaty of Paris on September 3, 1783 and ratification of the treaty by the Congress of the Confederation on May 12, 1784, that dust had settled on the determined resistance of the states to subjecting themselves to the power of a strong central government.

Because the Articles of Confederation gave very limited power to the central government, the Confederation Congress lacked enforcement power for any action taken by the Congress. Implementation of most decisions, including modifications to the Articles, required unanimous approval of all thirteen state legislatures. However, the primary problem was, as stated by George Washington, "no money." The taxes authorized were minimal and all of the states were derelict in paying their taxes, some of the states refusing to pay any of their assessed taxes. Accordingly, if the Confederation Congress borrowed money, it had no ability to pay it back. It had no ability to pay interest on debt owed to foreign governments, and defaulted on debts as they came due. The

United States had grossly inadequate funds to support an effective military and so it could not even defend its commercial shipping. Trade protection laws enacted by each state stifled interstate trade. Massachusetts had to raise funds from Boston merchants to minimally fund a volunteer army.

The Confederation Congress became largely non-functional. The dream of the founding fathers of a republic with all the representatives elected by the people at regular elections and no person obtaining power by inheritance seemed to be eluding them. James Madison was so disturbed by the status of the new nation that he openly questioned whether the Articles of Confederation was a binding compact or could ever provide for a viable government.

In view of the sad state of the union and with matters only getting worse, the Confederation Congress became desperate. On February 21, 1787, the Confederation Congress voted to call a convention of delegates from each of the 13 states at Philadelphia for the "sole and express purpose of revising the Articles of Confederation". The convention was intended to "render the federal constitution adequate to the exigencies of government and the preservation of the Union." By the end of May, 1787, convention delegates from 12 of the 13 states were seated and the convention was underway.

The convention delegates worked very diligently through the summer of 1787 on the articles of a new Constitution. The advocates of the new Constitution were anxious to obtain unanimous support of all twelve states represented in the Convention. At the end of the convention, although several of the delegates had misgivings about some of the provisions, the proposed Constitution was agreed to by eleven state delegations and the lone remaining delegate from New York, Alexander Hamilton. On September 17, 1787, the convention delegates voted to send the proposed constitution to the Confederation Congress with their endorsement, "Done in Convention, by the unanimous consent of the States present."

The proposed new Constitution was vigorously debated in the Confederation Congress between the Anti-Federalists, who opposed it, and the Federalists, who favored it. The principal, hotly contested issue was, of course, the proposed additional powers for the central government. The Anti-Federalists, relying on the vivid memories of British tyranny, warned of the people again fighting governmental tyranny. In particular, they warned of the possibility of a military takeover of the states by the federal government, if the Congress passed laws prohibiting states from arming citizens and prohibiting citizens from arming themselves. Despite these concerns, the abject failure of the Articles of Confederation and the Confederation form of government made the argument of the Federalists much easier. The mob rule observed in 1789 in the very violent French Revolution also contributed to a recognition of a need for a stronger and more stable central government.

On June 21, 1788, the Constitution had been ratified by the minimum of nine states required under Article VII. By the end of July, 1788, eleven states had ratified and the Confederation Congress passed a resolution on September 13, 1788, to put the new Constitution into operation. The federal government began operations under the new form of government on March 4, 1789. George Washington was inaugurated as the nation's first president on April 30, 1789. The final two states, North Carolina and Rhode Island, both subsequently

ratified the Constitution on November 21, 1789 and May 29, 1790,

respectively.

Since 1789, when the Constitution became effective, there have

been 27 amendments to the Constitution. The first ten amendments,

ratified by the States in 1791, are known collectively as the Bill of

Rights. These amendments offer specific protections of individual

liberty and justice and place restrictions on the powers of government.

The majority of the seventeen later amendments expand individual civil

rights protections, the needs for which were precipitated by changing

conditions within the nation since its formation.

We are concerned here with the Second Amendment. The

Second Amendment to the Constitution of the United States, is the

second member of the Bill of Rights. Obviously, it follows just after the

First Amendment, which reads as follows:

> Congress shall make no law respecting an establishment of
> religion, or prohibiting the free exercise thereof; or abridging the
> freedom of speech, or of the press; or the right of the people
> peaceably to assemble, and to petition the Government for a
> redress of grievances.

The First Amendment prohibits Congress from obstructing the

exercise of certain individual freedoms: freedom of religion, freedom of

speech, freedom of the press, freedom of assembly, and right to petition.

Its Free Exercise Clause guarantees a person's right to hold whatever

religious beliefs he or she wants, and to freely exercise that belief, and

its Establishment Clause prevents the federal government from creating

an official national church or favoring one set of religious beliefs over

another. The amendment guarantees an individual's right to express and to be exposed to a wide range of opinions and views. It was intended to ensure a free exchange of ideas, even unpopular ones. It also guarantees an individual's right to physically gather or associate with others in groups for economic, political or religious purposes. Additionally, it guarantees an individual's right to petition the government for a redress of grievances.

The text of the Second Amendment reads as follows:

A well-regulated Militia, being necessary to the security of a free State, the right of the people to keep and bear Arms, shall not be infringed.

It should be noted that the wording of the Second Amendment was arguably borrowed from very similar clauses in some of the original 13 state constitutions. The Second Amendment protects the right of individuals to keep and bear arms. Although, as will be discussed in detail below, the Supreme Court has ruled that this right applies to individuals, not merely to collective militias. It has also held, as will also be discussed in detail below, that the government may regulate or place certain limits on the manufacture, ownership and sale of firearms or other weapons. Requested by several states during the Constitutional ratification debates, the amendment reflected the lingering resentment over the widespread efforts of the British to confiscate the colonists' firearms at the outbreak of the Revolutionary War. Patrick Henry had rhetorically asked, shall we be stronger, "when we are totally disarmed, and when a British Guard shall be stationed in every house?" Muskets, cannons, mortars, musket balls, cannon balls, and gunpowder were essential to the fight of the colonists against British tyranny. How should and does that relate to the Second Amendment discussions?

SECOND AMENDMENT

The Second Amendment to the Constitution of the United States of America states as follows:

A well-regulated Militia, being necessary to the security of a free State, the right of the people to keep and bear Arms, shall not be infringed.

In 1791, when the Second Amendment was ratified as one of the ten amendments to the Constitution constituting the Bill of Rights, the Revolutionary War, and the conflict with the British Crown and the British Parliament that led to the war, was fresh on the minds and hearts of the members of the Congress of the United States. This was also true for the legislatures of each of the states that had to consider and ratify the Amendment. The fear of a runaway, intrusive, and oppressive power, reminiscent of the power asserted on the colonies by the British Crown, was an overriding concern of Congress and the state legislatures, as well as the rank and file citizens of the United States. The right of the people to bear arms, and thereby to support a militia, was appropriately deemed an essential for the security of the United States.

The controversy over Second Amendment rights seems to boil down to two questions. The first is to what extent each citizen of the United States was intended, by the Second Amendment, to be the beneficiary of the right to bear arms. Does "the right of the people" refer to a collective right of "the people" or to an individual right of each citizen. With a preamble reading "a well-regulated Militia, being necessary to the security of a free State", it is easy to support an argument that this amendment was solely about a collective right for "the people to keep and bear arms" for a "well-regulated Militia". It is easy to argue that this amendment, by its express language, does not address the right of a citizen who is not involved with a "well-regulated Militia" to have a musket in her or his closet or a cannon in her or his barn. It is further easy to argue that this is true whether the right is for the purpose of enabling the person to join an impromptu militia in the event of a threat to the security of the United States, or for the purpose of enabling the person to defend against domestic threats to her or his person, her or his family, or her or his home or property. At the time of adoption of the Second Amendment, when men were called for service in a militia, they were expected to appear bearing arms of their own of a type appropriate for the militia service.

There is nothing in the Second Amendment that expressly speaks to a right to keep and bear arms for purely personal concerns. On its face, it is about the security of the United States. Considering again what the framers of the Constitution and the citizens of the United States had just endured and the fears that were derived from that, the overriding intent of the Amendment is clear. However, notwithstanding the preamble and the obvious intent, the statement of the rights conferred by the amendment, "the right of the people to keep and bear Arms, shall not be infringed" is also arguably unequivocal. If "the people" is referring to each individual person and not to the citizenry collectively, then the right of each person to keep and bear Arms "shall not be infringed."

It is plausible, of course, that the Second Amendment has nothing to do with the right of an individual to keep and bear arms for the purpose of defending against domestic threats to her or his person, her or his family, or her or his home or property. It is plausible that the

Framers and the citizenry of the time would have considered such a right to be so basic and incontestable that it required no constitutional provision or amendment to address it, and that only the collective right to keep and bear arms for a militia needed protection.

Although the reader will likely have a general understanding of the meaning of the terms "Founding Fathers," and "Framers" (of the Constitution and the Bill of Rights), it may be helpful for a better understanding of the discussion below, to clarify the meaning of these and related terms.

A Committee of Five, composed of John Adams, Thomas Jefferson, Benjamin Franklin, Roger Sherman, and Robert Livingston, drafted and presented to the Continental Congress, the Declaration of Independence which was adopted on July 4, 1776.

The "Founding Fathers" were Patriots who united the Colonies, led the Patriot forces in the Revolutionary War, and shepherded the establishment of a democratic republic form of government for the United States of America. The term Founding Fathers is sometimes used in a more technical sense to refer to the "Signers" of the Declaration of Independence. Most of the Founding Fathers were former Loyalists who came from a wide range of backgrounds and occupations. They included plantation owners and businessmen, slave owners and abolitionists, wealthy landowners and humble tradesmen, politicians and non-politicians, philosophers and writers, lawyers and doctors. Seven persons, John Adams, Benjamin Franklin, Alexander Hamilton, John Jay, Thomas Jefferson, James Madison, and George Washington, have been recognized by historians as key Founding Fathers.

Jefferson, Madison and Washington, all wealthy Virginia plantation owners, were slave owners. Although they all repeatedly criticized the institution of slavery and expressed the need to end the practice over time, they remained slave owners for all of their lives. By contrast, Hamilton, Franklin and Jay were leading advocates for the abolition of slavery. Adams, Jefferson, and Franklin were members of the Committee of Five that drafted the Declaration of Independence. Washington, of course, was commander-in-chief of the Continental Army. Jay, Adams, and Franklin negotiated the Treaty of Paris (1783) that ended the American Revolutionary War.

The term "Framers" is usually defined as the 55 individuals who were appointed to be delegates to the 1787 Constitutional Convention and took part in drafting the proposed Constitution of the United States. George Washington, James Madison, Alexander Hamilton and Benjamin Franklin were among the delegates to the Constitutional Convention and George Washington was elected President of the Convention. Well known Founding Fathers who did not accept appointment or could not attend the Constitutional Convention include Patrick Henry, Thomas Jefferson, John Adams, Samuel Adams, John Jay, John Hancock and Richard Henry Lee. Although John Jay, who became the first Chief Justice of the Supreme Court, was not a delegate to the Constitutional Convention, and, hence, was not one of the signers of the Constitution, he did write a draft of the Constitution in 1787 and he spear-headed efforts to amend or replace the Articles of Confederation. Also, the constitutions drafted by John Jay for the State of New York (1777) and John Adams for the State of Massachusetts (1780) were heavily relied upon for the drafting of the U.S. Constitution, although neither was a Framer. Furthermore, Jay, along with Alexander Hamilton and James Madison who were signers of the Constitution, were authors of *The Federalist Papers* written to explain and advocate for ratification of the Constitution by the states.

Of the 55 Framers, only 39 were actual signers of the Constitution. Some left before the convention was concluded. Some were concerned that the Constitution gave too much power to the Federal Government. Three refused to sign because it did not contain an explicit Bill of Rights.

The foundation of the laws of the United States, at least in many respects, is the English Common Law. The English Bill of Rights of 1689 (also referred to as the Declaration of Rights) provides "that the subjects, which are protestants, may have arms for their defence suitable to their condition, and as allowed by law." Although without limiting the right to Protestants of course, the Second Amendment may be viewed as being derived, as least in part, from English law. Under English Common Law, the right to bear arms is regarded as an inherent right arising out of the right of the individual to personal security, personal liberty, and private property. Sir William Blackstone (1723-1780), an English barrister, judge and Tory politician of the eighteenth century, rose to notoriety with the publication in 1765 of his work the *Commentaries on the Laws of England*. This work was highly regarded and widely circulated in the American Colonies, and is recognized as having an immense influence on the perspective of the framers on matters of the rights of individuals.

Blackstone's description of the right to bear arms comes in his discussions of the rights of the subject. He begins by identifying three "absolute rights" - personal security, personal liberty, and private property – which leads to his discussion of five "auxiliary rights":

> In the three preceding articles we have taken a short view of the principal absolute rights [personal security, personal liberty, private property] which appertain to every Englishman. But in vain would these rights be declared, ascertained, and protected by the dead letter of the laws, if the constitution had provided no other method to secure their actual enjoyment. It has therefore established certain other auxiliary subordinate rights of the subject, which serve principally as outworks or barriers to protect and maintain inviolate the three great and primary rights, of personal security, personal liberty, and private property.
>
> 1. The constitution, powers, and privileges of parliament . . . .
>
> 2. The limitation of the king's prerogative . . . .
>
> 3. . . . [A]pplying to the courts of justice for redress of injuries.
>
> 4. . . . [T]he right of petitioning the king, or either house of parliament, for the redress of grievances.
>
> 5. The fifth and last auxiliary right of the subject, that I shall at present mention, is that of having arms for their defence, suitable to their condition and degree, and such as are allowed by law. Which is also declared by the same statute . . . and is indeed a public allowance, under due restrictions, of the natural right of resistance and self-preservation, when the sanctions of society and laws are found insufficient to restrain the violence of oppression.
>
> . . . [T]o vindicate [the three primary rights], when actually violated or attacked, the subjects of England are entitled, in the first place, to the regular administration and free course of justice in the courts of law; next, to the right of petitioning the king and parliament for redress of grievances; and, lastly, to the right of having and using arms for self-preservation and defence.

In regard to the right to have arms, there are two interpretations suggested for the English Bill of Rights of 1689. The Bill itself states that it is acting to restore "ancient rights" trampled upon by James II. Even so, some have argued that the English Bill of Rights created a new right to have arms, which developed out of a duty to have arms and to be prepared to serve in a militia. However, as described below, in *District of Columbia v. Heller*, 554 U.S. 570 (2008), the U.S. Supreme Court did not accept this view, observing that the right codified by the English Bill of Rights was "clearly an individual right, having nothing whatsoever to do with service in the militia."

The drafters of the Second Amendment were undoubtedly heavily influenced by the English Bill of Rights. However, what is not so clear is whether the drafters intended for the Second Amendment to severely restrict federal regulation of arms while reserving the right of states to regulate arms, as the English Parliament had reserved for itself as against the crown, or whether they intended to create a new right, like many others guaranteed by the Constitution and the Bill of Rights, for the individual to bear arms. The Supreme Court decided in *Heller* that it was the latter.

Beginning at least as early as the Stone Age, which spanned approximately 2.5 million years, and continuing through the Bronze Age (c.3500BC - 700BC), there was no question about the right and the necessity of individuals to keep and bear arms for the defense of person, family and community. Since long before mankind had developed the ability to record its history, humans have always armed themselves for the protection of themselves and others. Since humans have begun to gather in communities, weapons have been deemed necessary, and rightfully so, for the protection of the communities and its constituents collectively. As larger communities and nations began to form, the necessity and the right of individuals to keep and bear arms for the protection of the respective communities and the nations were inevitably recognized. Of course, there have also been many instances in recorded history of tyrannical powers and governments attempting to disarm the populace in order to control their power to resist or rebel. In England, for example, notwithstanding the English Bill of Rights, the ordinary citizens were generally disarmed during the 1700's, under the specious pretext of preserving game. Parliament was able to enlist the support of the land-owning aristocracy for such laws under this premise. The result of the game preservation laws was that only a small percentage of the ordinary citizens were able to keep a gun without violating the law.

Pre-revolutionary America was likewise the target of attempts by the Crown, enabled by the British Parliament, to disarm the citizenry. During the pre-revolutionary period of the 1760's and continuing into the early 1770's, the colonial militia in each of the colonies were initially composed of colonists who included Loyalists and Patriots, i.e. colonists who were loyal to Britain and colonists who favored independence from Britain. Much distrust developed between the two factions. This resulted in the Patriots forming militias that excluded Loyalists and they began stockpiling their own caches of weapons. This quickly aroused the attention of the British colonial forces and resulted in the British Parliament enacting an embargo against the colonies for firearms, ammunition and firearm parts. The British forces also began attempting to disarm colonists in areas that were considered the hotbeds of rebellion.

When confronted with British forces and Loyalist efforts to disarm the colonial Patriot militia, the Patriot colonists protesting by citing the British Bill of Rights, Blackstone's Summary of the

Declaration of Rights, and British Common Law regarding the right to self-defense. Blackstone states that the right of the people to bear arms ". . . is to be made use of when the sanctions of society and law are found insufficient to restrain the violence of oppression." Colonial pre-Revolutionary War publications referred to the right to bear arms, stating: "it is a natural right which the people have reserved to themselves, confirmed by the Bill of Rights, to keep arms for their own defence."

George Tucker, a law professor at the University of William and Mary and a Virginia state court judge, wrote *Blackstone's Commentaries: With Notes of Reference, to the Constitution and Laws, of the Federal Government of the United States; and of the Commonwealth of Virginia*, published in 1803 and considered the earliest preeminent commentary on the U.S. Constitution. In this work, he noted a very important difference between the English Bill of Rights and the Second Amendment to the U.S. Constitution, that ". . . the right of the people to keep and bear arms shall not be infringed" is guaranteed "without any qualification as to their condition or degree, as is the case in the British government." The absence of any such condition was very likely the result of the recent experience of the citizens of this fledgling country with attempts by the British forces and the Loyalists to disarm the Patriots. Tucker criticized the English Bill of Rights for allowing the limitation of gun ownership to the very wealthy under the premise of game protection, leaving the ordinary citizens effectively disarmed, and expressed the hope that Americans would "never cease to regard the right of keeping and bearing arms as the surest pledge of their liberty."

In determining the intent of the Framers of the Second Amendment, the intent of the Congress in proposing the Second Amendment for ratification by the States, and the intent of the States as they ratified the Amendment, we should consider the declarations of those involved at the time. Statements of the Framers, made before passage and ratification of the Second Amendment, confirm the general acceptance of the sentiment expressed by George Tucker.

James Madison, known as the "father of the Constitution", was a key figure in convening the Constitutional Convention and in accomplishing the purpose for which it was convened, the drafting and adoption of a Constitution to replace the Articles of Confederacy. He was preeminent in rebutting arguments against the adoption of a new constitution. After the Constitution was written, signed by the convention delegates, and transmitted to the States for ratification, Madison co-authored the *Federalist Papers* with Alexander Hamilton and John Jay, which were a collection of 85 essays written to explain the new Constitution and to persuade the states to ratify it.

George Mason, a delegate to the Constitutional Convention from Virginia, came to the Convention with grave concerns about the amount of power that would be ceded to the federal government under the new Constitution being proposed, and, surprisingly for a delegate from a slave state, about the convention's unwillingness to end the slave trade. George Mason had a unique role in regard to the Bill of Rights. He was one of three delegates not to sign the Constitution because it did not contain a strong bill of rights to protect individuals and the States from the new Federal government. Although James Madison ultimately took the lead role in drafting the Bill of Rights and in persuading the first

Congress convened under the new Constitution to adopt the Bill of Rights, Mason was the most determined proponent of an explicit bill of rights in the Constitutional Convention. When the Constitution was finalized, adopted and signed by the other delegates, Mason said "I would sooner chop off my right hand" than sign the Constitution without a Bill of Rights. Even though he did not participate in the drafting of the ten amendments of the Bill of Rights, Mason's determined advocacy for having the freedoms and rights of the country's citizens specifically stated in the Constitution was a primary catalyst for the drafting and adoption of the first 10 amendments to the Constitution, the Bill of Rights. In regard to the right to keep and bear arms guaranteed by the Second Amendment, Mason pointed to England's efforts to disarm the people, stating that "it was the best and most effectual way to enslave them ... by totally disusing and neglecting the militia." He also reminded that the militia consist ". . . now of the whole people, except a few public officers." Since all of the citizenry were members of the militia, they all must enjoy the right to individually bear arms so they would be prepared to serve in the citizens militia.

James Monroe, who ultimately served as fifth President of the United States from 1817 to 1825, was an American statesman, lawyer, diplomat, Founding Father and Revolutionary War officer. He also served as the governor of Virginia, a member of the United States Senate, the U.S. ambassador to France and Britain, the seventh Secretary of State, and the eighth Secretary of War. He is best remembered for the Monroe Doctrine, opposing European colonialism in the Americas. Writing after the ratification of the Constitution, but before the election of the first Congress, Monroe stated that "the right to keep and bear arms" must be included in a list of basic "human rights", which he proposed to be added to the Constitution.

Patrick Henry, a famous Patriot, attorney, planter, and orator best known for his declaration to the Second Virginia Convention of 1775, advocating for independence from England, "Give me liberty, or give me death!" A Founding Father, he served as the first and sixth post-colonial Governor of Virginia, from 1776 to 1779 and from 1784 to 1786. In 1774 and 1775, Henry served as a delegate to the First and Second Continental Congresses. The actions of the national government under the Articles of Confederation made Henry fear a strong federal government and he declined appointment as a delegate to the 1787 Constitutional Convention. Although he actively opposed ratification of the new Constitution, speaking on June 5, 1788 in the Virginia convention wherein ratification of the Constitution was being considered, Patrick Henry advocated for the right to bear arms as essential for the preservation of liberty. He stated, "Guard with jealous attention the public liberty. Suspect everyone who approaches that jewel. Unfortunately, nothing will preserve it but downright force. Whenever you give up that force, you are inevitably ruined."

Noah Webster (1758-1843) wrote that "Before a standing army can rule the people must be disarmed; as they are in almost every kingdom in Europe. The supreme power in America cannot enforce unjust laws by the sword; because the whole body of the people are armed, and constitute a force superior to any band of regular troops that can be, on any pretence, raised in the United States." Noah Webster, who first published *An American Dictionary of the English Language* in 1828, later editions of which were referred to for generations as the

Webster Dictionary, was an influential political writer, textbook publisher, spelling reformer and prolific author. The dictionary he created, now named the *Merriam-Webster Dictionary*, is still perhaps the most widely used dictionary in the United States. He is also called the "Father of American Scholarship and Education," largely due to his "Blue-backed Speller" books which were used by generations of early American children to learn how to read and spell.

Theodore Sedgwick (1746-1813) was an American attorney, politician and jurist, who served in elected state government and as a Delegate to the Continental Congress, a U.S. Representative, and a United States Senator from Massachusetts. He served as the fourth Speaker of the United States House of Representatives. He was appointed to the Massachusetts Supreme Judicial Court in 1802 and served there the rest of his life. Theodore Sedgwick stated that it is "a chimerical idea to suppose that a country like this could ever be enslaved ... Is it possible ... that an army could be raised for the purpose of enslaving themselves or their brethren? Or, if raised whether they could subdue a nation of freemen, who know how to prize liberty and who have arms in their hands?"

James Madison introduced his initial proposal for a bill of rights to the House of Representatives on June 8, 1789, during the first session of the newly constituted U.S. Congress.
The initial proposed passage relating to arms was:

> The right of the people to keep and bear arms shall not be infringed; a well-armed and well-regulated militia being the best security of a free country: but no person religiously scrupulous of bearing arms shall be compelled to render military service in person.

Madison again raised the issue of his proposed bill of rights on July 21 and he proposed the creation of a select committee to review and report on it. The House voted in favor of Madison's motion to refer the bill to a select committee, and the Bill of Rights entered committee for review. A revised version of the right to bear arms amendment was returned by the committee on July 28. That version was read into the House Journal on August 17:

> A well regulated militia, composed of the body of the people, being the best security of a free State, the right of the people to keep and bear arms shall not be infringed; but no person religiously scrupulous shall be compelled to bear arms.

The House finally debated the arms amendment in the latter part of August, which debate led to a further modification. The debates revolved primarily around the risk of the possible use of the "religiously scrupulous" clause to disempower the militia as Great Britain had attempted to do to the colonial militias at the commencement of the Revolution. These concerns were addressed by a further modification of the final clause, which was then approved by a vote in the House and sent to the Senate on August 24:

> A well regulated militia, composed of the body of the people, being the best security of a free state, the right of the people to keep and bear arms shall not be infringed; but no one religiously scrupulous of bearing arms shall be compelled to render military service in person.

The Senate received the proposed arms amendment from the House the next day, August 25, and entered it into the Senate Journal. However, the Senate scribe added a comma before "shall not be infringed" and

changed the semicolon separating that phrase from the religious
exemption portion to a comma:

> A well regulated militia, composed of the body of the people,
> being the best security of a free state, the right of the people to
> keep and bear arms, shall not be infringed, but no one religiously
> scrupulous of bearing arms shall be compelled to render military
> service in person.

By this time, each of the proposed rights enumerated in the proposed Bill
of Rights, including the proposed right to keep and bear arms, were in
separate proposed amendments. This was done to allow each
amendment to be separately considered and voted upon in Congress, and
separately considered for ratification by each State. It should be noted
that there were actually twelve amendments under consideration, the
right to bear arms amendment being the 4th Amendment at the time. On
September 4, the Senate voted to modify the language of the arms
amendment yet again by removing the definition of militia, and striking
the "religiously scrupulous" (conscientious objector) clause:

> A well regulated militia, being the best security of a free state, the
> right of the people to keep and bear arms, shall not be infringed.

On September 9, the Senate considered this amendment for a final time.
A proposal to insert the words "for the common defence" next to the
words "bear arms" was defeated. However, a proposal to replace the
words "the best," with "necessary to the" passed. The Senate then voted
to return the final version of the arms amendment to the House:

> A well regulated militia being necessary to the security of a free
> state, the right of the people to keep and bear arms, shall not be
> infringed.

The House voted on September 21, 1789 to accept the changes made by the Senate.

The enrolled original Joint Resolution passed by Congress on September 25, 1789, on permanent display in the Rotunda, reads as:

> A well regulated militia, being necessary to the security of a free State, the right of the People to keep and bear arms, shall not be infringed.

A little over two years later, on December 15, 1791, the first ten amendments to the Constitution, comprising the Bill of Rights, were ratified by the last of the eleven states required to constitute the three-fourths majority of the then fourteen states of the United States. All of the fourteen states then in existence except Connecticut, Massachusetts, and Georgia had ratified the amendments, making them part of the Constitution and hence the law of the land. Two amendments, the proposed first amendment dealing with the number of congressional representatives, and the proposed second amendment dealing with congressional salaries, were not ratified. The result was that the proposed 3rd Amendment providing for religious freedom, free speech, free press, and freedom of assembly became the 1st Amendment and the proposed 4th Amendment for the right to keep and bear arms became the 2nd Amendment. It is interesting to note that Connecticut, Massachusetts and Georgia symbolically ratified the ten Amendments of the Bill of Rights in 1939, the 150th anniversary of their adoption by Congress.

The right to bear arms is also enshrined in the State Constitutions of a number of states. For example, the Pennsylvania Constitution of 1776 states that, "the people have a right to bear arms for the defence of themselves and the state."

It is clear that George Mason, in vehemently advocating for a Bill of Rights, and James Madison, in drafting the Second Amendment, did not invent and did not believe they were inventing the right to keep and bear arms. The right was pre-existing in the common law, which had been acknowledged and expressly confirmed by many of the original state constitutions. They were merely proposing that the right be constitutionally guaranteed so that there would be no question that the common law right was preserved by the Constitution. However, some historians believe that the framers of the Bill of Rights sought to balance not just political power, but also military power, between the people, the states and the federal government. In that regard, Alexander Hamilton explained in his *Concerning the Militia* essay published in 1788:

> ... it will be possible to have an excellent body of well-trained militia, ready to take the field whenever the defence of the State shall require it. This will not only lessen the call for military establishments, but if circumstances should at any time oblige the Government to form an army of any magnitude, that army can never be formidable to the liberties of the People, while there is a large body of citizens, little, if at all, inferior to them in discipline and the use of arms, who stand ready to defend their own rights, and those of their fellow-citizens. This appears to me the only substitute that can be devised for a standing army, and the best possible security against it, if it should exist.

Alexander Hamilton also wrote in Federalist Paper No. 29 that "little more can be reasonably aimed at, with respect to the people at large, than to have them properly armed . . ."

The question then arises, did the Framers intend that the Second Amendment would provide for armed insurrection by the citizenry against a standing federal army that was deemed by the citizenry to be seeking to oppress individual rights or the States. There is and has been

considerable debate on this issue among historians and legal scholars.

Some have argued that our own Declaration of Independence boldly

confirms "the Right of the People to . . . institute new Government." The

second paragraph of the Declaration of Independence states:

> We hold these truths to be self-evident, that all men are created
> equal, that they are endowed by their Creator with certain
> unalienable Rights, that among these are Life, Liberty and the
> pursuit of Happiness.--That to secure these rights, Governments
> are instituted among Men, deriving their just powers from the
> consent of the governed, --***That whenever any Form of
> Government becomes destructive of these ends, it is the Right of
> the People to alter or to abolish it, and to institute new
> Government, laying its foundation on such principles and
> organizing its powers in such form, as to them shall seem most
> likely to effect their Safety and Happiness.*** Prudence, indeed,
> will dictate that Governments long established should not be
> changed for light and transient causes; and accordingly all
> experience hath shewn, that mankind are more disposed to suffer,
> while evils are sufferable, than to right themselves by abolishing
> the forms to which they are accustomed. ***But when a long train
> of abuses and usurpations, pursuing invariably the same Object
> evinces a design to reduce them under absolute Despotism, it is
> their right, it is their duty, to throw off such Government, and to
> provide new Guards for their future security.***--Such has been the
> patient sufferance of these Colonies; and such is now the
> necessity which constrains them to alter their former Systems of
> Government. The history of the present King of Great Britain is a
> history of repeated injuries and usurpations, all having in direct
> object the establishment of an absolute Tyranny over these States.
> To prove this, let Facts be submitted to a candid world. (*emphasis
> added*)

In reviewing the foregoing excerpt from the Declaration of

Independence, it seems compelling that the Founding Fathers believed in the right of the people to engage in insurrection, if necessary, to overthrow "any Form of Government" which "becomes destructive" of the rights of the people to "Life, Liberty and the pursuit of Happiness."

Many historians and scholars have argued, however, that the Founding Fathers intended to place their trust in the democratic government established by the Constitution to protect the inviolate rights of the people and to prevent the necessity of armed insurrection from ever developing. The Declaration of Independence further states, in the same second paragraph, that "Prudence, indeed, will dictate that Governments long established should not be changed for light and transient causes." There have been many serious ideological, political and social conflicts among the citizenry and governments of the United States. However, we have always found a workable solution. The disputes have and will likely always be "transient," because the form of government that the Founding Fathers and the Framers had the wisdom to form, provides for continuing, responsive change and adaptation. Though we may vehemently disagree on issues, at the end of the day, week, year or decade, we collectively come to our senses and strike an accord that we can all live with. None of us will ever be completely happy with all of the conditions and situations present in this great country. There will always be serious disagreement. However, we will coexist and persevere.

As the proposed Constitution was being drafted, debated, revised and adopted by the Constitutional Convention delegates, and as the proposed Bill of Rights were being drafted, debated, revised and adopted by the new Congress, some representatives were very concerned over the inherent risks of giving power to a central, federal government.

Federalists, including James Madison, initially argued that a bill of rights was unnecessary, apparently based on the belief that the federal government, at least the one they envisioned, would never be able to raise a standing (federal) army powerful enough to overcome a militia of the armed populace. Noah Webster, also a Federalist who advocated for the inviolate right of the people to bear arms, argued that an armed populace would have no trouble resisting the potential threat to liberty that could arguably arise from a standing army. Anti-Federalists, who feared otherwise, advocated amending the Constitution with clearly defined and enumerated rights providing more explicit constraints on the new government. They argued that explicit protection of those rights would allay the fears and were only defining rights that all, Federalists and Anti-Federalists alike, agreed were inherent and embodied in the common law anyway. Federalists countered that in listing only certain rights, unlisted rights might lose protection.

The fear that loomed large among the Anti-Federalists, based upon their recent experience with Britain, was that the new federal government would choose to try to disarm state militias. Ultimately, the Federalist delegates of the Constitutional Convention realized that there was insufficient support among the States for the ratification of the Constitution without a bill of rights. Accordingly, they offered the Anti-Federalists a commitment for the addition of a bill of rights by amendment to the Constitution following ratification. Apparently, in those days a representative's word must have meant something, both to the receiver and the giver, since the Federalists' commitment resulted in adoption of the Constitution by the Convention and ratification by the requisite three-fourths majority of the States.

The Constitution was declared ratified and became the law of the land on June 21, 1788 when the last of the required nine of the thirteen states had ratified it. The remaining four states did ultimately ratify the Constitution, but Rhode Island and North Carolina only did so after Congress had passed the Bill of Rights and sent it to the states for ratification. As described above, James Madison drafted what ultimately became the Bill of Rights, which was passed by the first Congress and sent to the States for ratification on June 8, 1789. Ten of the twelve proposed amendments of the Bill of Rights were ratified by the tenth of the then fourteen States on December 15, 1791. Vermont had been added as the fourteenth State in 1790, which resulted in a requirement for ten states to constitute a three-fourths majority for ratification.

William Rawle in his critically acclaimed work published in 1825, *A View of the Constitution of the United States of America*, agreed with Tucker in condemning England's "arbitrary code for the preservation of game," and its reservation for "[a] very small proportion of the people" the right to bear arms. Rawle refers to the second clause of the Second Amendment as the "corollary clause" which he said constituted a general prohibition against such a capricious abuse of government power:

> No clause could by any rule of construction be conceived to give to congress a power to disarm the people. Such a flagitious attempt could only be made under some general pretence by a state legislature. But if in any blind pursuit of inordinate power, either should attempt it, this amendment may be appealed to as a restraint on both.

Commentaries on the Constitution of the United States, written by U.S. Supreme Court Justice Joseph Story and published in 1833, was considered the leading treatise on the Constitution for the first half of the 19th century. In view of the success of and public interest in *Commentaries*, Justice Story wrote *Familiar Exposition of the Constitution of the United States*, a summary of the *Commentaries* for a general public audience which was published in 1840. The following excerpt is from *Familiar Exposition*.

The next amendment is, "A well-regulated militia being necessary to the security of a free state, the right of the people to keep and bear arms shall not be infringed." One of the ordinary modes, by which tyrants accomplish their purposes without resistance, is, by disarming the people, and making it an offence to keep arms, and by substituting a regular army in the stead of a resort to the militia. The friends of a free government cannot be too watchful, to overcome the dangerous tendency of the public mind to sacrifice, for the sake of mere private convenience, this powerful check upon the designs of ambitious men.

The importance of this article will scarcely be doubted by any persons, who have duly reflected upon the subject. The militia is the natural defence of a free country against sudden foreign invasions, domestic insurrections, and domestic usurpations of power by rulers. It is against sound policy for a free people to keep up large military establishments and standing armies in time of peace, both from the enormous expenses, with which they are attended, and the facile means, which they afford to ambitious and unprincipled rulers, to subvert the government, or trample upon the rights of the people. The right of the citizens to keep and bear arms has justly been considered, as the palladium of the liberties of a republic; since it offers a strong moral check against the usurpation and arbitrary power of rulers; and will generally, even if these are successful in the first instance, enable the people to resist and triumph over them. And yet, though this truth would seem so clear, and the importance of a well regulated militia would seem so undeniable, it cannot be disguised, that among the American people there is a growing indifference to any system of militia discipline, and a strong disposition, from a sense of its burthens, to be rid of all regulations. How it is practicable to keep the people duly armed

without some organization, it is difficult to see. There is
certainly no small danger, that indifference may lead to disgust,
and disgust to contempt; and thus gradually undermine all the
protection intended by this clause of our national bill of rights.

It would be well for Americans to reflect upon the
passage in Tacitus, (Hist. IV. ch. 74): "Nam neque quies sine
armis, neque arma, sine stipendiis, neque stipendia sine tributis,
haberi queunt." Is there any escape from a large standing army,
but in a well disciplined militia? There is much wholesome
instruction on this subject in 1 Black. Comm. ch. 13, p. 408 to
417.

A similar provision in favour of protestants (for to them
it is confined) is to be found in the bill of rights of 1688, it being
declared, "that the subjects, which are protestants, may have arms
for their defence suitable to their condition, and as allowed by
law." But under various pretences the effect of this provision has
been greatly narrowed; and it is at present in England more
nominal than real, as a defensive privilege.

Michigan Supreme Court Justice Thomas Cooley was the leading

constitutional commentator of the late 1800's. He was elected to the

Supreme Court of Michigan in 1864, during the fury of the Civil War,

and served as the Chief Justice of that Court for 20 years. He wrote a

constitutional commentary entitled *A Treatise on Constitutional

Limitations*, published in 1868, which he revised many times before the

end of the century. He also wrote an abridgment of the treatise

entitled *Principles of Constitutional Law*, which was published in 1898.

Judge Cooley wrote extensively about the Second Amendment in his

Treatise and in *Principles*.

Though the Supreme Court of Michigan was an elected body and

Judge Cooley remained a Republican all his life, he was an independent

thinker which led him to defy the Republican party and support Grover

Cleveland in 1884, and later in 1894. This earned him the title of "mugwump." This independence may have cost him an appointment to the U.S. Supreme Court, but it also had its rewards, aside from the peace of mind that naturally comes with being an uninhibited thinker. In 1887, President Cleveland nominated him to the Interstate Commerce Commission, one of the first independent agencies of the federal government.

Judge Cooley wrote the following in the *Treatise* in a section entitled *The Right to Bear Arms:*

> Among the other defences to personal liberty should be mentioned the right of the people to keep and bear arms. A standing army is peculiarly obnoxious in any free government, and the jealousy of one has at times been demonstrated so strongly in England as almost to lead to the belief that a standing army recruited from among themselves was more dreaded as an instrument of oppression than a tyrannical king, or any foreign power. So impatient did the English people become of the very army which liberated them from the tyranny of James II., that they demanded its reduction, even before the liberation could be felt to be complete; and to this day, the British Parliament render a standing army practically impossible by only passing a mutiny bill from session to session. The alternative to a standing army is "a well-regulated militia," but this cannot exist unless the people are trained to bearing arms. How far it is in the power of the legislature to regulate this right, we shall not undertake to say, as happily there has been very little occasion to discuss that subject by the courts. [fn1]
>
> *[fn1] In Bliss v. Commonwealth, 2 Lit. 90, the statute "to prevent persons wearing concealed arms" was held unconstitutional, as infringing on the right of the people to bear arms in defence of themselves and of the State. But See Nunn v. State, 1 Kelly, 243. As bearing also upon the right of self-defence, see Ely v. Thompson, 3 A. K. Marsh. 73, where it was held that the statute subjecting free persons of color to corporal*

punishment for "lifting their hands in opposition" to a white person was held unconstitutional.

Judge Cooley also wrote the following in *Principles* in a section entitled *The Right to Keep and Bear Arms*:

> *The Constitution.* -- By the Second Amendment to the Constitution it is declared that "a well regulated militia being necessary to the security of a free State, the right of the people to keep and bear arms shall not be infringed."
>
> The amendment, like most other provisions in the Constitution, has a history. It was adopted with some modification and enlargement from the English Bill of Rights of 1688, where it stood as a protest against arbitrary action of the overturned dynasty in disarming the people, and as a pledge of the new rulers that this tyrannical action should cease. The right declared was meant to be a strong moral check against the usurpation and arbitrary power of rulers, and as a necessary and efficient means of regaining rights when temporarily overturned by usurpation.
>
> *The Right is General.* -- It may be supposed from the phraseology of this provision that the right to keep and bear arms was only guaranteed to the militia; but this would be an interpretation not warranted by the intent. The militia, as has been elsewhere explained, consists of those persons who, under the law, are liable to the performance of military duty, and are officered and enrolled for service when called upon. But the law may make provision for the enrolment of all who are fit to perform military duty, or of a small number only, or it may wholly omit to make any provision at all; and if the right were limited to those enrolled, the purpose of this guaranty might be defeated altogether by the action or neglect to act of the government it was meant to hold in check. The meaning of the provision undoubtedly is, that the people, from whom the militia must be taken, shall have the right to keep and bear arms, and they need no permission or regulation of law for the purpose. But this enables the government to have a well regulated militia; for to bear arms implies something more than the mere keeping; it implies the learning to handle and use them in a way that makes those who keep them ready for their efficient

use; in other words, it implies the right to meet for voluntary discipline in arms, observing in doing so the laws of public order.

Standing Army. -- A further purpose of this amendment is, to preclude any necessity or reasonable excuse for keeping up a standing army. A standing army is condemned by the traditions and sentiments of the people, as being as dangerous to the liberties of the people as the general preparation of the people for the defence of their institutions with arms is preservative of them.

What Arms may be kept. -- The arms intended by the Constitution are such as are suitable for the general defence of the community against invasion or oppression, and the secret carrying of those suited merely to deadly individual encounters may be prohibited.

A century later, toward the end of the 1900's, the debate continued to rage over whether the Second Amendment protected a collective right to a militia or an individual right to keep and bear arms. Unsurprisingly, the debate continued to focus on the introductory clause, "A well regulated militia being necessary to the security of a free State", and whether a collective right to maintain a militia was the sole purpose of the amendment, with the operative second clause, "the right of the People to keep and bear arms shall not be infringed", merely for protecting the best and essential means to provide for the militia. The metamorphosis of alternative thought on this issue is intriguing and enlightening, as is vividly articulated by the scholarly articles, court decisions, and opinions summarized below.

In 1990, following his retirement as Chief Justice of the U.S. Supreme Court, Warren E. Burger, a conservative Republican appointed by President Richard Nixon, wrote:

"The Constitution of the United States, in its Second Amendment, guarantees a 'right of the people to keep and bear arms.' However, the meaning of this clause cannot be understood except by looking to the purpose, the setting and the objectives of the draftsmen ... People of that day were apprehensive about the new "monster" national government presented to them, and this helps explain the language and purpose of the Second Amendment ... We see that the need for a state militia was the predicate of the 'right' guaranteed; in short, it was declared 'necessary' in order to have a state military force to protect the security of the state."

In 1991, the former Chief Justice Burger further stated:

If I were writing the Bill of Rights now, there wouldn't be any such thing as the Second Amendment . . . that a well regulated militia being necessary for the defense of the state, the peoples' rights to bear arms. This has been the subject of one of the greatest pieces of fraud - I repeat the word 'fraud' - on the American public by special interest groups that I have ever seen in my lifetime.

In a 1992 opinion published in the <u>Washington Post</u>, six former American attorneys general wrote:

For more than 200 years, the federal courts have unanimously determined that the Second Amendment concerns only the arming of the people in service to an organized state militia; it does not guarantee immediate access to guns for private purposes. The nation can no longer afford to let the gun lobby's distortion of the Constitution cripple every reasonable attempt to implement an effective national policy toward guns and crime.

As noted in the comments of the Founding Fathers and the Framers presented above, as well as the commentaries of scholars of the 1800's and 1900's, the potential entity or institution feared most and the establishment of which was strongly opposed, was a "standing army." Merriam-Webster defines a standing army as "a permanent army of paid soldiers." A standing army is a permanent, professional army, composed of full-time soldiers and is not disbanded during times of peace. It differs from army reserves, who may be enrolled for the long term, but activated only during wars or natural disasters, and temporary armies, referred to historically as militias, which are raised from the civilian population only during a war or threat of war and disbanded once the war or threat is over. The earliest known use of the term "standing army" was in 1603 in reference to the actions of King James. However, standing armies have been used throughout history by untold numbers of totalitarian and repressive regimes to control the people. Declan Leary wrote in *National Review* on July 19, 2019, "In exercising the dispensing power, maintaining a *standing army*, dissolving Parliaments, and any of the other acts to which Parliament objected, James was simply ruling within the bounds and precedents of the crown."

The experience of the Founding Fathers and the Framers with Britain, as well as their knowledge of British history, left them with the unshakeable conviction that standing armies were to be avoided like the plague by the United States. The militia was to be a safeguard against the establishment of a repressive standing army. The armed populace, ready for the call to arms, was the anticipated and intended militia. Hence, the right of the people to keep and bear arms was deemed essential for the preservation and safeguarding of liberty.

Notwithstanding the ostensible primary purpose of the Second Amendment as stated in the initial prefatory clause, "A well-regulated Militia, being necessary to the security of a free State," it is the Courts that have the authority and the responsibility to interpret the law. In the case of the U.S. Constitution, including the Bill of Rights, it is, of course, the U.S. Supreme Court that has the final word on interpretation. The Court of Appeals for the various Federal Circuits also issue decisions on Constitutional matters that stand, at least within the Circuit, unless and until the U.S. Supreme Court subsequently issues a decision on the matter. In that regard, the question of whether the right to bear arms is a collective right or an individual right has arguably been resolved, by recent court decisions, in favor of the individual rights position.

The decisions of the U.S. Supreme Court, as well as other courts, both recent and historical, on the right to bear arms are discussed in detail below. Those decisions include the 2001 Fifth Circuit Court decision in *United States v. Emerson*, the 2008 U.S. Supreme Court decisions in *District of Columbia v. Heller*, and the 2010 U.S. Supreme Court decision in *McDonald v. Chicago*. In *Heller*, the Supreme Court resolved any inconsistencies arising from prior Circuit Court decisions by ruling that the Second Amendment protects the right of each individual to keep and bear arms. In *McDonald*, the Supreme Court ruled that the Second Amendment was incorporated by the due process section of the Fourteenth Amendment and individuals, in each of the 50 U.S. states, were therefore granted a constitutional right to keep firearms in their homes for self-protection. The Court ruled that this right was greater than the states' power to restrict it.

The majority and dissent opinions in *Heller* enlighten on the most recent thinking of the Justices of the U.S. Supreme Court to be embodied in a Second Amendment case decision. Recently deceased, conservative Justice Antonin Scalia, writing for the majority in *Heller*, stated:

In _Nunn v. State_, 1 Ga. 243, 251 (1846), the Georgia Supreme Court construed the Second Amendment as protecting the 'natural right of self-defence' and therefore struck down a ban on carrying pistols openly. Its opinion perfectly captured the way in which the operative clause of the Second Amendment furthers the purpose announced in the prefatory clause, in continuity with the English right.

Nor is the right involved in this discussion less comprehensive or valuable: "The right of the people to bear arms shall not be infringed." The right of the whole people, old and young, men, women and boys, and not militia only, to keep and bear arms of every description, not such merely as are used by the militia, shall not be infringed, curtailed, or broken in upon, in the smallest degree; and all this for the important end to be attained: the rearing up and qualifying a well-regulated militia, so vitally necessary to the security of a free State. Our opinion is, that any law, State or Federal, is repugnant to the Constitution, and void, which contravenes this right, originally belonging to our forefathers, trampled under foot by Charles I. and his two wicked sons and successors, reestablished by the revolution of 1688, conveyed to this land of liberty by the colonists, and finally incorporated conspicuously in our own Magna Charta [sic]! And Lexington, Concord, Camden, River Raisin, Sandusky, and the laurel-crowned field of New Orleans, plead eloquently for this interpretation! And the acquisition of Texas may be considered the full fruits of this great constitutional right.

Justice Scalia further stated:

Nowhere else in the Constitution does a "right" attributed to "the people" refer to anything other than an individual right. What is more, in all six other provisions of the Constitution that mention "the people," the term unambiguously refers to all members of the political community, not an unspecified subset. This contrasts markedly with the phrase "the militia" in the prefatory clause. As we will describe below, the "militia" in colonial America consisted of a subset of "the people" – those who were male, able bodied, and within a certain age range. Reading the Second Amendment as protecting only the right to "keep and bear Arms" in an organized militia therefore fits poorly with the operative clause's description of the holder of that right as "the people."

According to the majority in *Heller*, there were several different reasons for this amendment, and protecting militias was only one of them; if protecting militias had been the only reason then the amendment could have instead referred to "the right of the *militia* to keep and bear arms" instead of "the right of the *people* to keep and bear arms." Justice Scalia specifically rejected the view that the term "to bear arms" implies only the military use of arms:

> Before addressing the verbs "keep" and "bear," we interpret their object: "Arms." The term was applied, then as now, to weapons that were not specifically designed for military use and were not employed in a military capacity. Thus, the most natural reading of "keep Arms" in the Second Amendment is to "have weapons." At the time of the founding, as now, to "bear" meant to "carry." In numerous instances, "bear arms" was unambiguously used to refer to the carrying of weapons outside of an organized militia. Nine state constitutional provisions written in the 18th century or the first two decades of the 19th, which enshrined a right of citizens "bear arms in defense of themselves and the state" again, in the most analogous linguistic context – that "bear arms" was not limited to the carrying of arms in a militia. The phrase "bear Arms" also had at the time of the founding an idiomatic meaning that was significantly different from its natural meaning: "to serve as a soldier, do military service, fight" or "to wage war." But it unequivocally bore that idiomatic meaning only when followed by the preposition "against." Every example given by petitioners' amici for the idiomatic meaning of "bear arms" from the founding period either includes the preposition "against" or is not clearly idiomatic. In any event, the meaning of "bear arms" that petitioners and Justice Stevens propose is not even the (sometimes) idiomatic meaning. Rather, they manufacture a hybrid definition, whereby "bear arms" connotes the actual carrying of arms (and therefore is not really an idiom) but only in the service of an organized militia. No dictionary has ever

adopted that definition, and we have been apprised of no source that indicates that it carried that meaning at the time of the founding. Worse still, the phrase "keep and bear Arms" would be incoherent. The word "Arms" would have two different meanings at once: "weapons" (as the object of "keep") and (as the object of "bear") one-half of an idiom. It would be rather like saying "He filled and kicked the bucket" to mean "He filled the bucket and died."

In a dissent, joined by Justices Souter, Ginsburg, and Breyer, Justice Stevens wrote:

When each word in the text is given full effect, the Amendment is most naturally read to secure to the people a right to use and possess arms in conjunction with service in a well-regulated militia. So far as appears, no more than that was contemplated by its drafters or is encompassed within its terms. Even if the meaning of the text were genuinely susceptible to more than one interpretation, the burden would remain on those advocating a departure from the purpose identified in the preamble and from settled law to come forward with persuasive new arguments or evidence. The textual analysis offered by respondent and embraced by the Court falls far short of sustaining that heavy burden. And the Court's emphatic reliance on the claim "that the Second Amendment ... codified a pre-existing right," ante, at 19 [refers to p. 19 of the opinion], is of course beside the point because the right to keep and bear arms for service in a state militia was also a pre-existing right.

Justice Stevens further stated:

The Amendment's text does justify a different limitation: the "right to keep and bear arms" protects only a right to possess and use firearms in connection with service in a state-organized militia. Had the Framers wished to expand the meaning of the phrase "bear arms" to encompass civilian possession and use, they could have done so by the addition of phrases such as "for the defense of themselves."

Unsurprisingly, the decision in *Heller*, as stated for the majority by Justice Scalia, has received a lot of scrutiny, including a lot of criticism from Constitutional scholars. One of those is Robert James Spitzer, distinguished service professor and chair of the political science department at the State University of New York (SUNY) at Cortland. He has taught at SUNY Cortland since 1979, and as a visiting professor at Cornell University since 1988. His areas of specialty include the American presidency and gun politics. He is the author of numerous books, including five books on gun control: *The Politics of Gun Control; The Right to Bear Arms; Gun Control: A Documentary and Reference Guide; Guns across America: Reconciling Gun Rules and Rights;* and co-author of *Encyclopedia of Gun Control and Gun Rights.* He also has written numerous articles, essays, papers, and op-eds for newspapers on many topics related to American politics. His written work on the subject has appeared in the *Washington Post* and the *New York Daily News.*   He has appeared on numerous radio and television shows about gun control, including NPR's *Fresh Air With Terry Gross* and on MSNBC's *Countdown with Keith Olbermann.*

On the basis of research completed by Robert Spitzer, he determined that every law journal article discussing the Second Amendment through 1959 "reflected the Second Amendment affects citizens only in connection with citizen service in a government organized and regulated militia." Not until 1960 was an "individualist" view of gun ownership rights first advocated in law journal articles.

Spitzer argues that history and prior law do not support the individualist interpretation of the Second Amendment reflected in *Heller* and *McDonald.* Since the cases were decided, Spitzer wrote:

"The *Heller* and *McDonald* rulings established, as a matter of law, an individual rights interpretation of the Second Amendment. But while judges can change the law, they cannot change history, and the historical record largely contradicts the bases for these two recent rulings." Spitzer has suggested that one approach to "breaking the political deadlock over gun control" would be to treat it like international arms relations and "renounce disarmament but embrace arms control, especially for weapons of military origin."

Dennis Baron, a professor of English and linguistics at the University of Illinois at Urbana-Champaign, has done extensive research and writing on the technologies of communication; language legislation and linguistic rights; language reform; gender issues in language; language standards and minority languages and dialects; English usage; and the history and present state of the English language. Baron has held a Fulbright Fellowship and a National Endowment for the Humanities Fellowship. He twice chaired the National Council of Teachers of English Committee on Public Language. His works include *A Better Pencil: Readers, Writers, and the Digital Revolution*; *The English-Only Question: An Official Language for Americans?*; *Guide to Home Language Repair*; *Declining Grammar and Other Essays on the English Vocabulary*; *Grammar and Gender*; *and Grammar and Good Taste: Reforming the American Language*. *The New York Times*, *The Washington Post*, the *Los Angeles Times*, the *Chicago Tribune* and other newspapers have published articles by Baron on language matters and he has been interviewed on NPR, the BBC, CBC and CNN. Baron has been identified as an English language expert in a number of publications by others and has been a legal expert witness, interpreting the language of contracts and advertising materials.

Of particular note, Baron was the lead author, along with two colleagues, of an amicus brief, referred to as "Brief for Professors of Linguistics and English" and as "the Linguists' Brief," filed with the Supreme Court in *Heller*. The brief provided an interpretation of the Second Amendment based on language usage common in the time of the Framers, as well as dictionaries and other references demonstrating that the interpretation was still valid at the time of *Heller*. Baron offered the opinion that the common and essentially exclusive usage of term "bear arms" at the time of the drafting of the Second Amendment, was confined to a military context. However, while the Linguists' Brief was referred to favorably by Justice Stevens in the minority opinion, Justice Scalia, in writing for the majority, disputed the Linguistics' Brief and chose instead to rely upon the research and conclusions of Clayton E. Cramer and Joseph Edward Olson in their work "What Did "Bear Arms" Mean in the Second Amendment?" The work of Clayton E. Cramer is discussed in detail below.

On May 21, 2018, based on further research completed after the *Heller* decision, Baron wrote, in an article published in the *Washington Post*, entitled "Antonin Scalia was wrong about the meaning of 'bear arms' ":

> In his opinion in *Heller*, Justice Antonin Scalia, who said that we must understand the Constitution's words exactly as the framers understood them, disconnected the right to keep and bear arms from the need for a well-regulated militia, in part because he concluded that the phrase "bear arms" did not refer to military contexts in the founding era.

By Scalia's logic, the natural meaning of "bear arms" is simply to carry a weapon and has nothing to do with armies. He explained in his opinion: "Although ['bear arms'] implies that the carrying of the weapon is for the purpose of 'offensive or defensive action,' it in no way connotes participation in a structured military organization. From our review of founding-era sources, we conclude that this natural meaning was also the meaning that 'bear arms' had in the 18th century. In numerous instances, 'bear arms' was unambiguously used to refer to the carrying of weapons outside of an organized militia."

But Scalia was wrong. Two new databases of English writing from the founding era confirm that "bear arms" is a military term. Non-military uses of "bear arms" are not just rare — they're almost nonexistent.

A search of Brigham Young University's new online Corpus of Founding Era American English, with more than 95,000 texts and 138 million words, yields 281 instances of the phrase "bear arms." BYU's Corpus of Early Modern English, with 40,000 texts and close to 1.3 billion words, shows 1,572 instances of the phrase. Subtracting about 350 duplicate matches, that leaves about 1,500 separate occurrences of "bear arms" in the 17th and 18th centuries, and only a handful don't refer to war, soldiering or organized, armed action. These databases confirm that the natural meaning of "bear arms" in the framers' day was military.

A well-researched and persuasive article, entitled "What Did "Bear Arms" Mean in the Second Amendment?" written by Clayton E. Cramer and Joseph Edward Olson in 2008, was cited by Judge Scalia in *Heller* and seems to seriously undermine the conclusions of Baron cited in the Linguists' Brief in *Heller* and the conclusions of Baron and the data he relied upon for the 2018 *Washington Post* article referenced above.

Clayton E. Cramer is an American historian, gun rights advocate, and software engineer whose rise to prominence was sparked in 1996 while he was working on a master's thesis for his M.A. in History at Sonoma State University. His thesis included a discussion of the development of concealed weapon laws in the early years of the United States. While working on his thesis, Cramer read a paper entitled "Arming America: The Origins of a National Gun Culture" written by Michael A. Bellesiles, historian and history professor at Emory University, on early gun laws, and published in the *Journal of American History* in 1996. Cramer's attention was aroused as he noted that Bellesiles' article appeared to contradict Cramer's own knowledge of gun ownership, possession and access in early America, derived from his prior reading and research.   However, at the time, Cramer assumed that the contradictions were due to Bellesiles having relied on different references than those Cramer was familiar with.

At the time Bellesiles' book, *Arming America: The Origins of a National Gun Culture*, an expansion of the 1996 article, was ready for publication in 2000, Cramer received an advance review copy. This time around, it appeared clear to Cramer that Belleside's purported research results and his own knowledge of the time period around the time of the Revolutionary War, were irreconcilable. Cramer could no longer attribute contradictions between Bellesiles' research and conclusions and his own knowledge to differences in references. In particular, Cramer was immediately convinced that Bellesiles' conclusions that guns were uncommon during peacetime and that ordinary citizens had very limited ownership, possession and access to guns in the early years of the United States prior to Civil War times were incorrect.

Cramer followed up on his initial concerns by checking facts and he discovered that many of Bellesiles' reference citations and quotes were at odds with the historical records Bellesiles purportedly relied upon. Cramer describes that initial investigation: "I sat down with a list of bizarre, amazing claims that Bellesiles had made, and started chasing down the citations at Sonoma State University's library. I found quotations out of context that completely reversed the author's original intent. I found dates changed. I found the text of statutes changed - and the changes completely reversed the meaning of the law. It took me twelve hours of hunting before I found a citation that was completely correct." But Cramer was, after all, a minimally educated gun rights partisan who possessed only a lowly M.A. and had no honors or credits to his name, or so Bellesiles was soon to be urging.

While intensive critical examination of Bellesile's research and conclusions was underway behind the scenes, *Arming America* was garnering favorable and enthusiastic peer and professional reviews. The favorable reviews included a review by Roger Lane appearing in the September 2001 edition of the *Journal of American History*. He wrote that Bellesiles had "attacked the central myth behind the National Rifle Association's interpretation of the Second Amendment." Lane further wrote that Bellesile's research was "meticulous and thorough," and that Bellesiles' evidence so formidable that "if the subject were open to rational argument," the debate would be over.

Even more impressive than the many favorable peer reviews, Bellesiles won the coveted Bancroft Prize in 2001 for this work. Unsurprisingly, the book also garnered a lot of political attention, as well as the ire of the NRA. The provocative conclusions dragged the book and Bellesiles into the ongoing political turmoil over gun rights and the Second Amendment. The NRA's famous president, actor Charton

Heston, characterized Bellesiles' conclusions as "ludicrous." As it turned out, Charlton Heston was right.

In view of Bellesiles' exalted position in the academic community and the glowing initial peer and professional reviews of *Arming America*, Cramer's critical review was initially met with skepticism from other historians and journal editors. Still, Cramer marched on with his shocking allegations of professional turpitude against Bellesiles. Soon, James Lindgren of Northwestern University and other historians lined up to support Cramer's claims. Accordingly, within a few months following Bellesiles receipt of the Bancroft Prize, the serious questions about the research purportedly completed by Bellesiles which he reported in *Arming America* and upon which he based the conclusions presented in the book, began to gain traction. As a result of the questions, Emory University commissioned an ad hoc Investigative Committee, comprised of Stanley N. Katz, Chair (Professor of Public and International Affairs, Princeton University), Hanna H. Gray (Judson Distinguished Professor of History Emeritus, University of Chicago), and Laurel Thatcher Ulrich (James Duncan Phillips Professor of History, Harvard University) to investigate the allegations against Bellesides. The committee issued its final report, the "Report of the Investigative Committee in the matter of Professor Michael Bellesiles," in July, 2002.

In its conclusions, the committee stated:

> In summary, we find on Questions 1 and 2, that despite serious failures of and carelessness in the gathering and presentation of archival records and the use of quantitative analysis, we cannot speak of intentional fabrication or falsification. On Question 3, we find that the strained character of Professor Bellesiles'

explanation raises questions about his veracity with respect to his account of having consulted probate records in San Francisco County. On Question 4, dealing with the construction of the vital Table One, we find evidence of falsification. And on Question 5, which raises the standard of professional historical scholarship, we find that Professor Bellesiles falls short on all three counts.

Upon release of the Committee Report, Bellesiles immediately resigned his position at Emory University. Bellesile's Bancroft Prize was soon thereafter rescinded following a decision of Columbia University's Board of Trustees that Bellesiles had "violated basic norms of scholarship and the high standards expected of Bancroft Prize winners."

After the release of the Report and the resignation of Bellesiles, Cramer suggested that the reason "why historians swallowed *Arming America*'s preposterous claims so readily is that it fit into their political worldview so well... *Arming America* said things, and created a system of thought so comfortable for the vast majority of historians, that they didn't even pause to consider the possibility that something wasn't right." Other historians who acceded to the request of the publisher of *Arming America* to provide a support statement "were ecstatic in part because the book knocked the gun lobby."

Bellesiles attempted to use the political turmoil over gun rights and side taking in that conflict as a smoke screen against confirmation of his subterfuge. He arrogantly replied to Charlton Heston's criticism by suggesting to Heston that he needed to earn his own Ph.D. before daring to invade the province of learned academics and scholars. He referred to Cramer as "a long time advocate of unrestricted gun ownership" while pointing out that he, as a professional, had "certain obligations of accuracy that transcend current political benefit." Bellesiles added, to his arrogance laced defense, claims of being victimized by a barrage of hate mail. These claims prompted the American Historical Association and the Organization of American Historians to endorse a resolution condemning the alleged harassment. Historian Peter Charles Hoffer, although a renowned advocate for gun control measures, wrote, in 2004, that Bellesiles "was convinced that whether the entire profession agreed with "his stance on gun ownership (and I suspect most did), surely academic historians would not let their expertise be impugned by a rank and partisan amateur like Cramer."

The article written by Cramer and Joseph Edward Olson in 2008 entitled "What Did "Bear Arms" Mean in the Second Amendment?" was cited by Judge Scalia in *Heller* and in *McDonald*. Olson is a Professor of Law at Hamline University, president of Academics for the Second Amendment, and a member of the Board of Directors of the NRA. Cramer has written a regular column on gun owners' rights and related issues for *Shotgun News*. Cramer also manages an online blog titled *'Civilian Gun Self-Defense Blog'* which records civilian use of firearms in self-defense through citing news articles across the nation. Clearly, Cramer and Olson are gun rights partisans with a pro-gun agenda. However, the research and conclusions presented in "What Did "Bear Arms" Mean in the Second Amendment?" appear to be well founded and considerably more persuasive than that of the Linguistics' Brief of Banon et al, cited in *Heller*.

The reason the present author elected to present the foregoing detailed discussion of the Cramer investigation of Bellesiles and the fall of Bellesiles was to point up the inadvisability of buying in to a controlling ideology on the gun rights-gun control issue. It is possible to invest in either side of the ideological argument to the point that logic, reason and truth become secondary concerns. Although it is easy to surmise that Bellesiles was motivated solely by desire for professional recognition and financial gain in writing *Arming America*, in the abstract it is equally plausible that he was motivated by a desire to advance a gun control agenda.

In the opening paragraphs of "What Did "Bear Arms" Mean in the Second Amendment?", Cramer and Olson write:

> Among the many heated controversies concerning the Second Amendment is the meaning of the phrase "keep and bear arms." Those who argue that the original meaning of the Second Amendment was only to protect a collective right, either of the states to maintain militias, or perhaps of citizens to jointly form militias, assert that "bear arms" refers exclusively or at least overwhelmingly, to the collective, military carrying of weapons. Some have claimed that even "keep arms" was exclusively military in its meaning, although the Rhode Island Supreme Court has argued that "keep arms" was non-military, while "bear arms" referred to military use. While one might challenge the overly narrow focus on "bear arms" instead of the entire phrase "keep and bear arms," those arguing for a collective right have thrown down the gauntlet by making this strong claim about just two words. This paper demonstrates that the Founding Generation, and at least two generations after them, did not understand "bear arms" as limited to military or collective militia duty.

> If "bear arms" referred *only* to the military carrying or use of arms, then the right protected by the Second Amendment would not be an individual right to possess or carry arms for personal self-defense. The right would be for a government organized militia, or at best, to exercise what the Tennessee Supreme Court in *Aymette* acknowledged was a right to revolution. After explaining

that the Tennessee Constitution's guarantee included the qualifier "for their common defence" (explicitly rejected by the U.S. Senate for the Second Amendment) the Court articulated an individual *right* that existed to serve a collective *purpose*, "[t]he object then, for which the right of keeping and bearing arms is secured, is the defence of the public. The free white men may keep arms to protect the public liberty, to keep in awe those who are in power, and to maintain the supremacy of the laws and the constitution."

Previous scholarly examination of the phrase "bear arms" in English language documents published around the time of the Constitution does show almost entirely military uses or contexts. But this is perhaps reflective of a selection bias problem. Consider Dorf's statement that, "Searching for the phrase 'bear arms' in the Library of Congress's database of congressional and other documents from the founding era produces a great many references, nearly all of them in a military context." This should be no surprise; Dorf's footnote recommends that readers "click on 'Political Science and Law,' and choose a database." If you look in databases consisting almost entirely of government documents, it should not be a surprise that most of the uses will be governmental in nature.

In view of the foundation of American arms laws arising from British law, including the failure of British law to provide adequate protections for the rights of ordinary citizens, Cramer and Olson cite a number of examples of usage of the phrase "bear arms" in English, Scottish, and Welsh settings. The following excerpt from "What Did "Bear Arms" Mean in the Second Amendment?" is illustrative.

In debates in the House of Lords on June 19, 1780, in the aftermath of the Gordon Riots in London, Lord Richmond objected to certain parts of the King's speech concerning the actions taken to suppress the riots:

> His next object of censure was the conduct of the
> Commander in Chief of the army, for the letters he sent to
> Colonel Twisleton, who commanded the military force in
> the City, ordering him to disarm the citizens, who had
> taken up arms, and formed themselves in to associations,
> for the defence of their lives and properties. These letters
> he considered as a violation of the constitutional right of
> Protestant subjects to *keep and bear arms* for their own
> defence.

Lord Amherst agreed that the disarming order was
intended only for the rioters, "but no passage in his letter could
be construed to mean, that the arms should be taken away from
the associated citizens, who had very properly armed themselves
for the defence of their lives and property."

> Earl Bathurst stated the difference between the right of
> *bearing arms* for personal defence, and that of bodies of
> the subjects arraying themselves, without a commission
> from the king; the latter he declared to be unlawful.

The duality of the contemporary usage was shown by a
contemporaneous pronouncement by the Recorder of London --
the city's chief legal officer -- when asked if right to *have arms* in
the English Declaration of Rights protected armed groups as well
as armed individuals. He wrote:

> The right of his majesty's Protestant subjects, to **have**
> arms for their own defence, and to **use** them for lawful
> purposes, is most clear and undeniable. It seems, indeed,
> to be considered, by the ancient laws of this kingdom, not
> only as a *right*, but as a *duty*; for all the subjects of the
> realm, who are able to **bear arms**, are bound to be ready,
> at all times, to assist the sheriff, and other civil
> magistrates, in the execution of the laws and the
> preservation of the public peace. And **that right, which
> every Protestant most unquestionably possesses,**

individually, may, and in many cases *must,* be exercised collectively, is likewise a point which I conceive to be most clearly established by the authority of judicial decisions and ancient acts of parliament, as well as by reason and common sense. (emphasis added *by Cramer and Olson*)

The common law was in agreement. Edward Christian's edition of Blackstone's Commentaries that appeared in the 1790's described the rights of Englishmen (which every American colonist had been promised) in these terms "everyone is at liberty to keep or carry a gun, if he does not use it for the [unlawful] destruction of game." This right was separate from militia duties.

In looking then at evidence from American sources and transactions regarding the question of a collective versus an individual right to bear arms, Cramer and Olson referred to the following events.

The Framers' generation used "bear arms" in both civilian and military contexts. Just four short years before he penned the first draft of the Bill of Rights, James Madison himself presented to the Virginia General Assembly, in October of 1785, a Bill for the Preservation of Deer drafted by Thomas Jefferson. The bill prohibited the hunting of deer under certain circumstances and ends with the following restriction:

[A]nd, if, within twelve months after the date of the recognizance he shall bear a gun out of his inclosed ground, unless whilst performing military duty, it shall be deemed a breach of the recognizance, and be good cause to bind him a new, and every such bearing of a gun shall be a breach of the new recognizance and cause to bind him again.

In 1789, one would expect Madison to retain these same linguistic habits regarding the use of "bear" in a legislative context. Madison and Jefferson, at least, understood "bear" as a word not locked into a military or militia usage. And, as shall be demonstrated, so did other men who were present during the debates over the language of the Bill of Rights.

. . .

In a discussion of the history of Bologna in *A Defence of the Constitutions of Government of the United States of America*, John Adams describes how "these new magistrates in Bologna were obliged to adopt" various measures:

> In order to purge the city of its many popular disorders, they were obliged to forbid a great number of persons, under grievous penalties, to enter the palace: nor was it permitted them to go about the city, nor to *bear arms*.

There is nothing in the context that would suggest that this ordinance was a limitation on military service or duty, or that these disorderly persons were engaged in an organized rebellion. These were simply disorderly and troublesome persons. It is rather difficult to imagine that Adams would use the phrase "bear arms" rather than "carry arms" in such a context if he believed that phrase was exclusively military in nature.

James Wilson was a member of the Constitutional Convention, one of the authors of the 1790 Pennsylvania Constitution, a University of Pennsylvania law professor, and a U.S. Supreme Court associate justice until his death in 1798. In writing about homicide and self-defense:

> With regard to the first, it is the great natural law of self preservation, which, as we have seen, cannot be repealed, or superseded, or suspended by any human institution. This law, however, is expressly recognized in the constitution of Pennsylvania. "The right of the citizens to *bear arms* in the defence of themselves shall not be questioned." This is one of our many renewals of the Saxon regulations. "They were bound," says Mr. Selden, "to keep arms for the preservation of the kingdom, and *of their own persons*."

When the a law professor who was one of the authors of a state constitution tells you what a clause means—and explicates that "bear arms" included defense "of their own persons"—it is best to assume that he knows what he is talking about.

Since some of these Americans were lawyers—and one could even say "superlawyers," considering their positions—it strains credulity to believe that they casually and incorrectly used the phrase "bear arms."

. . .

Unsurprisingly, most of the state constitutions adopted in the early Republic period contain guarantees of a right to bear arms—and many of them are identical to, or very similar to, the guarantees in the Pennsylvania Constitutions of 1776 and 1790. Vermont's 1777, 1786, and 1793 Constitutions, "[t]hat the people have a right to bear arms for the defence of themselves and the State . . . ." Ohio Constitution of 1802 and Indiana Constitution of 1816 use identical language, with only slight differences in capitalization and punctuation. The similarity to the Pennsylvania Constitution of 1790 is quite striking, "[t]hat the right of citizens to bear arms, in defence of themselves and the State, shall not be questioned."42 Kentucky's 1792 and 1799 Constitutions are somewhat more specific to citizens, "[t]hat the rights of the citizens to bear arms in defence of themselves and the State shall not be questioned." Missouri Constitution of 1820 uses language similar to that of the Pennsylvania Constitution—but tied the right more closely to a clearly individual right:

> That the people have the right peaceably to assemble for their common good, and to apply to those vested with the powers of government for redress of grievances by petition or remonstrance; and that their right to *bear arms* in defence of themselves and of the State cannot be questioned.

Other state constitutions of the era also use "bear arms" and in language that is even more clearly individual. The Mississippi Constitution of 1817 declares, "[e]very citizen has a right to bear arms, in defence of himself and the State." The Connecticut Constitution of 1818 also declares, "[e]very citizen has a right to bear arms in defense of himself and the State" as does the Alabama Constitution of 1819. The Michigan Constitutions of 1835 and 1850, "[e]very citizen has a right to bear arms in defense of himself and the State." Whatever one might want to claim about the state constitutions that used the Pennsylvania language protecting the right of the people to bear arms "for the defence of themselves and the State," it is self-evident that, "[e]very citizen has a right to bear arms in defense of himself" refers to an individual right to self-defense—and thus, "bear arms" was not always military in its meaning.

In light of Justice Wilson's exposition of what this right means, it is no surprise to see that there are many antebellum decisions that recognized that the right to bear arms was individual in nature (although often subject to regulation), and not specific to military duty. Eleven of these decisions were cases where the court determined the limits of the right to bear arms. Two other decisions did not dispute that the right was individual in nature—sometimes just not applicable, because the defendant was the wrong color. Most of these decisions upheld statutes that sought to regulate either the carrying of certain *categories* of arms (usually edged weapons and pistols), or certain *ways* of carrying them (such as concealed carry). If "bear arms" was widely understood to refer only to militia duty, or military purposes, the courts could have greatly shortened the decisions upholding these regulatory measures with a simple statement: The guarantee of a right to "bear arms" refers only to militia duty under the direction of the government, and has no relevance to an individual carrying arms.

An apology to the reader if it seems that I have devoted an inordinate amount of attention to Cramer and to his work with Olson, "What Did "Bear Arms" Mean in the Second Amendment?". However, the majority, and Justice Scalia in writing for the majority, in *Heller* and Justice Alito in writing for the majority in *McDonald*, the most important Court decisions dealing with the Second Amendment, seem to have relied substantially on the research of Cramer in regard to the historical precedence for the use and meaning of the phrase "bear arms." I also need to confess that I did not expect to be impressed by the work of Cramer. After all, he was only a master's degree holding, gun toting, gun rights blogger from Idaho. But I was. In particular, I was impressed by the thorough scholarship of his research and the reasonable conclusions he reached from the references he identified and relied upon. But more importantly, Justice Scalia and Justice Alito were impressed.

The syllabus for the *Heller* decision, as published by the Supreme Court, contains an introductory summary history of the case as presented to the Supreme Court, and the holding (decision) of the Supreme Court for the case. The syllabus is reproduced below.

Argued March 18, 2008 - Decided June 26, 2008

District of Columbia law bans handgun possession by making it a crime to carry an unregistered firearm and prohibiting the registration of handguns; provides separately that no person may carry an unlicensed handgun, but authorizes the police chief to issue 1-year licenses; and requires residents to keep lawfully owned firearms unloaded and disassembled or bound by a trigger lock or similar device. Respondent Heller, a D. C. special policeman, applied to register a handgun he wished to keep at home, but the District refused. He filed this suit seeking, on Second Amendment grounds, to enjoin the city from enforcing the bar on handgun registration, the licensing requirement insofar as it prohibits carrying an unlicensed firearm in the home, and the trigger-lock requirement insofar as it prohibits the use of functional firearms in the home. The District Court dismissed the suit, but the D. C. Circuit reversed, holding that the Second

Amendment protects an individual's right to possess firearms and that the city's total ban on handguns, as well as its requirement that firearms in the home be kept nonfunctional even when necessary for self-defense, violated that right.

Held:

1.	The Second Amendment protects an individual right to possess a firearm unconnected with service in a militia, and to use that arm for traditionally lawful purposes, such as self-defense within the home. Pp. 2–53.

(a) The Amendment's prefatory clause announces a purpose, but does not limit or expand the scope of the second part, the operative clause. The operative clause's text and history demonstrate that it connotes an individual right to keep and bear arms. Pp. 2–22.

(b) The prefatory clause comports with the Court's interpretation of the operative clause. The "militia" comprised all males physically capable of acting in concert for the common defense. The Antifederalists feared that the Federal Government would disarm the people in order to disable this citizens' militia, enabling a politicized standing army or a select militia to rule. The response was to deny Congress power to abridge the ancient right of individuals to keep and bear arms, so that the ideal of a citizens' militia would be preserved. Pp. 22–28.

(c) The Court's interpretation is confirmed by analogous arms-bearing rights in state constitutions that preceded and immediately followed the Second Amendment. Pp. 28–30.

(d) The Second Amendment's drafting history, while of dubious interpretive worth, reveals three state Second Amendment proposals that unequivocally referred to an individual right to bear arms. Pp. 30–32.

(e) Interpretation of the Second Amendment by scholars, courts and legislators, from immediately after its ratification through the late 19th century also supports the Court's conclusion. Pp. 32–47.

(f) None of the Court's precedents forecloses the Court's interpretation. Neither *United States* v. *Cruikshank*, 92 U. S. 542, 553, nor *Presser* v. *Illinois*, 116 U. S. 252, 264–265, refutes the individual rights interpretation. *United States* v. *Miller*, 307 U. S.

174, does not limit the right to keep and bear arms to militia purposes, but rather limits the type of weapon to which the right applies to those used by the militia, *i.e.*, those in common use for lawful purposes. Pp. 47–54.

2.   Like most rights, the Second Amendment right is not unlimited. It is not a right to keep and carry any weapon whatsoever in any manner whatsoever and for whatever purpose: For example, concealed weapons prohibitions have been upheld under the Amendment or state analogues. The Court's opinion should not be taken to cast doubt on longstanding prohibitions on the possession of firearms by felons and the mentally ill, or laws forbidding the carrying of fire- arms in sensitive places such as schools and government buildings, or laws imposing conditions and qualifications on the commercial sale of arms. *Miller*'s holding that the sorts of weapons protected are those "in common use at the time" finds support in the historical tradition of prohibiting the carrying of dangerous and unusual weapons. Pp. 54–56.

3.   The handgun ban and the trigger-lock requirement (as applied to self-defense) violate the Second Amendment. The District's total ban on handgun possession in the home amounts to a prohibition on an entire class of "arms" that Americans overwhelmingly choose for the lawful purpose of self-defense. Under any of the standards of scrutiny the Court has applied to enumerated constitutional rights, this prohibition - in the place where the importance of the lawful defense of self, family, and property is most acute - would fail constitutional muster. Similarly, the requirement that any lawful firearm in the home be disassembled or bound by a trigger lock makes it impossible for citizens to use arms for the core lawful purpose of self-defense and is hence unconstitutional. Because Heller conceded at oral argument that the D. C. licensing law is permissible if it is not enforced arbitrarily and capriciously, the Court assumes that a license will satisfy his prayer for relief and does not address the licensing requirement. Assuming he is not disqualified from exercising Second Amendment rights, the District must permit Heller to register his handgun and must issue him a license to carry it in the home. Pp. 56–64.

478 F. 3d 370, affirmed.

The Supreme Court held in *McDonald et al v. City of Chicago et al* that the Fourteenth Amendment, in particular the Due Process clause of Section 1 of the Fourteenth Amendment which states: "No State shall make or enforce any law which shall . . . deprive any person of life, liberty, or property, without due process of law . . ." mandates that the Second Amendment applies to the States. Accordingly, the prohibition against infringement of the right of the people to keep and bear arms applies to the states and to political subdivisions (e.g. cities and counties) of the states. Following are the introductory summary history of the case, as it was presented to the Supreme Court, and excerpts from the holding, as they appear in the case syllabus published by the Supreme Court for this case.

Argued March 2, 2010—Decided June 28, 2010

Two years ago, in *District of Columbia* v. *Heller*, 554 U. S. ___, this Court held that the Second Amendment protects the right to keep and bear arms for the purpose of self-defense and struck down a District of Columbia law that banned the possession of handguns in the home. Chicago (hereinafter City) and the village of Oak Park, a Chicago suburb, have laws effectively banning handgun possession by almost all private citizens. After *Heller*, petitioners filed this federal suit against the City, which was consolidated with two related actions, alleging that the City's handgun ban has left them vulnerable to criminals. They sought a declaration that the ban and several related City ordinances violate the Second and Fourteenth Amendments. Rejecting petitioners' argument that the ordinances are un-constitutional, the court noted that the Seventh Circuit previously had upheld the constitutionality of a handgun ban, that *Heller* had explicitly refrained from opining on whether the Second Amendment applied to the States, and that the court had a duty to follow established Circuit precedent. The Seventh Circuit affirmed, relying on three 19th-century cases - *United States* v.

Cruikshank, 92 U. S. 542, *Presser* v. *Illinois*, 116 U. S. 252, and *Miller* v. *Texas*, 153 U. S. 535 - which were decided in the wake of this Court's interpretation of the Fourteenth Amendment's Privileges or Immunities Clause in the *Slaughter-House Cases,* 16 Wall. 36.

Held: The judgment is reversed, and the case is remanded. 567 F. 3d 856, reversed and remanded.

JUSTICE ALITO delivered the opinion of the Court with respect to Parts I, II–A, II–B, II–D, III–A, and III–B, concluding that the Fourteenth Amendment incorporates the Second Amendment right, recognized in *Heller,* to keep and bear arms for the purpose of self- defense. Pp. 5–9, 11–19, 19–33.

. . .

(b) The Bill of Rights, including the Second Amendment, originally applied only to the Federal Government, not to the States . . .

(c) Whether the Second Amendment right to keep and bear arms applies to the States is considered in light of the Court's precedents applying the Bill of Rights' protections to the States. Pp. 11–19.
(1) In the late 19th century, the Court began to hold that the Due Process Clause prohibits the States from infringing Bill of Rights pro- tections. See, *e.g., Hurtado* v. *California*, 110 U. S. 516 . . .

(2) Justice Black championed the alternative theory that §1 of the Fourteenth Amendment totally incorporated all of the Bill of Rights' provisions, see, *e.g., Adamson* v. *California*, 332 U. S. 46, 71– 72 (Black, J., dissenting), but the Court never has embraced that the- ory. Pp. 13–15.
(3) The Court eventually moved in the direction advocated by Justice Black, by adopting a theory of selective incorporation by which the Due Process Clause incorporates particular rights contained in the first eight Amendments. See, *e.g., Gideon* v. *Wainwright*, 372 U. S. 335, 341. These decisions

abandoned three of the characteristics of the earlier period. The Court clarified that the governing standard is whether a particular Bill of Rights protection is fundamental to our Nation's particular scheme of ordered liberty and system of justice. *Duncan, supra,* at 149, n. 14. The Court eventually held that almost all of the Bill of Rights' guarantees met the requirements for protection under the Due Process Clause. The Court also held that Bill of Rights protections must "all . . . be enforced against the States under the Fourteenth Amendment according to the same standards that protect those personal rights against federal encroachment." *Malloy* v. *Hogan,* 378 U. S. 1, 10. Under this approach, the Court overruled earlier decisions holding that particular Bill of Rights guarantees or remedies did not apply to the States. See, *e.g., Gideon, supra,* which overruled *Betts* v. *Brady,* 316 U. S. 455. Pp. 15–19.

(d) The Fourteenth Amendment makes the Second Amendment right to keep and bear arms fully applicable to the States. Pp. 19–33.

(1) The Court must decide whether that right is fundamental to the Nation's scheme of ordered liberty, *Duncan* v. *Louisiana,* 391 U. S. 145, 149, or, as the Court has said in a related context, whether it is "deeply rooted in this Nation's history and tradition," *Washing- ton* v. *Glucksberg,* 521 U. S. 702, 721. *Heller* points unmistakably to the answer. Self-defense is a basic right, recognized by many legal systems from ancient times to the present, and the *Heller* Court held that individual self-defense is "the central component" of the Second Amendment right. 554 U. S., at   ,   . Explaining that "the need for defense of self, family, and property is most acute" in the home, *ibid.,* the Court found that this right applies to handguns because they are "the most preferred firearm in the nation to 'keep' and use for protection of one's home and family," *id.,* at , – . It thus concluded that citizens must be permitted "to use [handguns] for the core lawful purpose of self-defense." *Id.,* at . *Heller* also clarifies that this right is "deeply rooted in this Nation's history and traditions," *Glucksberg, supra,* at 721. . .

(2) A survey of the contemporaneous history also demonstrates clearly that the Fourteenth Amendment's Framers and ratifiers counted the right to keep and bear arms among those

fundamental rights necessary to the Nation's system of ordered liberty. Pp. 22–33.

(i) By the 1850's, the fear that the National Government would disarm the universal militia had largely faded, but the right to keep and bear arms was highly valued for self-defense . . .

Evidence from the period immediately following the Amendment's ratification confirms that that right was considered fundamental. Pp. 22–31.

(ii) . . . The right to keep and bear arms must be regarded as a substantive guarantee, not a prohibition that could be ignored so long as the States legislated in an evenhanded manner. Pp. 30–33.

. . .

JUSTICE THOMAS agreed that the Fourteenth Amendment makes the Second Amendment right to keep and bear arms that was recognized in *District of Columbia* v. *Heller*, 554 U. S. 570, fully applicable to the States. However, he asserted, there is a path to this conclusion that is more straightforward and more faithful to the Second Amendment's text and history. The Court is correct in describing the Second Amendment right as "fundamental" to the American scheme of ordered liberty, *Duncan* v. *Louisiana*, 391 U. S. 145, 149, and "deeply rooted in this Nation's history and traditions," *Washington* v. *Glucksberg*, 521 U. S. 702, 721. But the Fourteenth Amendment's Due Process Clause, which speaks only to "process," cannot impose the type of substantive restraint on state legislation that the Court asserts. Rather, the right to keep and bear arms is enforceable against the States because it is a privilege of American citizenship recognized by §1 of the Fourteenth Amendment, which provides, *inter alia:* "No State shall make or enforce any law which shall abridge the privileges or immunities of citizens of the United States." In interpreting this language, it is important to recall that constitutional provisions are " 'written to be understood by the voters.' " *Heller*, 554 U. S., at ___. The objective of this inquiry is to discern what "ordinary citizens" at the time of the Fourteenth Amendment's ratification would have understood that Amendment's Privileges or Immunities Clause to mean. *Ibid.* A survey of contemporary legal authorities plainly shows that, at that time, the ratifying public understood the Clause to protect constitutionally enumerated rights, including the right to keep and bear arms. Pp. 1–34.

It appears that the Supreme Court has spoken decisively on the Second Amendment in *Heller* and *McDonald*. Notwithstanding the prefatory clause, "A well-regulated Militia, being necessary to the security of a free State," the Supreme Court has unequivocally decided that "the right of the people to keep and bear Arms" is an individual right and neither the federal government nor any state or local government can take away that right. As noted above, Justice Alito, in writing for the majority in McDonald states:

> *Heller* points unmistakably to the answer. Self-defense is a basic right, recognized by many legal systems from ancient times to the present, and the *Heller* Court held that individual self-defense is "the central component" of the Second Amendment right. 554 U. S., at ___. Explaining that "the need for defense of self, family, and property is most acute" in the home, *ibid.*, the Court found that this right applies to handguns because they are "the most preferred firearm in the nation to 'keep' and use for protection of one's home and family," *id.*, at , ___. It thus concluded that citizens must be permitted "to use [handguns] for the core lawful purpose of self-defense." *Id.*, at . *Heller* also clarifies that this right is "deeply rooted in this Nation's history and traditions, "
>
> . . .
>
> (2) A survey of the contemporaneous history also demonstrates clearly that the Fourteenth Amendment's Framers and ratifiers counted the right to keep and bear arms among those fundamental rights necessary to the Nation's system of ordered liberty. Pp. 22–33.

(i) By the 1850's, the fear that the National
Government would disarm the universal militia had largely
faded, but the right to keep and bear arms was highly valued for
self-defense . . .

The Court in *McDonald* makes it clear that the Second Amendment guarantee of the right of the people to keep and bear arms of Second Amendment had a two-fold purpose, to contravene the possibility that "the National Government would disarm the universal militia" and to provide for "self-defense." The McDonald Court further acknowledged that the former purpose, to prevent the federal government from disarming the "universal militia", was no longer relevant, thus leaving the second purpose, namely keeping and bearing arms for self-defense, as the remaining operative purpose of the Second Amendment.

For those gun control advocates that are disheartened by the *Heller* and *McDonald* decisions, I suggest that you ponder for a moment how the alternative interpretation and its implications could have developed. Let's suppose that the Supreme Court had decided that the "right of the people to keep and bear arms" was a collective right of the people to have arms for service in the "universal militia." Then wouldn't the logical result of such a ruling be that the weapons that the people would keep and bear would be military type weapons. Semi-automatic assault rifles would be mere child's play under possible extensions of such an interpretation. I suggest to gun control advocates that the best possible scenario for your point of view is for the Supreme Court to rule, as it has in *Heller* and *McDonald,* that the right of the people to keep and bear arms so that they might support the militia in contravening an oppressive federal government and its standing army is no longer relevant, and that the sole remaining purpose of the Second Amendment is to empower individuals in providing for their self-defense.

The types of arms that are reasonable, at present, for individuals to "keep and bear" for self-defense are inherently much more limited than the weapons that would be reasonable for service in a militia. Accordingly, as we will discuss later, federal, state and local governments have successfully legislated and successfully issued regulations substantially controlling the types of arms that individuals may keep and bear. Except when states or local governments have attempted to prohibit weapons that are clearly suitable for self-defense, or have attempted to impose significant impediments on their usefulness for self-defense, such as prohibiting the possession of hand guns in the home or requiring a trigger lock on a weapon kept in a home, the statutes and regulations have generally been upheld. A summary of the significant court decisions regarding the Second Amendment follows in the next chapter.

So, how do we, you and I, as ordinary citizens decide what we think the Second Amendment means? Do we try to decide what the Framers meant when they wrote it? Do we try to decide what the States understood it to mean when they ratified it? Do we interpret the amendment in view of the world as it is today? Do we defer to the U.S. Supreme Court to tell us what it means? Do we really care what it means – i.e. is the interpretation of the Second Amendment really all that important?

For starters, let's summarize what we may have learned from the foregoing references and analyses relating to each of these questions and see where it takes us.   First, let's recall what we learned about what the Framers meant when they wrote the Second Amendment.

James Madison's initial proposal for the Bill of Rights included the following proposed passage relating to arms:

> The right of the people to keep and bear arms shall not be infringed; a well-armed and well-regulated militia being the best security of a free country: but no person religiously scrupulous of bearing arms shall be compelled to render military service in person.

There were changes to the proposed amendment before passage by the First Congress convened under the new Constitution. Following are the changes made, in chronological order.

> A well regulated militia, composed of the body of the people, being the best security of a free State, the right of the people to keep and bear arms shall not be infringed; but no person religiously scrupulous shall be compelled to bear arms.

> A well regulated militia, composed of the body of the people, being the best security of a free state, the right of the people to keep and bear arms shall not be infringed; but no one religiously scrupulous of bearing arms shall be compelled to render military service in person.

> A well regulated militia, composed of the body of the people, being the best security of a free state, the right of the people to keep and bear arms, shall not be infringed, but no one religiously scrupulous of bearing arms shall be compelled to render military service in person.

> A well regulated militia, being the best security of a free state, the right of the people to keep and bear arms, shall not be infringed.

> A well regulated militia, being necessary to the security of a free State, the right of the People to keep and bear arms, shall not be infringed.

The form of the original arms provision of the proposed Bill of Rights drafted by James Madison makes abundantly clear the concern intended to be addressed by the provision. The Framers, and the citizens of this fledgling country, were very concerned about the possible oppression by the new federal government, particularly with the possible development of a standing federal army.   They understood the necessity of a well-armed populace at the ready to fulfill their duty as members of a militia. The concern over the need for individuals to be able to keep and bear arms for their personal defense is not expressly addressed in any version of the arms provision that ultimately became the Second Amendment.

Among the statements by the Founding Fathers and Framers discussed previously, statements by George Mason, Alexander Hamilton and Patrick Henry are illustrative. George Mason pointed to England's efforts to disarm the people, stating that "it was the best and most effectual way to enslave them ... by totally disusing and neglecting the militia." He also reminded that the militia consist ". . . now of the whole people, except a few public officers." Since all of the citizenry were members of the militia, they all must enjoy the right to individually bear arms so they would be prepared to serve in the citizens militia.

Alexander Hamilton explained in his *Concerning the Militia* essay published in 1788:

> ... it will be possible to have an excellent body of well-trained militia, ready to take the field whenever the defence of the State shall require it. This will not only lessen the call for military establishments, but if circumstances should at any time oblige the Government to form an army of any magnitude, that army can never be formidable to the liberties of the People, while there is a

large body of citizens, little, if at all, inferior to them in discipline and the use of arms, who stand ready to defend their own rights, and those of their fellow-citizens. This appears to me the only substitute that can be devised for a standing army, and the best possible security against it, if it should exist.

Alexander Hamilton also wrote in Federalist Paper No. 29 that "little more can be reasonably aimed at, with respect to the people at large, than to have them properly armed . . ."

Speaking on June 5, 1788 in the Virginia convention as ratification of the Constitution was being considered, Patrick Henry advocated for the right to bear arms as essential for the preservation of liberty. He stated, "Guard with jealous attention the public liberty. Suspect everyone who approaches that jewel. Unfortunately, nothing will preserve it but downright force. Whenever you give up that force, you are inevitably ruined."

While the Second Amendment to the U.S. Constitution does not expressly address the right of the people to bear arms for their personal defense, arms provisions in state constitutions adopted both before and after ratification of the Bill of Rights Amendments to the U.S. Constitution, do expressly provide for the right to bear arms to extend to personal defense. As described previously, a typical provision, which was incorporated in the Pennsylvania State Constitution in 1776, and in a number of state constitutions within a few years after that, is:

> Article XIII. That the people have a right to bear arms for the defense of themselves and the state; . . .

The U.S. Supreme Court found in *Heller* that the Framers intended the Second Amendment to protect the right of the people to keep and bear arms for service in the militia and for self-defense, and that it was an individual right, not a collective right. The Court further recognized in *McDonald* that only the latter purpose, self-defense, remained as a viable purpose for the Second Amendment. The Court relied, in *Heller* and *McDonald*, upon Cramer's work in deciding that the term "bear arms" was used, prior to and at the time of the drafting and ratification of the Second Amendment, in both military and non-military settings.

CHAPTER 3

KEEP AND BEAR ARMS COURT CASES

The principal decisions of the US Supreme Court affecting the current status of the law have been discussed previously. However, a review of the decisions described below will help the reader appreciate the impressive variability in the decisions of the Court relating to the interpretation and application of the Second Amendment. The stark contrast of the decisions in *Heller* and *McDonald* with the historical precedence of prior decisions by the U.S. Supreme Court in the years leading up to the *Heller* and *McDonald* decisions is very interesting and instructive.

Dred Scott v. Sandford, 60 U.S. 393 (1857).

The *Dred Scott* decision is generally considered one of the most infamous, if not the most infamous of all, in the history of the Supreme Court. Fortunately, the *Dred Scott* decision was nullified merely a decade later by the Thirteenth Amendment and the Fourteenth Amendment to the U.S. Constitution. The opinion was written by Chief Justice Taney, who had been appointed by Democrat Andrew Jackson to the Supreme Court in 1836. Taney was from a wealthy plantation family in Maryland. Taney had freed the slaves he inherited, but he was an avowed proponent of states' rights. It is important to remember that the decision simply rationalized a social ideology that prevailed in a large part of the United States at the time. Taney was enraged by Northern attacks on slavery, and he apparently believed he could use the *Dred Scott* decision to permanently remove slavery as a subject of national debate. This far reaching decision deeply angered many Northerners and strengthened the anti-slavery Republican Party, substantially contributing to the victory of Republican Abraham Lincoln in the 1860 presidential election. After Lincoln's election, Taney sympathized with the seceding Southern states, but he did not resign from the Supreme Court.

Dred Scott was born a slave in the State of Virginia, most likely in the year 1799. Scott's owner at the time of his birth was Peter Blow. Peter Blow moved to Alabama in 1818, taking Scott with him, where Blow and Scott remained until 1830, when Blow moved to St. Louis, Missouri. Blow operated a boarding house in St. Louis until his death in 1832. Virginia, Alabama, and Missouri were all slave states.

Immediately before or just after Blow's death, Dr. John Emerson, an Army surgeon, bought Scott and in 1834 relocated to Illinois, taking Scott with him. Illinois was a free state and so slavery was prohibited. Approximately two years later, in 1836, Emerson relocated again and took Scott with him to Fort Snelling in Wisconsin Territory where the Missouri Compromise had outlawed slavery. In 1837, while in Wisconsin, Scott was allowed to marry, and his wife Harriet, a slave also, was acquired by Emerson at the time of their marriage.

Scott remained in the Wisconsin Territory for approximately two years, until February, 1838, when Emerson moved Scott to Louisiana, which had been admitted to the Union as a slave state in 1812. In October, 1838, Emerson moved back to the Wisconsin Territory, taking Scott with him. When Emerson was discharged from the Army in 1842, Emerson moved back to Missouri, again taking Scott, as well as his wife and children, with him.

Scott had remained in the State of Illinois and the Wisconsin Territory for an aggregate total of approximately 4 years during the first stint, and had remained in the Wisconsin territory for a total of 4 years during the second stint. Thus, except for the few months in Louisiana during 1838, he had lived in a free state or territory for eight years. For unknown reasons, Dred Scott and his wife Harriet never tried to run away or sue for freedom while living in or traveling through free states and territories. It was not until after the death of Emerson in 1843 that Scott sued Emerson's widow, by whom he was then purportedly owned, asserting that he had become a free man when he had been transported to and lived in the free state of Illinois.

In this time, immediately before the Civil War, of very serious conflict in the U.S. over the slavery issue, it is perhaps unsurprising that the US Supreme Court decided:

> 4. **A free negro of the African race, whose ancestors were brought to this country and sold as slaves, is not a "citizen"** within the meaning of the Constitution of the United States.

> 5. When the Constitution was adopted, they were not regarded in any of the States as members of the community which constituted the State, and were not numbered among its "people or citizens." **Consequently, the special rights and immunities guaranteed to citizens do not apply to them.** And not being "citizens" within the meaning of the Constitution, they are not entitled to sue in that character in a court of the United States, and the Circuit Court has not jurisdiction in such a suit.

> 6. The only two clauses in the Constitution which point to this race treat them as persons whom it was morally lawfully to deal in as articles of property and to hold as slaves.

> 7. Since the adoption of the Constitution of the United States, **no State can by any subsequent law make a foreigner or any**

**other description of persons citizens of the United States, nor
entitle them to the rights and privileges secured to citizens by
that instrument.**

8. A State, by its laws passed since the adoption of the
Constitution, may put a foreigner or any other description of
persons upon a footing with its own citizens as to all the rights
and privileges enjoyed by them within its dominion and by its
laws. But that will not make him a citizen of the United States,
nor entitle him to sue in its courts, nor to any of the privileges
and immunities of a citizen in another State.

9. The **change in public opinion** and feeling in relation to the
African race which has taken place **since the adoption of the
Constitution cannot change its construction and meaning**, and
it **must be construed and administered now according to its
true meaning and intention when it was formed and adopted**.

Having decided that Dred Scott was not a citizen of the U.S., it is further
unsurprising that the Court also decided that Scott did not have the
protection of the Bill of Rights. In the provision of the *Dred Scott*
decision that is most pertinent to our discussion here, the Court stated
that if the Bill of Rights were applicable to Mr. Scott:

> It would give to persons of the negro race, . . . the right to enter
> every other State whenever they pleased, . . . the full liberty of
> speech in public and in private upon all subjects upon which its
> own citizens might speak; to hold public meetings upon political
> affairs, and **to keep and carry arms wherever they went**. (P.
> 417)
> *(emphasis added)*

Thus, the Court clearly stated that all citizens have the right to "keep and
carry arms" wherever they go. It is clear that the Court deemed the right
to be **an individual right and not a right confined to association with**

a militia. It is also significant that the Court defined **"bear" to mean "carry"**.

United States v. Cruikshank, 92 U.S. 542 (1875). This is the first post-Civil War case addressing the Second Amendment. The case arose out of the disputed1872 Louisiana gubernatorial election and the subsequent 1873 massacre in Colfax, Louisiana, in which a group of armed whites killed approximately 150 African American men. Federal charges were brought against several white men, who were members of the Ku Klux Klan, for violating the Federal 1870 Enforcement Act which prohibited conspiracies to deny the constitutional rights of citizens. This Act was primarily intended to control Ku Klux Klan violence. Three men were convicted under the Act in Federal Court for conspiring to deprive the black victims of their constitutional rights, which were their First Amendment right to freely assemble and their Second Amendment right to keep and bear arms. The convicted defendants appealed on the grounds that their indictments were insufficient and the U.S. Supreme Court agreed. The Court overturned the Federal Court convictions, holding that neither the First Amendment nor the Second Amendment applied to the actions of state governments against individuals or to the actions of individuals against other individuals.

The Supreme Court thus held that the Second Amendment did not apply to state regulation of firearms. **The Court stated that the Second Amendment "was not intended to limit the powers of the State Governments in respect to their own citizens," and further, that the Second Amendment "has no other effect than to restrict the powers of the national government."** Accordingly, the Court ruled that the federal government could not charge nor prosecute citizens in federal court for alleged violations of other citizens' constitutional rights. Only the states could provide protection of a citizen's fundamental rights and only the states could provide remedies to that citizen for violation of those rights by other citizens.

The Cruikshank decision allowed the states to disarm African American residents while it protected Ku Klux Klan members from federal prosecution. Accordingly, it left African Americans in the South grossly unprotected from hostile state governments dominated by white Democratic legislatures and from the Ku Klux Klan. It allowed the Ku Klux Klan and other white supremacy groups to continue to use paramilitary force to suppress black voting.

It is worth noting that a plaque installed at the site of Colfax Massacre in 1951, seventy-eight years after the massacre, read as follows:

> COLFAX RIOT
> On this site occurred the
> Colfax Riot in which three
> white men and 150 negroes
> were slain. This event on
> April 13, 1873 marked the
> end of carpetbag misrule
> in the South.

It is true that the Reconstruction that ensued in the South after the Civil War basically fizzled about the time of the *Cruikshank* decision. *Cruikshank* enabled that demobilization and greatly emboldened the KKK.

Presser v. Illinois, 116 U.S. 252 (1886). This is the second post-Civil War U.S. Supreme Court case addressing Second Amendment rights. **The Court ruled that the Second Amendment right to keep and bear arms was a right of individuals, not militias, and was not a right to form or belong to a militia. Instead, the right to bear arms provided for each individual to keep and bear arms**, who would then be equipped to serve as a member of a militia if called to service by the Government. Accordingly, the Court ruled that the provisions of the Illinois statute being challenged that prohibited citizens from forming paramilitary organizations, and from drilling or parading, was constitutional. The Court ruled that prohibiting the formation of paramilitary organizations and parading by such groups did not constitute an infringement of the personal right of individuals to keep and bear arms.

In this regard, the Court stated:

> We think it clear that there are no sections under consideration, which only forbid bodies of men to associate together as military organizations, or to drill or parade with arms in cities and towns unless authorized by law, do not infringe the right of the people to keep and bear arms.

The Court also reiterated what had been stated in *Cruikshank*, that the Second Amendment only restrained the federal government from regulating gun ownership, not the individual states.

> The second amendment declares that it shall not be infringed, but this, as has been seen, means no more than that it shall not be infringed by congress. **This is one of the amendments that has no other effect than to restrict the powers of the national government**, leaving the people to look for their protection against any violation by their fellow-citizens of the rights it recognizes to what is called in City of New York v. Miln, 11 Pet.

[116 U.S. 252, 102] 139, the 'powers which relate to merely municipal legislation, or what was perhaps more properly called internal police,' 'not surrendered or restrained' by the constitution of the United States.

(emphasis added)

United States v. Miller, 307 U.S. 174 (1939). In a setting of a dangerous world in turmoil and the beginning of World War II, the Supreme Court ruled, in perhaps the most often cited case on the Second Amendment, that **the "obvious purpose" of the Second Amendment was to "assure the continuation and render possible the effectiveness of" the state militia, and the Amendment "must be interpreted and applied with the end in view."** The Court stated:

> In the absence of any evidence tending to show that possession or use of a "shotgun having a barrel of less than eighteen inches in length" at this time has some reasonable relationship to the preservation or efficiency of a well-regulated militia, we cannot say that the Second Amendment guarantees the right to keep and bear such an instrument. Certainly, it is **not within judicial notice that this weapon is any part of the ordinary military equipment, or that its use could contribute to the common defense**. Aymette v. State, 2 Humphreys (Tenn.) 154, 158. The signification attributed to the term Militia appears from the debates in the Convention, the history and legislation of Colonies and States, and the writings of approved commentators. These show plainly enough that the Militia comprised all males physically capable of acting in concert for the common defense. 'A body of citizens enrolled for military discipline.' And further, that **ordinarily when called for service these men were expected to appear bearing arms supplied by themselves and of the kind in common use at the time.**

(emphasis added)

From the stark perspective of another looming World War for a world which was still very much in recovery from the devastation of World War I, the **Court seemingly departs from the holding of *Presser v. Illinois*.** The Court ruled in *Miller* that the **Second Amendment was intended to protect the rights of states to form militias, not the rights of individuals to own guns**, and that the right to keep and bear arms provided by the Second Amendment arises from the need to **facilitate the formation and maintenance of militias by the states. However, the Court seems to imply that a right for individuals to own a firearm gun may exist to facilitate their participation in the common defense.** The Court specifically ruled that a sawed-off shotgun had no "reasonable relationship to the preservation or efficiency of a well-regulated militia," and, thus, was not protected by the Second Amendment. **The decision in *Miller* is widely believed to have supported the proposition that only those guns usable in militia service and held for the purpose of militia service were protected by the Second Amendment.**

Duncan v. Louisiana, 391 U.S. 145 (1968). The tumultuous year 1968, the height of the civil rights movement against racial discrimination in the United States, the year of the assassinations of Martin Luther King, Jr., the nation's foremost civil rights leader, and presidential candidate Robert F. Kennedy, and the enactment of the Civil Rights Act of 1968, provides the setting for *Duncan v. Louisiana*.

The Court held:

1. Since trial by jury in criminal cases is fundamental to the American scheme of justice, the Fourteenth Amendment

guarantees a right of jury trial in all criminal cases which, were they tried in a federal court, would come within the Sixth Amendment's guarantee of trial by jury. Pp. 391 U. S. 147-158.

2. The penalty authorized for a particular crime is of major relevance in determining whether it is a serious one subject to the mandates of the Sixth Amendment, and it is sufficient here, without defining the boundary between petty offenses and serious crimes, to hold that a crime punishable by two years in prison is a serious crime, and that appellant was entitled to a jury trial. Pp. 391 U. S. 159-162.

The Supreme Court thus held that the Fourteenth Amendment mandated that the Sixth Amendment right to a jury trial applied to criminal trials in the state courts of each state. Justice Hugo Black in his concurring opinion, referred to a statement by Senator Howard, who introduced the proposed Fourteenth Amendment to Congress, to support the Court's ruling that the **Fourteenth Amendment requires the states, not just the federal government, to protect the individual rights enumerated in the Bill of Rights**:

> "Such is the character of the privileges and immunities spoken of in the second section of the fourth article of the Constitution [the Senator had just read from the old opinion of *Corfield v. Coryell,* 6 Fed.Cas. 546 (No. 3,230) (E. D.Pa. 1825)]. To these privileges and immunities, whatever they may be -- for they are not and cannot be fully defined in their entire extent and precise nature to these should be added the personal rights guarantied and secured by the first eight amendments of the Constitution; such as the freedom of speech and of the press; the right of the people peaceably to assemble and petition the Government for a redress of grievances, a right appertaining to each and all the people; **the right to keep and to bear arms**; the right to be exempted from the quartering of soldiers in a house without the consent of the owner; the right to be exempt from unreasonable searches and seizures, and from any search or seizure except by virtue of a warrant issued upon a formal oath or affidavit; the right of an

accused person to be informed of the nature of the accusation against him, and his right to be tried by an impartial jury of the vicinage, and also the right to be secure against excessive bail and against cruel and unusual punishments."

(*emphasis added*)

It should be noted that *Duncan* is a bold departure from the decision of the Court in the 1875 *Cruikshank* case. The Fourteenth Amendment was found to impose an obligation upon the states to protect the individual rights of its citizens as conferred by the Bill of Rights. This included the Second Amendment right to keep and bear arms.

Lewis v. United States, 445 U.S. 55 (1980). The Supreme Court ruled that Congress may prohibit felons from possessing firearms. The Court stated:

> This Court has recognized repeatedly that a legislature constitutionally may prohibit a convicted felon from engaging in activities far more fundamental than the possession of a firearm. ... These legislative restrictions on the use of firearms are neither based upon constitutionally suspect criteria nor do they trench upon any constitutionally protected liberties. **See United States v. Miller, 307 U. S. 174, 307 U. S. 178 (1939) (the Second Amendment guarantees no right to keep and bear a firearm that does not have "some reasonable relationship to the preservation or efficiency of a well regulated militia")** (*emphasis added*)

It should be noted that in the 1980 decision in *Lewis*, the Supreme Court, is still following the precedence established in *Miller* in early World War II 1939.

United States v. Verdugo-Urquidez, 494 U.S. 259 (1990). This case dealt with the question of whether nonresident aliens have rights under the Fourth Amendment.

> After the Government obtained an arrest warrant for respondent -- a Mexican citizen and resident believed to be a leader of an organization that smuggles narcotics into this country -- he was apprehended by Mexican police and transported here, where he was arrested. Following his arrest, Drug Enforcement Administration agents, working with Mexican officials, searched his Mexican residences and seized certain documents. The District Court granted his motion to suppress the evidence, concluding that the Fourth Amendment -- which protects "the people" against unreasonable searches and seizures -- applied to the searches, and that the DEA agents had failed to justify searching the premises without a warrant.

This led to the Supreme Court to determine who "the people," referred to several times in the Constitution and the Amendments, including the Second Amendment. The Court stated:

> The Fourth Amendment phrase "the people" seems to be a term of art used in select parts of the Constitution, and contrasts with the words "person" and "accused" used in Articles of the Fifth and Sixth Amendments regulating criminal procedures. This suggests that **"the people" refers to a class of persons who are part of a national community or who have otherwise developed sufficient connection with this country to be considered part of that community.**

The decision by the Supreme Court in this case seems to make it clear that citizenship is not required to be included within the group of persons identified as "the people". Persons who are "part of a national community" or who have "developed sufficient connection" to be part of the national community would presumably include at least legal permanent residents and other persons in the country legally, such as persons holding work or student visas. **The obvious implication is that these classes of non-citizen, legal residents would presumably have the same Second Amendment right to bear arms as citizens.**

Farmer v. Higgins, 907 F.2d 1041 (11th Cir. 1990), cert. denied, 498 U.S. 1047 (1991). The Court notes that 18 U.S.C.A. §922(o) of The Firearms Owners' Protection Act of 1986 states:

> (1) Except as provided in paragraph (2), it shall be unlawful for any person to transfer or possess a machinegun.
> (2) This subsection does not apply with respect to –
> (A) a transfer to or by, possession by or under the authority of, the United States or any department or agency thereof or a State, or a department, agency, or political subdivision thereof; or
> (B) any lawful transfer or lawful possession of a machinegun that was lawfully possessed before the date this subsection takes effect.

The effective date of §922(o) was May 19, 1986.

On October 24, 1986, five months after the effective date of §922(o), Farmer filed an application with the Bureau of Alcohol, Tobacco & Firearms for a permit to make and register a machinegun for his private collection. When the Bureau denied the permit, Farmer filed a declaratory judgment action with the U.S. District Court for the Northern District of Georgia.

The U.S. District Court for the Northern District of Georgia concluded that the Act's first exemption from the machine gun prohibition, which permits possession of a machine gun "under the authority" of a governmental unit, allows a private person, who complies with the National Firearms Act's application and registration requirements, to manufacture and possess a machine gun. The U.S. District Court for the

Northern District of Georgia concluded that the Act's first exemption from the machine gun prohibition, which permits possession of a machine gun "under the authority" of a governmental unit, allows a private person, who complies with the National Firearms Act's application and registration requirements, to manufacture and possess a machine gun.

The Eleventh Circuit reversed the District Court, finding that the legislative history made it clear that Congress intended to prohibit the private possession of machineguns not lawfully possessed prior to May 19, 1996. The U.S. Supreme Court Denied Cert, i.e. refused to review the Eleventh Circuit decision, and thus let that decision stand.

It is worth noting that the attorneys handling the case on behalf of Farmer were purportedly affiliated with the NRA, and this decision was an apparent defeat of the NRA's present position that the Second Amendment right to bear arms is unlimited.

United States v. Rock Island Armory, 773 F. Supp. 117 (C.D. Ill. 1991). This was a Federal District Court case in the United States District Court for the Central District of Illinois. Rock Island Armory was charged, among other things, with violation of the registration and taxation requirements of the National Firearms Act of 1934, for a machine gun made after May 19, 1986. The Court stated:

> Since its passage in 1934, the registration, taxation, and other requirements of the National Firearms Act ("NFA") have been upheld by the courts under the power of Congress to raise revenue. However, 18 U.S.C. § 922(*o*), which became effective on May 19, 1986, prohibits possession of machineguns, and thereby repealed or rendered unconstitutional the portions of the National Firearms Act which provided for the raising of revenue

from the making, possession, and transfer of machineguns made after such date. As the government conceded at oral argument, the United States refuses to register or accept tax payments for the making or transfer of machineguns made after 1986. Thus, § 922(*o*), as applied to machineguns made after May 19, 1986, left the registration and other requirements of the National Firearms Act without any constitutional basis.

. . .

In sum, since enactment of 18 U.S.C. § 922(*o*), the Secretary has refused to accept any tax payments to make or transfer a machinegun made after May 19, 1986, to approve any such making or transfer, or to register any such machinegun. As applied to machineguns made and possessed after May 19, 1986, the registration and other requirements of the National Firearms Act, Chapter 53 of the Internal Revenue Code, no longer serve any revenue purpose, and are impliedly repealed or are unconstitutional. Accordingly, Counts 1(a) and (b), 2, and 3 of the superseding indictment are DISMISSED.

The District Court thus ruled that Rock Island Armory could not be prosecuted for failing to comply with any taxation, registration or other requirements of the 1934 National Firearms Act in regard to a machinegun produced after May 19, 1986. The manufacturing, transfer or registration of machineguns after May 19, 1986, was unquestionably prohibited by 18 U.S.C. § 922(*o*), which was an amendment to the Gun Control Act of 1968.

A discussion of the development and history of Federal and State Statutes relating to firearm rights and control follows in Chapter 5.

United States v. Warner (10th Cir. 1993). Mr. Warner was arrested in Utah for possession of a machine gun made after May 19, 1986 and convicted in the Federal District Court for the District of Utah under the federal statute, 18 U.S.C. § 922(o). Mr. Warner appealed to the 10th Circuit Court of Appeals, claiming that the Utah constitution allows its citizens to bear arms, and therefore that he was exempt based on 18 U.S.C. § 922(o)(2)(A), since his possession of the machine gun was "under authority of the State." However, the Tenth Circuit Court disagreed, citing the *Farmer* case and confirming that **machine guns made after the May 19, 1986 effective date of § 922(o) could not be possessed by private citizens**. The Court Stated:

> **Moreover, § 922(*o*)(2)(A) is properly read to permit only lawful possession of machine guns by federal or state agents acting in an official capacity**. As noted by the court in *Farmer,* the legislative history of the exemption clarifies § 922(*o*)(2)(A) was enacted so that military personnel and police officers, when acting officially, could utilize and possess machine guns. *Id.* 907 F.2d at 1045. To read this subsection to permit an exception for private citizens would essentially eliminate the federal prohibition entirely. In *United States v. Aiken,* 974 F.2d 446, 449 (4th Cir. 1992), the court stated, "Congress made it illegal for anyone other than government personnel to possess . . . a machine gun in 1986, 18 U.S.C. § 922(*o*)(1)." The explicit language of the subsection coupled with the legislative history permits no other interpretation.
> (emphasis added)

United States v. Lopez, 514 U.S. 549 (1995). On March 10, 1992, Lopez, a 12th grade student at Edison High School in San Antonio, Texas, carried a concealed .38 caliber handgun and five bullets into the school. Based upon an anonymous tip, he was arrested and charged under Texas law with firearm possession on school premises. The next day, the state charges were dismissed after federal agents charged Lopez with violating the federal Gun Free School Zones Act of 1990. He was indicted by a federal grand jury for knowing possession of a firearm at a school zone in violation of §922(q) of the Gun Free School Zones Act. Lopez filed a Motion to Dismiss the federal indictment on the ground that §922(q) "is unconstitutional as it is beyond the power of Congress to legislate control over our public schools." The District Court denied the motion. Lopez waived his right to a jury trial and was convicted in a bench trial for knowing possession of a firearm at a school zone. He was sentenced to 6 months imprisonment and 2 years of supervised release.

Lopez appealed, claiming that that §922(q) exceeded Congress' power to legislate under the Commerce Clause. The U.S. Court of Appeals for the Fifth Circuit agreed and reversed Lopez's conviction. The Government then appealed the reversal to the U.S. Supreme Court.

The decision by the Supreme Court in this case was the first post New Deal case to establish limits on Congress' powers under the Commerce Clause. In ruling that the Gun-Free School Zones Act of 1990 was unconstitutional, the Court, in an opinion by Chief Justice Rehnquist, stated:

> **We start with first principles. The Constitution creates a Federal Government of enumerated powers. See U. S. Const., Art. I, §8. As James Madison wrote, "[t]he powers delegated by the proposed Constitution to the federal government are few and defined. Those which are to remain in the State governments are numerous and indefinite."** The Federalist No. 45, pp. 292-293 (C. Rossiter ed. 1961). This constitutionally mandated division of authority "was adopted by the Framers to ensure protection of our fundamental liberties." *Gregory* v. *Ashcroft*, 501 U.S. 452, 458 (1991) . . . . The Constitution delegates to Congress the power "[t]o regulate Commerce with foreign Nations, and among the several States . . . The Court, through Chief Justice Marshall, first defined the

nature of Congress' commerce power in *Gibbons* v. *Ogden*, 9 Wheat. 1, 189-190 (1824):

"Commerce, undoubtedly, is traffic, but it is something more: it is intercourse. It describes the commercial intercourse between nations, and parts of nations, in all its branches, and is regulated by prescribing rules for carrying on that intercourse."

. . .

We pause to consider the implications of the Government's arguments. The Government admits, under its "costs of crime" reasoning, that Congress could regulate not only all violent crime, but all activities that might lead to violent crime, regardless of how tenuously they relate to interstate commerce . . . **. under the Government's "national productivity" reasoning, Congress could regulate any activity that it found was related to the economic productivity of individual citizens: family law (including marriage, divorce, and child custody) . . . Thus, if we were to accept the Government's arguments, we are hard pressed to posit any activity by an individual that Congress is without power to regulate.**

Although Justice Breyer argues that acceptance of the Government's rationales would not authorize a general federal police power, he is unable to identify any activity that the States may regulate but Congress may not . . .

Justice Breyer focuses, for the most part, on the threat that firearm possession in and near schools poses to the educational process and the potential economic consequences flowing from that threat. *Post*, at 5-9. Specifically, the dissent reasons that (1) gun related violence is a serious problem; (2) that problem, in turn, has an adverse effect on classroom learning; and (3) that adverse effect on classroom learning, in turn, represents a substantial threat to trade and commerce. *Post*, at 9. This analysis would be equally applicable, if not more so, to subjects such as family law and direct regulation of education.

. . .

To uphold the Government's contentions here, we would have to pile inference upon inference in a manner **that would bid fair to convert congressional authority under the Commerce Clause**

to a general police power of the sort retained by the States. . .
This we are unwilling to do.

For the foregoing reasons the judgment of the Court of Appeals is
Affirmed
.

(emphasis added)

An apology to the reader for the amount of detail presented for this case, which is not one usually cited as particularly decisive on gun rights issues. However, I found this decision, written by Chief Justice Rehnquist, appointed to the Court by Richard Nixon in 1972 and elevated to the Chief Justice position by Ronal Reagan in 1986, instructive on several levels. First is a reminder that the powers of the Federal Government are enumerated powers, while the powers of the state governments are non-enumerated and indefinite. Second, the Court made it clear that regulation of the possession of otherwise legal firearms, even in such obviously sensitive locations such as school zones, was not going to be permissible under the Commerce Clause of the Constitution. Finally, the decision seemed to be intended to put an end to a trend toward allowing increasingly broad regulation under the Commerce Clause affecting activities having a tenuous effect on interstate trade and commerce.

United States v. Rybar (3d Cir. 1996). Rybar was a federally licensed firearms dealer who had conditionally pleaded guilty to possessing two machine guns at a gun show in Monroeville, Pennsylvania. The Court noted that:

> "Machinegun," in turn, is defined in 26 U.S.C. § 5845(b), part of the National Firearms Act, as any weapon which shoots, is

designed to shoot, or can be readily restored to shoot, **automatically more than one shot, without manual reloading, by a single function of the trigger**. The term shall also include the frame or receiver of any such weapon, **any part designed and intended solely and exclusively, or combination of parts designed and intended, for use in converting a weapon into a machinegun, and any combination of parts from which a machinegun can be assembled if such parts are in the possession or under the control of a person.**

The weapons in question were a Chinese, Type 54, 7.62-millimeter machine gun, and a U.S. Military, M-3, .45 caliber submachine gun, both of which were illegal under the Firearm Owners Protection Act of 1986. Rybar was convicted of two felonies. Rybar claimed on appeal to the United States Court of Appeals for the Third Circuit that these convictions violated his Second Amendment rights as well as the Commerce Clause of the United States Constitution.

In view of, or arguably notwithstanding, the 1993 decision of the United States Court of Appeals for the Tenth Circuit in *Warner* and the 1995 decision of the Supreme Court in *Lopez*, in this case, the United States Court of Appeals for the Third Circuit ruled, in a 2-1 decision, with future Supreme Court Justice Samuel Alito dissenting, that **Congress did have the power to regulate possession of homemade machine guns under the Commerce Clause**, thereby affirming Rybar's conviction.

It should be noted that although Justice Alito dissented, he did not challenge Congress' power to enact §922(o), prohibiting the transfer or possession of a machine gun. Indeed, rather than asserting that the Act was unconstitutional, Alito asserted that Congress had not made findings sufficient to justify the application of the Commerce Clause for this Act, suggesting that, had Congress made sufficient findings to support the invocation of the Commerce Clause for the Act, or alternatively had the DOJ assembled "empirical evidence documenting such a link," he would have deferred to those findings.

Navegar Incorporated, d/b/a Intratec, and Penn Arms, Incorporated v. United States (DC Cir. 1999). Navegar, Inc., doing business as Intratec ("Intratec"), and Penn Arms, Inc. ("Penn Arms") were licensed by the United States Bureau of Alcohol, Tobacco and Firearms ("BATF") to manufacture firearms. In 1994, Congress passed the Violent Crime Control and Law Enforcement Act. Subtitle A of Title XI of the Act, which regulated assault weapons, was entitled the "Public Safety and Recreational Firearms Use Act." Section 110102(a) of the Act made it "unlawful for a person to manufacture, transfer, or possess a semiautomatic assault weapon." Intratec was the sole manufacturer of the TEC-9, TEC-DC9[1] and TEC-22 semiautomatic pistols and Penn Arms was the sole manufacturer of the Striker 12, 12S, 12E and 12SE, 12-gauge revolving cylinder shotguns. These were two of the categories of guns prohibited by the statute. Under a "grandfather" clause which exempted from the Act semiautomatic assault weapons lawfully possessed on the date of enactment, the BATF sent letters to all federally licensed firearm manufacturers, including Intratec and Penn Arms, giving notice of the "grandfather" provision, and that the BATF would permit seven additional days of weapon manufacturing before it would take a final inventory identifying all grandfathered weapons. When the additional seven-day window for grandfathering weapons closed, Intratec held in its inventory over 40,000 TEC-DC9 and TEC-22 frames and thousands of dollars of gun parts which it could no longer assemble. Penn Arms was unable to take advantage of the seven-day window and was left with an inventory of $58,000 worth of gun parts for the Striker 12 series of shotguns.

Intratec and Penn Arms brought a declaratory judgment action under 28 U.S.C. § 2201 in the United States District Court for the District of Columbia, claiming that certain provisions of section 110102 of the Violent Crime Control and Law Enforcement Act of 1994 exceeded Congress' Commerce Clause power, and, therefore, were unconstitutional. The District Court granted the Government summary judgment, dismissing the claims of Intratec and Penn Arms.

The United States Court of Appeals for the DC Circuit affirmed the District Court decision, finding that **"the Act readily falls within category 3 as a regulation of activities having a substantial effect on interstate commerce," and that "The legislative history and congressional hearings conducted prior to the Act clearly manifest a congressional intent to restrict the interstate flow of "semiautomatic assault weapons,"** especially across the borders of states which had laws prohibiting such weapons."

United States v. Emerson, 270 F.3d 203 (5th Cir. 2001), cert. denied, 536 U.S. 907 (2002). This is a decision by the United States Court of Appeals for the Fifth Circuit holding that the Second Amendment to the United States Constitution guarantees individuals the right to bear arms. The case involved a challenge to the Constitutionality of 18 U.S.C. § 922(g)(8)(C)(ii), a federal statute which prohibited the transportation of firearms or ammunition in interstate commerce by persons subject to a court order that, by its explicit terms, prohibits the use of physical force against an intimate partner or child. The Fifth Circuit engaged in an extensive analysis of the text and history of the Second Amendment and its attendant caselaw (including many state supreme court decisions), and it **ultimately determined that the Second Amendment "protects the right of individuals to privately" keep and bear arms**. Nonetheless, the court held that the particular deprivation of the right to bear arms in the case before it did not violate the Constitution, while also acknowledging the federal government's sharp limitations on disarming of individual Americans. **The U.S. Supreme Court Denied Cert., i.e. declined to review the Fifth Circuit's decision**.

Silveira v. Lockyer, 312 F.3d 1052 (9th Cir. 2002). This is a decision by the United States Court of Appeals for the Ninth Circuit ruling that the **Second Amendment to the United States Constitution did not guarantee individuals the right to bear arms.** This decision was **contrary to the decision of the 5th Circuit in *United States v. Emerson*.** The case involved a challenge to the constitutionality of a California Statute, the Roberti-Roos Assault Weapons Control Act of 1989 (AWCA), which banned the manufacture, sale, transportation, or importation of specified semi-automatic firearms. The plaintiffs alleged that various provisions of the AWCA infringed upon their constitutionally guaranteed right to keep and bear arms as individuals. The court engaged in an extensive analysis of the history of the Second Amendment and its attendant case law in concluding that the Second Amendment does not guarantee individuals the right to keep and bear arms. The court concluded that the **Second Amendment provides "collective" rights, which is limited to the arming of state militia. The U.S. Supreme Court denied review**.

United States v. Stewart (348 F.3d 1132 (2003) and 451 F.3d 1071 (2006). Stewart, a convicted felon, **sold parts kits that an undercover ATF agent determined could be "readily . . . converted" into an unlawful firearm**, in violation of 18 U.S.C. § 922(a)(1)(A) and 18 U.S.C. § 921(a)(3)(A). The ATF agent then applied for and received a **federal search warrant** for Stewart's residence, which led to the discovery of thirty-one firearms, including **five machine guns which Stewart had machined and assembled**. Stewart was convicted in Arizona Federal Court of one count for being a felon in possession of a firearm under 18 U.S.C. § 922(g)(1) and 18 U.S.C. § 924(a)(2), and five counts for unlawful possession of a machine gun in violation of 18 U.S.C. § 922(o) and of possessing several unregistered, home-made machine guns. **Stewart was sentenced to five years in federal prison**. Stewart appealed his conviction under 18 U.S.C. § 922(o), claiming it exceeds Congress's commerce clause power and violates the Second Amendment.

In 2003, the United States Court of Appeals for the Ninth Circuit vacated, on Commerce Clause grounds, Stewart's conviction for possession of an unregistered machine gun (18 U.S.C. §922(o)). The Department of Justice then appealed to the U.S. Supreme Court. Following the Supreme Court's decision in *Gonzales v. Raich*, the Supreme Court vacated the Ninth Circuit decision and remanded *Stewart* to the Ninth Circuit for further consideration in light of its decision in *Raich*. The Ninth Circuit then upheld Stewart's conviction, concluding that **Congress had a rational basis for concluding that in the aggregate, possession of homemade machine guns could substantially affect interstate commerce in machine guns.**

District of Columbia v. Heller, 554 U.S. 570 (2008). *Heller* is discussed in detail in a previous chapter. The District of Columbia had banned all handguns from the city and required that all other guns be kept in homes unloaded and disassembled or trigger-locked. The Supreme Court, in a 5-4 decision, ruled that **the Second Amendment guarantees an individual right to possess a firearm unconnected with service in a militia, and to use that firearm for traditionally lawful purposes, such as self-defense within the home**. *Heller* settled the long-term uncertainty over whether the right to keep and bear arms conferred by the Second Amendment was an individual right or a collective right, i.e. whether the Second Amendment guarantees an individual right to own and bear arms, or a collective right for the people to bear arms for service in a militia. The Supreme Court had, in *Dred Scott* (1857) and *Presser* (1886) given strong indications that the right was an individual right, not limited by or derived from the individual's service or potential service in a militia. However, in *Miller* (1939), the Court had ruled that the "obvious purpose" of the Second Amendment was to "assure the continuation and render possible the effectiveness of" the state militia, and the Amendment "must be interpreted and applied with the end in view." ***Heller* has seemingly put the issue to rest, and has solidified the indications of the earlier *Dred Scott* and *Presser* holdings, that the right was an individual right and not a collective**

right, and was not limited by or derived from the individual's service or potential service in a militia.

The Supreme Court stated that blanket prohibitions on entire categories of guns that could be used for lawful purposes and restrictions that essentially prevented the use of a gun for lawful purposes were not constitutional. However, the Court emphasized that the individual right to bear arms was not unlimited and certain forms of federal regulation remain permissible. In that regard, the Court stated that:

> . . . nothing in our opinion should be taken to cast doubt on longstanding prohibitions on the possession of firearms by felons and the mentally ill, or laws forbidding the carrying of firearms in sensitive places such as schools and government buildings, or laws imposing conditions and qualifications on the commercial sale of arms.

McDonald v. Chicago, 561 U.S. 742 (2010). *McDonald* is also discussed in detail above. Shortly after the *Heller* decision, the Supreme Court ruled that the **rights guaranteed by the Second Amendment are subject to the Fourteenth Amendment, and, accordingly, that the states are prohibited from abridging the right of individuals to keep and bear arms**. In the decision, the Court stated:

> In Heller, we held that the Second Amendment protects the right to possess a handgun in the home for the purpose of self-defense. Unless considerations of stare decisis counsel otherwise, a provision of the Bill of Rights that protects a right that is fundamental from an American perspective applies equally to the Federal Government and the States. We therefore hold that the **Due Process Clause of the Fourteenth Amendment incorporates the Second Amendment right recognized in Heller.**
> (*emphasis added*)

McDonald **extends the right of individuals to keep and bear arms to individuals in all 50 states**. The Court ruled that individuals were therefore granted a constitutional right to keep firearms in their homes for self-protection. This right, the Court stated, was greater than the states' power to restrict it. As in its holding in *Heller*, the Supreme Court indicated that **state and federal laws prohibiting possession of firearms by felons and the mentally ill and the possession of firearms inside public schools were constitutional**.

A STATE COURT CASE

People v. Aguilar, 2 N.E. 3d 321 (Ill. 2013). In 2013, the Illinois Supreme Court in *People v. Aguilar* held that a **total ban on carrying firearms outside the home violated the Second Amendment** and was unconstitutional.

Applying *Heller*, *McDonald*, and *Moore v. Madigan* (a Seventh Circuit decision), the Illinois Supreme Court overturned the conviction of Aguilar, stating that the **right to self-defense was at the core of the Second Amendment**.

Nordyke v. King, 644 F.3d 776 (9th Cir. 2011). Alameda County, California had passed an **ordinance making it a misdemeanor to bring onto or to possess a firearm or ammunition on County property**. Gun show promoters (Nordyke) challenged the ordinance. In April 2009, a three-judge panel of the Ninth Circuit affirmed the district court ruling which upheld the Alameda County ordinance. The court accepted Nordyke's argument that the Second Amendment was incorporated through the Due Process Clause of the

Fourteenth Amendment and so that it applied to the states and local governments. The court found that the right to keep and bear arms is "deeply rooted in this Nation's history and tradition." However, the court ruled that the ordinance was constitutional, finding the ban of guns on county property to fall under *Heller*'s doctrine allowing governments to restrict possession in "sensitive" places. After a delay in subsequent proceedings pending the Supreme Court's decision in *McDonald*, the case was reheard en banc (the full court) in March 2012. During oral arguments the county stated that gun shows were not banned, and could be held with unloaded firearms if they were secured with cables. In June 2012, the full court ruled that the **county law was constitutional, since it allowed gun shows to take place on the fairgrounds, with tight restrictions**.

Henderson v. United States, 135 S. Ct. 1780 (2015). In *Henderson*, the Court addressed whether federal law gives felons the right to transfer their lawfully owned firearms to a third party. In a unanimous ruling, the court held that the **transfer of a felon's lawfully owned firearms from government custody to a third party is not barred by §922(g) if the court is satisfied that the recipient will not give the felon control over the firearms during or after the transfer**. The Court's holding allows felons to ask the government to transfer their firearms to an independent third party, including transfers to dealers for sale on the open market and directed transfers to specific people.

Caetano v. Massachusetts, 136 S. Ct. 1027 (2016). The Supreme Court held that a Massachusetts state law prohibiting the personal possession of

stun guns was contrary to the Court's decisions in *Heller* and *McDonald.* The Court concluded that the **Second Amendment extends to "all instruments that constitute bearable arms, even those that were not in existence at the time of the founding" and that this right arising out of the Second Amendment is applicable to the States.**

New York State Rifle & Pistol Association Inc. v. City of New York, New York, 86 F. Supp. 3d 249 (S.D.N.Y. 2015); aff'd, 883 F.3d 45 (2d Cir. 2018); cert. granted, S. Ct. No. 18-280 (2019); 590 U.S ___ (2020).

In this case, the Petitioners, three individual residents of New York City and the New York State Rifle & Pistol Association, Inc., challenge the constitutionality of a New York City law that prohibited the transport of firearms from one's residence to anywhere other than one of seven shooting ranges within the City. It must be noted that, on July 16, 2019, after the Supreme Court granted certiorari on January 22, 2019, and before Oral Argument on December 2, 2019, New York Governor Andrew Cuomo signed into law a bill passed by the New York Legislature amending New York Penal Law and authorizing premises licensees to transport their handguns between residences, places of business, shooting ranges, competitions, and any other locations for which they are licensed to possess a handgun. A few days later, on July 21, 2019, New York City followed the lead of the State legislature and amended its law to authorize premises licensees to transport their handguns between residences or places of business for which they are licensed to possess such a handgun, and to transport their handguns to and from shooting ranges and competitions both within and outside of

the City. The City of New York notified the Court of the changes made
to the NYC law as well as the New York State Statute, and took the
position that these changes to the City and State laws give the Petitioners
the relief they sought in the lawsuit and render the Petitioners' appeal to
the Supreme Court moot. The Petitioners disagreed, arguing that unless
the Court finds that the prior laws of the State of New York and the City
of New York were unconstitutional, the City and the State could
reinstitute the prior laws at any time.

It is important to understand that the firearms laws of the State of
New York are highly restrictive and New York City's ordinances are
even more restrictive than the State statutes. The State of New York law
prohibits the possession of firearms without a license. To obtain a
handgun license, an individual must submit an application to a local
licensing officer, who in New York City is the Police Commissioner, the
application including submission to a mental health history, criminal
history, and moral character investigation. There are two primary types
of handgun licenses, "carry" licenses and "premises" licenses. This case
involves premises licenses.

Except for a few professions for which gun ownership is
considered a necessity and for which the owner may obtain a "carry
license", gun owners in New York City may possess a gun within their
home only under a "premises license," and the gun must be kept
unloaded and in a locked container. Under the former New York City
law which triggered the District Court lawsuit, gun owners could not
transport the guns, except directly to and from one of seven small arms
ranges or shooting clubs located in New York City. Guns could not be
transported outside the city limits, even to an external shooting range or

to a second residence of the gun owner. Violations of this ordinance could result in a sentence of up to a year in prison.

The three individuals, who along with New York State Rifle & Pistol Association filed the initial lawsuit, had premises licenses and sought to transport their handguns to shooting ranges and competitions outside New York City. One of the individuals also sought to transport his handgun between the premises in New York City for which it was licensed and his second home in Hancock, New York. These individuals and New York State Rifle & Pistol Association, Inc., filed suit against the City in 2013 in the United States District Court for the Southern District of New York after confirming with the New York City Police that they could not take guns they owned in the city to shooting competitions in New Jersey nor to a second home outside the city. They claimed that the City's ordinance violated their Second Amendment rights as affirmed by *Heller*, as well as the Dormant Commerce Clause and the freedom to travel. The "Dormant" Commerce Clause provides that since Congress has power over interstate commerce, states cannot unduly burden interstate commerce, even in the absence of federal legislation regulating the activity.

The District Court found that the City had a compelling public safety interest in limiting firearms transport, and further found that gun owners are not prevented from traveling out of the city, without their guns, or from using shooting ranges outside the city with guns purchased out of the city. The District Court thus found that the rule "merely regulates rather than restricts the right to possess a firearm in the home and is a minimal, or at most, modest burden on the right" and thus did not violate plaintiffs' Second Amendment rights. The District Court also found that the rule did not violate the Dormant Commerce Clause, the First Amendment right of expressive association, or the fundamental right to travel. The District Court issued summary judgment for the City in 2015, dismissing the plaintiffs' claims.

The plaintiffs appealed to the U.S. Court of Appeals for the Second Circuit in 2015. The Second Circuit affirmed the District Court's findings in early 2018, holding that *Heller* and *McDonald* affirmed the constitutional right to own guns only in defense of one's home, not for transport or use outside of the home. The Second Circuit confirmed that the law served the important governmental interest of promoting public safety and that "the City has met its burden of showing a substantial fit between the Rule and the City's interest in promoting public safety."

As mentioned above, after the Second Circuit decision, after the Supreme Court granted certiorari, and before Oral Argument before the Supreme Court, the New York Legislature amended New York Penal Law authorizing premises licensees to transport their handguns between residences, places of business, shooting ranges, competitions, and any other locations for which they are licensed to possess a handgun. A few days later, New York City followed the lead of the State legislature and amended its law to authorize premises licensees to transport their handguns between residences or places of business for which they are licensed to possess such a handgun, and to transport their handguns to and from shooting ranges and competitions both within and outside of the City. Since this arguably gave the Petitioners the relief they sought in the lawsuit, the question was whether this rendered the appeal moot.

A decision was issued by the Supreme Court on April 27, 2020. Excerpts from the Supreme Court decision is presented below:

PER CURIAM

. . . .

In the District Court, petitioners challenged a New York City rule regarding the transport of firearms. Petitioners claimed that the rule violated the Second Amendment. Petitioners sought declaratory and injunctive relief against enforcement of the rule insofar as the rule prevented their transport of firearms to a second home or shooting range outside of the city. The District Court and the Court of Appeals rejected petitioners' claim. See 883 F. 3d 45 (CA2 2018). We granted certiorari. 586 U. S. ___ (2019). **After we granted certiorari, the State of New York amended its firearm licensing statute, and the City amended the rule so that petitioners may now transport firearms to a second home or shooting range outside of the city, which is the precise relief that petitioners requested in the prayer for relief in their complaint.** App. 48. **Petitioners' claim for declaratory and injunctive relief with respect to the City's old rule is therefore moot.** Petitioners now argue, however, that the new rule may still infringe their rights. In particular, petitioners claim that they may not be allowed to stop for coffee, gas, food, or restroom breaks on the way to their second homes or shooting ranges outside of the city. The City responds that those routine stops are entirely permissible under the new rule. We do not here decide that dispute about the new rule; as we stated in *Lewis* v. *Continental Bank Corp.*, 494 U. S. 472, 482-483 (1990):

"Our ordinary practice in disposing of a case that has become moot on appeal is to vacate the judgment with directions to dismiss. See, *e.g.*, *Deakins* v. *Monaghan*, 484 U. S., at 204; *United States* v. *Munsingwear, Inc.*, 340 U. S. 36, 39-40 (1950). However, in instances where the mootness is attributable to a change in the legal framework governing the case, and where the plaintiff may have some residual claim under the new framework that was understandably not asserted previously, our practice is to vacate the judgment and remand for further proceedings in which the parties may, if necessary, amend their pleadings or develop the record more fully.

See *Diffenderfer* v. *Central Baptist Church of Miami, Inc.*, <u>404 U. S. 412, 415</u> (1972)."

Petitioners also argue that, even though they have not previously asked for damages with respect to the City's old rule, they still could do so in this lawsuit. Petitioners did not seek damages in their complaint; indeed, the possibility of a damages claim was not raised until well into the litigation in this Court. The City argues that it is too late for petitioners to now add a claim for damages. **On remand, the Court of Appeals and the District Court may consider whether petitioners may still add a claim for damages in this lawsuit with respect to New York City's old rule.** The judgment of the Court of Appeals is vacated, and the case is remanded for such proceedings as are appropriate.

JUSTICE KAVANAUGH, concurring.

I agree with the *per curiam* opinion's resolution of the procedural issues before us—namely, that petitioners' claim for injunctive relief against New York City's old rule is moot and that petitioners' new claims should be addressed as appropriate in the first instance by the Court of Appeals and the District Court on remand.

I also agree with JUSTICE ALITO's general analysis of *Heller* and *McDonald. Post*, at 25; see *District of Columbia* v. *Heller*, <u>554 U. S. 570</u> (2008); *McDonald* v. *Chicago*, <u>561 U. S. 742</u> (2010); *Heller* v. *District of Columbia*, <u>670 F. 3d 1244</u> (CADC 2011) (Kavanaugh, J., dissenting). And **I share JUSTICE ALITO's concern that some federal and state courts may not be properly applying *Heller* and *McDonald*. The Court should address that issue soon, perhaps in one of the several Second Amendment cases with petitions for certiorari now pending before the Court.**

JUSTICE ALITO, with whom JUSTICE GORSUCH joins, and with whom JUSTICE THOMAS joins except for Part IV-B, dissenting.

By incorrectly dismissing this case as moot, the Court permits our docket to be manipulated in a way that should not be countenanced. Twelve years ago in *District of Columbia* v. *Heller*, <u>554 U. S. 570</u> (2008), we held that the Second Amendment protects the right of ordinary Americans to keep and bear arms. Two years later, our decision in *McDonald* v. *Chicago*, <u>561 U. S. 742</u> (2010), established that this right is fully applicable to the States. Since then, the lower courts have decided numerous cases involving Second Amendment challenges to a variety of federal, state, and local laws. Most have failed. We have been asked to review many of these decisions, but until this case, we denied all such requests.

On January 22, 2019, we granted review to consider the constitutionality of a New York City ordinance that burdened the right recognized in *Heller*. Among other things, the ordinance prohibited law-abiding New Yorkers with a license to keep a handgun in the home (a "premises license") from taking that weapon to a firing range outside the City. Instead, premises licensees wishing to gain or maintain the ability to use their weapons safely were limited to the seven firing ranges in the City, all but one of which were largely restricted to members and their guests.

In the District Court and the Court of Appeals, the City vigorously and successfully defended the constitutionality of its ordinance, and the law was upheld based on what we are told is the framework for reviewing Second Amendment claims that has been uniformly adopted by the Courts of Appeals. One might have thought that the City, having convinced the lower courts that its law was consistent with *Heller,* would have been willing to defend its victory in this Court. But once we granted certiorari, both the City and the State of New York sprang into action to prevent us from deciding this case. Although the City had previously insisted that its ordinance served important public safety purposes, our grant of review apparently led to an epiphany of sorts, and the City quickly changed its ordinance. And for good measure the State enacted a law making the old New York City ordinance illegal.

. . . .

Regrettably, the Court now dismisses the case as moot . . .

In sum, the City's travel restriction burdened the very right recognized in *Heller*. History provides no support for a restriction of this type. The City's public safety arguments were weak on their face, were not substantiated in any way, and were accepted below with no serious probing. And once we granted review in this case, the City's public safety concerns evaporated.

We are told that the mode of review in this case is representative of the way *Heller* has been treated in the lower courts. If that is true, there is cause for concern.

. . . .

This case is not moot. The City violated petitioners' Second Amendment right, and we should so hold. I would reverse the judgment of the Court of Appeals and remand the case to the District Court to provide appropriate relief. I therefore respectfully dissent.

(emphasis added)

The author suggests that, despite the Court dismissing the appeal as being moot, based upon the changes to the NYC Rule and the New York Statute, the Concurring opinion of Kavanaugh and the Dissent of Alito, joined by Gorsuch and by Thomas in part, are very instructive. With the recently added conservative justices to the Supreme Court, namely Justice Gorsuch and Justice Kavanaugh, it seems clear that the *Heller* and *McDonald* decisions are likely to be firmly institutionalized in regard to Second Amendment and firearm control/rights issues.

CHAPTER 4

TYPES OF ARMS

This leads us to the second question arising in the controversy over Second Amendment rights.   Assuming the Second Amendment does confer, as the U.S. Supreme Court has ruled in *Heller* and *McDonald*, the right to keep and bear arms upon each individual, what if any restrictions or regulations may be imposed on those rights. The Amendment says that the right "shall not be infringed." Muskets, cannons, mortars, musket balls, cannon balls, and gunpowder were essential for the colonial militias and the Continental Army in the Revolutionary War. Surely then, a citizen, at the time of ratification of the Second Amendment, could keep and bear a musket, gunpowder, and shot. "Keep" would surely include owning and possessing the musket and "bear" would surely include carrying the musket on the person of the bearer. There would generally be no issue about concealing a musket. But would there have been a potential issue about carrying a concealed a flintlock pistol? "To bear" would likely have been interpreted at the time as meaning "to carry on the person." If that right could not be infringed, was there an uninfringeable right to carry a concealed weapon. Also, if the right could not be infringed, were there any limits on the "arms" that the individual citizens could have? For instance, would the original beneficiaries of the Second Amendment have been entitled to keep a cannon or a mortar? As time passed, would a citizen of the 1800's be entitled to keep a Gatling gun?   Would a citizen of the 1900's be entitled to keep a 50-caliber machine gun, a Howitzer or a tank? What about an F-15 Fighter Jet, a 750-pound bomb, or even a nuclear weapon? Does "shall not be infringed" mean that there can be no limits placed on the right by law?

It might not have been an enormous stretch to imagine that a cannon capable of firing a 10-pound cannon ball would be within the "arms" of the Second Amendment, and, therefore, that the right of the citizenry to keep and bear the cannon could not be infringed. However, such a stretch is beyond the pale for other more modern weapons.

Although the Supreme Court has ruled that this right applies to individuals, not merely to collective militias, it has also held that the government may regulate or place limits on the manufacture, ownership and sale of firearms or other weapons. Requested by several states during the Constitutional ratification debates, the amendment reflected the lingering resentment over the widespread efforts of the British to confiscate the colonists' firearms at the outbreak of the Revolutionary War. Patrick Henry had rhetorically asked whether we would be stronger, "when we are totally disarmed, and when a British Guard shall be stationed in every house?"

What has the Supreme Court, or any of the respective Circuit Courts of Appeal, decided about the restrictions that may constitutionally be imposed on the types of weapons protected by the Second Amendment?

In deciding *Heller*, the Supreme Court noted that in *United States v. Miller*, 307 U.S. 174 (1939), the Court had addressed only the type of weapons eligible, at that time, for Second Amendment protection. The fact that the Court in *Miller* had apparently found that the Second Amendment guarantees no right to keep and bear a firearm that does not have "some reasonable relationship to the preservation or efficiency of a well regulated militia," did not deter the *Heller* Court, 70 years later. In *Heller*, the Court, found that the fact that *Miller* determined that a specific type of weapon, a sawed-off shotgun, was unlawfully possessed, supported the Court in its conclusion that the Second Amendment protects an individual right, noting that "it would have been odd to examine the character of the weapon rather than simply note that the two crooks were not militiamen." Nor, the Court added, did *Miller* "purport to be a thorough examination of the Second Amendment," and thus, the Court reasoned, it cannot be read to mean more than "say[ing] only that the Second Amendment does not protect those weapons not typically possessed by law-abiding citizens for lawful purposes, such as short-barreled shotguns."

After stating that the Second Amendment protects an individual's right to possess firearms, the *Heller* Court explained that, "[l]ike most rights, the right secured by the Second Amendment is not unlimited." The Court elected to leave an analysis of the full scope of the rights arising under the Second Amendment for subsequent decision, while noting that "nothing in our opinion should be taken to cast doubt on longstanding prohibitions on the possession of firearms by felons and the mentally ill, or laws forbidding the carrying of firearms in sensitive places such as schools and government buildings, or laws imposing conditions and qualifications on the commercial sale of firearms," or other "presumptively lawful" regulations. In regard to the types of weapons that are subject to Second Amendment protection, the Court noted that *Miller* limits Second Amendment coverage to weapons "in common use at the time" and that the prohibition of the particular weapon reviewed, the sawed-off shotgun, "is fairly supported by the historical tradition of prohibiting the carrying of dangerous and unusual weapons."

CHAPTER 5

FEDERAL AND STATE STATUTES

In January 1989, a gunman with an extensive criminal history used a semi-automatic AK-47 rifle to attack the Cleveland Elementary School in Stockton, California. Five children died and thirty-one other children and a teacher were wounded. In response to the horrific attack, in March 1989, Republican President George H.W. Bush issued an executive order banning the import of semi-automatic rifles. He made the import ban permanent in July 1989.

Subsequent mass shootings, including the Luby's Cafeteria shooting in Texas in October 1991, which left 23 people dead and 27 wounded, and the July 1993 California Street shooting in San Francisco, California, in which the shooter killed eight people and wounded six, caused support to increase for a federal legislative assault weapon ban. Two of the three firearms used by the California Street shooter were TEC-9 semi-automatic handguns with Hell-Fire triggers.

In November 1993, during the first year of the eight years of the presidency of Democratic President Bill Clinton, the proposed Public Safety and Recreational Firearms Use Protection Act (later referred to as the Assault Weapons Ban) passed the United States Senate. The author of the proposed ban, Democratic Senator Dianne Feinstein from California, and other sponsors decried the fact that it was a weakened version of their original proposal. In May of 1994, when the bill had still not been passed by the House of Representatives, former Republican President Gerald Ford, former Democratic President Jimmy Carter, and former Republican President Ronald Reagan wrote to the United States House of Representatives in support of banning "semi-automatic assault guns." They referred to the 1993 CNN/USA Today/Gallup Poll that found 77 percent of Americans supported a ban on the manufacture, sale, and possession of assault weapons. Democratic Representative Jack Brooks from Texas, then chairman of the House Judiciary committee, made a failed attempt to remove the assault weapons ban from the bill.

The Public Safety and Recreational Firearms Use Protection Act, thereafter commonly referred to as the federal "Assault Weapons Ban", was enacted in September 1994, as a subsection of the Violent Crime Control and Law Enforcement Act of 1994. The Assault Weapons Ban was applicable to firearms that met the criteria for what it defined as a "semi-automatic assault weapon", as well as magazines that met the criteria for what it defined as a "large capacity ammunition feeding device." The Assault Weapons Ban generally prohibited magazines with a capacity of more than 10 rounds. The Assault Weapons Ban had a 10-year sunset provision and expired in September 2004. That was two months before the November 2004 Presidential and Congressional elections. Incumbent Republican President George W. Bush was running for re-election. It was also three years following the September 11, 2001 terrorist attack on the United States. George bush was re-elected and the Republican majorities in both houses of Congress was increased in the 2004 elections.

The Violent Crime Control and Law Enforcement Act of 1994 enacted during the administration of Democratic President Bill Clinton, in addition to the Assault Weapons Ban, also instituted background checks for handgun purchases. As mentioned previously, former President George H. W. Bush, President George W. Bush's father, had offered an unequivocal letter of support for the Assault Weapons Ban that undoubtedly aided its passage. However, gun rights took a significant step forward during the eight years of the George W. Bush Administration that followed the Bill Clinton Administration.

In the 2000 and the 2004 presidential campaign debates, George W. Bush indicated his support for background checks for gun buyers and for trigger locks. In the 2000 campaign, he called for Congress to appropriate $325 million in matching funds to enable state and local governments across the country to implement voluntary trigger lock programs like he had implemented as Governor of Texas. President Bush even went so far as stating at one point during the 2000 campaign that he would sign a law requiring trigger locks for all handguns. He further stated his support for a minimum age of 21 for carrying a handgun.

During the 2000 campaign, candidate Bush did not commit to push for or even to sign, if passed by Congress, a renewal of the Assault Weapons Ban. However, as the September 2004 expiration date approached, the Bush administration signaled the willingness of the President to sign legislation that either extended the ban or made it permanent. "[The President] supports reauthorization of the current law," White House spokesman Scott McClellan told reporters in 2003, as the debate over the gun ban began to heat up. President Bush's position on the ban represented a break from the National Rifle Association, which had been one of his administration's staunchest allies. But the September 2004 deadline for renewing the ban came and went without an extension making it to the President's desk. The Republican majority in both houses of Congress simply declined to take up the matter.

President Bush felt serious criticism from both sides, the gun owners who felt betrayed and the gun ban proponents who felt he did not do enough to pressure Congress into passing the Assault Weapons Ban extension. For example, for the gun rights advocates, *keepandbeararms.com* publisher Angel Shamaya complained to the New York Times, "There are a lot of gun owners who worked hard to put President Bush into office, and there are a lot of gun owners who feel betrayed by him." For the gun control advocates, Bush's opponent in the looming 2004 presidential election, Sen. John Kerry, stated, "In a secret deal, [Bush] chose his powerful friends in the gun lobby over the police officers and families he promised to protect."

The end result of the George W. Bush Administration was several substantial advancements of gun rights at the federal level. This was especially true in the courts which were shaped by Bush's Supreme Court appointments of Justices John Roberts and Samuel Alito. The 5 to 4 decisions in *Heller* and *McDonald*, as described above, were enabled by those appointments. There was also a Republican majority in both houses of Congress during the entire eight years of the George W. Bush Administration. As it turned out, President Bush's support for background checks was limited to instant checks at the point of sale that did not require waiting periods of three or five days. Further, his support for trigger locks ultimately extended only to voluntary programs.

President Bush was also an ardent opponent of state and federal lawsuits against firearms manufacturers. President Clinton had made gun safety a major issue for the latter years of his Administration. In the year 2000, Clinton proposed legislation for gun safety and design standards, locking devices, restrictions on magazine sizes, and limits on the sales and distribution of firearms. Smith & Wesson, a well-known U.S. firearms manufacturer founded in 1852, was one of the standard issuers of firearms for the police and U.S. armed forces. Upon being prodded by the Clinton Administration, Smith & Wesson took a bold position and elected to cooperate with the federal government in its gun control efforts. In particular, Smith & Wesson agreed to include trigger locks with all its handguns and to implement smart gun technology. This was the first-ever compromise in which a major gun manufacturer committed to fundamentally changing the way guns are made, distributed and sold. Smith & Wesson also anticipated that the company would achieve a public relations benefit and would enhance its brand by becoming the firearms company that cared about safety. To say they were shocked by the actual result is a gross understatement.

The NRA promptly called for a boycott of Smith & Wesson products. Other gun manufacturers, Smith & Wesson's competitors, as well as dealers and other companies involved in the gun industry, were happy to jump on the NRA bandwagon. With the NRA, competitors and other industry businesses portraying Smith & Wesson as a disloyal traitor, gun enthusiasts heeded the NRA call for a boycott. The company experienced a sales decline of nearly 40 percent in 2001, the year following the deal with the Clinton Administration. In view of the devastation Smith & Wesson was experiencing at the hands of the NRA, President Bush's stance on gun industry lawsuits prompted Smith & Wesson to withdraw from the deal made with the Clinton Administration. In 2005, President Bush signed legislation providing the gun industry federal protection against lawsuits.

Despite the broad dissatisfaction from all sides about President George W. Bush's overall stance, and the actions and omissions on gun rights by his administration, the lasting legacy of the Bush administration will be his appointments to the U.S. Supreme Court. John Roberts was nominated by Bush to replace William Rehnquist in 2005. Later that same year, Bush nominated Samuel Alito to replace Sandra Day O'Connor on the high court. As discussed previously, three years later in 2008, in *Heller*, a critical case revolving around the District of Columbia's 25-year handgun ban, the court struck down the ban as unconstitutional and ruled for the first time that the Second Amendment applies to individuals, providing a right to own guns for self-defense inside the home. Both Roberts and Alito voted with the majority in a narrow 5-4 decision.

As also discussed previously, just 12 months after the *Heller* decision, the Supreme Court in *McDonald* struck down a gun ban in the city of Chicago as unconstitutional, ruling for the first time that the gun rights protections of the Second Amendment apply to states as well as to the federal government. Again, Roberts and Alito sided with the majority in a 5-4 decision.

Legislation to renew or replace the assault weapons ban has been proposed numerous times since 2004, all unsuccessfully. Between 2003 and 2008, Democratic Senator Dianne Feinstein from California, Republican Representative Michael Castle from Delaware, Democratic Representative Alcee Hastings from Florida, and Republican Representative Mark Kirk from Illinois, introduced bills to reauthorize the ban. During the same time period, Democratic Senator Frank Lautenberg from New Jersey and Democratic Representative Carolyn

McCarthy from New York introduced bills for a new assault weapons ban with a revised definition for the assault weapons. None of those bills made it out of committee.

After the November 2008 election, the website of President-elect Barack Obama presented a detailed agenda for his forthcoming administration. The agenda included making the expired federal Assault Weapons Ban permanent. In early 2009, the new Attorney General, Eric Holder, confirmed the Obama administration's commitment to reinstate the Assault Weapons Ban, stating in a press conference that "there are just a few gun-related changes that we would like to make, and among them would be to reinstitute the ban on the sale of assault weapons."

Approximately nine months later on December 14, 2012, 20-year old Adam Lanza shot and killed his mother at their Newton, Connecticut, home, and then drove to Sandy Hook Elementary School in his mother's car. Around 9:30 a.m., using a Bushmaster XM15-E2S rifle, a semi-automatic assault rifle similar to the AR-15, legally purchased by his mother, and ten magazines with 30 rounds each, Lanza shot his way through a glass panel next to the locked front entrance doors of the school, which had heightened security measures in place. Lanza then shot and killed 26 people, including 20 children between six and seven years old, and six adult staff members. When police arrived at the school, Lanza committed suicide by shooting himself in the head. A report issued by the Office of the Child Advocate in November 2014 said that Lanza had Asperger Syndrome and as a teenager suffered from depression, anxiety and obsessive-compulsive disorder, but concluded that they had "neither caused nor led to his murderous acts." The report went on to say, "his severe and deteriorating internalized mental health problems ... combined with an atypical preoccupation with violence ... (and) access to deadly weapons ... proved a recipe for mass murder".

The Sandy Hook shooting prompted renewed debate about gun control. Immediate discussions mostly centered around proposals for universal background checks, and for new federal and state gun legislation banning the manufacture and sale of certain types of semi-automatic firearms and of magazines for more than ten rounds of ammunition.

Two months after the horrific Sandy Hook tragedy, on January 24, 2013, Senator Feinstein introduced the proposed Assault Weapons Ban of 2013 (AWB 2013). The bill was similar to the 1994 ban, but differed in that the ban would not expire after 10 years, and incorporated a one-feature test for a firearm to qualify as an assault weapon rather than the two-feature test of the 1994 ban. Unsurprisingly, the GOP Congressional delegation from Texas and the NRA condemned Feinstein's bill. On March 14, 2013, the Senate Judiciary Committee approved a version of the bill along party lines. On April 17, 2013, AWB 2013 failed on a Senate vote of 40 to 60.

The proposed Assault Weapons Ban of 2015, was introduced to Congress on December, sponsored by Representative David N. Cicilline of Rhode Island along with 123 original co-sponsors. It currently has 149 co-sponsors. This legislation states that its purpose is "To regulate assault weapons, to ensure that the right to keep and bear arms is not unlimited, and for other purposes." The proposed legislation also targets various firearm accessories, including the barrel shroud (a safety covering for the barrel of the firearm to prevent the operator from burning his or her hands as the barrel becomes heated after the firing of multiple rounds), pistol grip, and certain types of firearm stocks such as telescoping or collapsing stocks. Also included are lists of various classes and models of firearms, including certain types of semi-automatic firearms, AR-15 style rifles, assault weapons, semi-automatic pistols, semi-automatic shotguns, and others, some of which have already been banned or restricted under existing legislation including grenade launchers. The legislation also would prohibit high-capacity magazines.

On the night of October 1, 2017 at about 10 p.m., an open-air country music concert was nearing conclusion at the Las Vegas Village outdoor performance site on the Las Vegas Strip. Stephen Paddock, a 64-year-old former auditor and real estate businessman, and big stakes gambler, opened fire on the concertgoers from his suite on the 32nd floor of the nearby Mandalay Bay Hotel. He killed 58 people and wounded 422. Another 429 persons were injured in the panic as the frantic concertgoers tried to flee to safety, bringing the total number of the injured to 851. He reportedly fired more than 1,100 rounds of ammunition in less than 10 minutes. About an hour later, Paddock was found dead in his room from a self-inflicted gunshot wound. Although evidence was found that Paddock had investigated other possible venues for mass shootings, no motive has been determined for the massacre at Las Vegas. It was the deadliest mass shooting committed by an individual in the history of the United States.

Paddock had checked in at Mandalay Bay on September 25, 2017. Because he was a high stakes gambler well known to the resort, he was given a complimentary room on the 32nd floor facing the outdoor concert site. He subsequently rented a connecting room also facing the concert site. Between September 25 and October 1, the day of the shooting, with the unknowing assistance of Mandalay Bay employees, he transported fourteen AR-15 rifles, eight AR-10 rifles, a .308 caliber bolt-action rifle, and a revolver, as well as prodigious amounts of ammunition, to the two rooms. All of the AR-15's were equipped with bump stocks and twelve of the AR-15's had 100-round magazines. A bump stock enables a semi-automatic rifle to shoot in rapid succession, at nearly the speed of a fully automatic weapon.

Unsurprisingly, the Las Vegas shooting reenergized the debate on firearms, focusing attention once again on semi-automatic assault rifles and large magazines, and calling heightened attention to bump stocks. Bump stocks were banned by a regulation issued by the U.S. Department of Justice Department in December 2018, which became effective in March 2019. No changes have followed for assault rifles or large magazines.

Largely due to a perceived unwillingness or inability of the U.S. Congress to enact appropriate assault weapon legislation, a number of states have adopted their own bans. The following table has been extracted from an article appearing in *Wikipedia* entitled "Assault Weapons legislation in the United States."

Three of these states, namely California in 1989, New Jersey in 1990, and Connecticut in 1993, enacted assault weapons bans before Congress passed the federal Assault Weapons Ban of 1994. Hawaii, Maryland, Massachusetts and New York passed assault weapons bans before AWB 1994 expired in 2004.

U.S. assault weapons bans by jurisdiction

Jurisdiction	Status	- By make/ model	Semiauto rifles	Semiauto Pistols	Shotguns	Features Test	Magazine capacity
California	In force	X	X	X	X	X	X
Connecticut	In force	X	X	X	X	X	X
District of Columbia	In force	X	X	X	X	X	X
Hawaii	In force			X		X	X
Maryland	In force	X	X	X	X	X	X
Massachusetts	In force	X	X	X	X	X	X
New Jersey	In force	X	X	X	X	X	X
New York	In force	X	X	X	X	X	X

State laws regulating the sale, ownership, possession and use of firearms vary considerably from state to state. Forty-four states have a provision in their state constitutions similar to the Second Amendment which protect the right to keep and bear arms. The exceptions are California, Iowa, Maryland, Minnesota, New Jersey, and New York. Civil rights statutes of New York contain a provision which is essentially identical to the Second Amendment. More fundamentally, the U.S. Supreme Court decision in *McDonald* mandates that the right to keep and bear arms guarantees of the Second Amendment apply to all 50 states, and the respective local governments of each state, under the

Fourteenth Amendment. States and local governments may not take from the citizens the rights guaranteed by the Second Amendment. And the Supreme Court decision in *Heller* clarifies that the rights guaranteed by the Second Amendment are individual and not collective, and that they specifically include keeping and bearing arms for personal defense.

The Supreme Court confirmed in *McDonald*, what was perhaps fundamentally obvious, that the principal stated purpose of the Second Amendment, namely to protect the right of the people to keep and bear arms for service in a militia, was no longer a valid purpose. The Court confirmed that the remaining purpose of the Second Amendment was to protect the right of the individual to keep and bear arms for self-defense. With that purpose being the limiting factor for federal or state laws regulating firearms sale, ownership, possession and use, a wide variety of restrictions are likely to pass constitutional muster. The result is that laws vary from very restrictive in some states to minimally restrictive in other states. In a number of states, firearms laws are considerably less restrictive than federal firearms laws. This does not mean that the residents of those states are immune to prosecution for violations of the more stringent federal firearms laws. However, under the U.S. Supreme Court's ruling in *Printz v. United States*, 521 U.S. 898 (1997), state and local police departments are not obligated to enforce federal firearms laws.

Wherever a person in possession of a firearm goes in the United States, he or she is subject to federal firearms laws. Upon crossing a state line and entering a state, he or she is also immediately subject to the firearms laws of the state being entered, not the state of her or his residency. Reciprocity may or may not exist between the entered state and the residency state in regard to certain firearms matters, such as concealed carry permits. Some states recognize an out-of-state concealed carry permit from a state that does not recognize their permits. Some states do not require a permit for an open carry or concealed carry firearm in a vehicle, deeming the vehicle to be a habitation that the person has a right to defend with a firearm. In view of the drastic differences in firearms laws from state to state, it is essential for a person intending to travel with a firearm, particularly a concealed firearm, to investigate the current firearms laws of each state to be entered or traversed.

Examples of firearm laws that vary from state to state are:

State Preemption. Some states have state preemption for some or all aspects of firearm laws. In states with state preemption, local governments are prohibited from enacting ordinances relating to firearms, at least in regard to matters that the state has chosen to preempt. In states that have not preempted firearm laws, local governments may enact their own firearm laws which are more restrictive than those of the state.

License. Some states and local governments require a license or permit to purchase or possess firearms.

Firearm Registration. Some states and local governments require that each firearm be registered with a law enforcement agency.

Background Checks. Federal law only requires background checks for sales by licensed gun dealers, and for any interstate sales. Some states require a background check of the buyer when a firearm is sold by a private party.

Assault Weapons. Some states and local governments ban or place restrictions on certain semi-automatic firearms that are defined by state statute or local ordinance as assault weapons, or on magazines that can hold more than a certain number of rounds of ammunition. NFA weapons are weapons that are heavily restricted at a federal level by the National Firearms Act of 1934 and the Firearm Owners Protection Act of 1986. These include automatic firearms (such as machine guns), short-barreled shotguns, and short-barreled rifles, as well as suppressors (silencers). Some states and localities place additional restrictions on such NFA weapons. Semi-automatic assault rifles and large capacity magazines have received much public and political attention at the state and local government level in many states since the 2004 expiration of the federal Assault Weapons Ban of 1994 and the occurrence of the mass shootings that have horrified this great nation.

Concealed Carry. Although every state allows concealed carry of certain firearms by certain persons in certain situations, some states and local governments are much more restrictive than others.

Open Carry. Many states allow some form of open carry of an unconcealed firearm in public or in a vehicle.

Peaceable Journey. Peaceable Journey laws vary from state to state. Accordingly, a potential dilemma arises when a person who lawfully possesses, and perhaps is licensed to conceal carry, a firearm in one state, desires to pass through another state which does not allow, for lack of a permit or license in that state or for some other reason, the person to possess or transport the firearm, to another state where the possession, and perhaps the concealed carry, of the firearm is lawful. The interstate transportation of firearms is addressed by federal law in 18

U.S. Code § 926A, of the Firearms Owners Protection Act of 1986 aka "The Peaceable Journey Law." 18 U.S. Code § 926A, Interstate Transportation of Firearms, states as follows:

> Notwithstanding any other provision of any law or any rule or regulation of a State or any political subdivision thereof, any person who is not otherwise prohibited by this chapter from transporting, shipping, or receiving a firearm shall be entitled to transport a firearm for any lawful purpose from any place where he may lawfully possess and carry such firearm to any other place where he may lawfully possess and carry such firearm if, during such transportation the firearm is unloaded, and neither the firearm nor any ammunition being transported is readily accessible or is directly accessible from the passenger compartment of such transporting vehicle: Provided, That in the case of a vehicle without a compartment separate from the driver's compartment the firearm or ammunition shall be contained in a locked container other than the glove compartment or console.

This federal statute allows a person to transport a firearm through a state in which he or she does not hold a valid permit and is not otherwise entitled to possess and transport the firearm, as long as he or she may lawfully possess and carry in the state of origin as well as the destination state. The owner of the firearm must be in transit and is not entitled to stay in the state where possession would be illegal. Unless the transited state allows otherwise, the firearm must be unloaded and contained outside the passenger compartment or in a locked box and out of the reach of any occupant of the vehicle. Some states require that the vehicle must pass through the state without stopping, and other states allow only short stops. The federal statute does not enable the owner to use his or her firearm for defense during transit unless permitted by the transited state.

Castle Doctrine and Stand-Your-Ground Laws. Some states have enacted a castle doctrine law, which allows the use of deadly force against an intruder in one's home or yard without attempting to retreat, or a stand-your-ground law, which allows the use of deadly force in self-defense in public places, without attempting to retreat.

Red Flag Laws. Some states have enacted red flag laws that enable a judge to issue a temporary confiscation order for the firearms of a person who is found to constitute an imminent threat to others or to themselves.

A question which arises from the discussion of the foregoing firearms control measures which have been implemented with varying degrees of non-uniformity across the US, is the extent to which firearms regulation should be the subject exclusively of Federal law and accordingly preempted by Federal law. Further discussion on possible Federal preemption follows.

CHAPTER 6

THE NATIONAL RIFLE ASSOCIATION (NRA)

The National Rifle Association ("NRA") is much maligned by gun control advocates. The NRA was founded in 1871 by two Union Civil War veterans and a former *New York Times* reporter. The most famous of the founders, Ambrose Everett Burnside, was a Union Army general in the Civil War. He led successful campaigns in North Carolina and Tennessee, as well as successful defenses to the raids of Confederate General John Hunt Morgan. However, his forces suffered resounding defeats at the Battle of Fredericksburg and the Battle of the Crater. His distinctive style of facial hair, which connected the hair on his head to his mustache, became known as sideburns, derived from an alteration of his last name. Burnside was the first president of the NRA.

Initially the NRA was conceived as sort of a club which was intended to improve the marksmanship of 'urban yankees'. The purported inferiority of union soldier marksmanship to that of confederates was widely believed to have prolonged the civil war. The initial motto of the NRA was "Firearms Safety Education, Marksmanship Training, Shooting for Recreation." Concern over protecting gun rights, under the purview of the Second Amendment, was nowhere in sight.

Although the NRA continues its involvement in firearms training, it is now primarily a gun rights advocacy group. According to the NRA, it had nearly 5 million members as of December 2018. The NRA is viewed as one of the most influential lobbying groups in Washington, D.C. It is certainly the most strident. The NRA Institute for Legislative

Action is its lobbying division, which manages its political action committee ("PAC"), the Political Victory Fund. Over its history the organization has influenced legislation, participated in or initiated lawsuits, and endorsed or opposed various candidates at local, state and federal levels. The NRA has been criticized by gun control and gun rights advocacy groups, political commentators, and politicians. The organization has been the focus of intense criticism in the aftermath of high-profile mass shootings because of its apparent insensitivity, alas even apparent complete indifference, to the humanity concerns when they conflict with the economic concerns of the gun industry.

The early NRA was very much a Republican institution. In view of the NRA distancing itself from its own history, the NRA's early history has been largely forgotten, just as the history of the Republican party has been lost. Republicans, in the days of the early 1900's, were much in favor of government action in the service of social reform. Ambrose Burnside would likely be appalled at the NRA policies and activities of today.

Believe it or not, in the 1920's and 1930's, the NRA helped write and lobby for the first federal gun control laws, the very kinds of laws that the NRA has vigorously opposed since the latter part of the 1900's. In the early 1920's, the National Revolver Association, the arm of the NRA involved in handgun training, proposed model legislation for the states that included requiring a permit to carry a concealed weapon, adding five years to a prison sentence if a gun was used in a crime, banning non-citizens from buying a handgun, requiring that gun dealers turn over sales records to police, and instituting a one-day waiting period between buying a gun and taking possession of the gun. These latter two provisions are among those presently vigorously opposed by the NRA.

The setting for these NRA proposals was the 1920 ratification of the 17th Amendment (Prohibition) outlawing alcohol and the almost immediate appearance of big city gangsters who outgunned rivals and the police with sawed-off shotguns and machine guns. The gangster crime spree of the 1930's prompted President Franklin Roosevelt to make gun control a feature of the New Deal. President Roosevelt relied on the willing assistance of the NRA in drafting the 1934 National Firearms Act and the 1938 Gun Control Act, the first federal gun control laws.

Those laws imposed stiff regulations and heavy taxes on firearms that were associated with crime, such as sawed-off shotguns, machine guns and silencers. Gun dealers and owners were required to register with the federal government and felons were banned from owning weapons. Those federal laws were unanimously upheld by the Supreme Court in 1939 (*United States v. Miller*). However, what is shocking to read, considering the present disposition of the NRA, is the testimony of Karl T. Frederick, the president of the NRA, before Congress. He testified, "I have never believed in the general practice of carrying weapons. I do not believe in the general promiscuous toting of guns. I think it should be sharply restricted and only under licenses."

For the next 30 years, the NRA continued to support gun control.

On Nov. 22, 1963, President John F. Kennedy was assassinated by Lee Harvey Oswald using an Italian military surplus rifle purchased from an NRA member mail-order advertisement. NRA Executive Vice-President Franklin Orth testified at a subsequent congressional hearing that mail-order sales should be banned. He testified, "We do think that any sane American, who calls himself an American, can object to placing into this bill the instrument which killed the president of the United States."

In the late 1960's, the Black Panthers, a militant black nationalist group, resorted to their understanding and criticism of California's gun laws to support their political statements about the subjugation of African-Americans. On May 2, 1967, thirty members of the Black Panthers staged an impromptu march on the California State Capitol, armed with .357 Magnums, 12-gauge shotguns and .45-caliber pistols. They exclaimed on the steps of the Capitol Building, "The time has come for black people to arm themselves." The event so frightened California politicians, including particularly Republican California Governor Ronald Reagan, that it prompted passage of the Mulford Act, a state law prohibiting the open carry of loaded firearms and prohibiting loaded firearms in the state Capitol. The NRA enthusiastically supported enactment of the Mulford Act, which initiated California's march toward some of the strictest gun laws in America.

The Mulford Act was one of a series of federal and state laws enacted in the late 1960's regulating firearms, with the specific unwritten intent of targeting African-Americans. This included the federal Gun Control Act of 1968. That Act incorporated provisions prohibiting certain people from owning guns, providing for increased licensing and inspections of gun dealers, and restricting the importation of the cheap pocket pistols referred to as Saturday night specials, a type of weapon that was prevalent in some urban communities, particularly poor black communities.

In contrast to the NRA's stonewall opposition to gun control of any variety in today's America, the NRA was all-in with the federal and state efforts for stricter gun regulations in the 1960's. This was undeniably part of an effort to keep guns out of the hands of African-Americans as racial tensions in the nation grew. As noted above, the NRA was especially fearful of the Black Panthers.

The summer riots of 1967 and the assassinations of Martin Luther King Jr. and Robert F. Kennedy in 1968 prompted Congress to enact the Gun Control Act of 1968. That Act included a reenactment of some of the FDR-era gun control laws which the NRA had supported. This act extended the gun ownership ban to include the mentally ill and drug addicts and included minimum age and serial number requirements. Certain types of ammunition could only be purchased with a show of an ID. It also restricted the shipping of guns across state lines to collectors and federally licensed dealers.

Although the NRA was apparently supportive of most of the provisions of the Gun Control Act of 1968, in what heralded in the era of NRA opposition to gun control, the NRA opposed and succeeded in blocking the most stringent part of the legislation, which would have mandated a national registry of all guns and a federal license for all gun carriers. However, even then, in an interview in *American Rifleman*, Franklin Orth, the current President of the NRA, stated that despite portions of the law which appeared "unduly restrictive, the measure as a whole appears to be one that the sportsmen of America can live with."

A major about-face in the NRA's platform was triggered by a 1971 event when the Bureau of Alcohol, Tobacco, Firearms and Explosives ("ATF"), during a house raid, shot and paralyzed a longtime

NRA member who was suspected of stockpiling illegal weapons. The NRA swiftly condemned the ATF for this event. William Loeb, an NRA board member and the editor of New Hampshire's *Manchester Union Leader,* referred to the ATF agents in this incident as "Treasury Gestapo". This incident also apparently led to the NRA following the lead of the Black Panthers in claiming that the Second Amendment constitutionally protected the gun rights of individuals.

On May 20, 2000, Charlton Heston, one of the most famous American actors of all time and then president of the NRA, addressed the NRA convention attendees at its 129th annual convention. In concluding his speech, Heston raised a replica of a flintlock rifle over his head and declared, in the dramatic fashion of Moses raising the stone tablets of the Ten Commandments, that anyone who wanted to take his gun would have to pry it "from my cold, dead hands." This dramatic expression by the NRA's famous president became a formative event casting the platform of the NRA in stone. The NRA has become the leading pro-gun advocacy group in America politics. It is relentless and seems to be lacking any heart or soul. It countenances no contravention of any right related to the manufacture, sale, possession or use of firearms or firearm accessories, including bump stocks and 100 round clips. It takes the position that crazy, deranged people commit the horrific mass shootings, not the guns, and access to the guns is guaranteed by the Second Amendment. Gun control laws are characterized as an unconstitutional intrusion on the Second Amendment right to bear arms, and politicians who support them are characterized as traitors to the Constitution. Indeed, the NRA's present day creed reflects the words uttered by the Black Panthers in the 1960's, "the gun

is the only thing that will free us - gain us our liberation."

Illustrative of the extreme approach of the NRA is their response

to the recent policy changes by Walmart. As discussed in greater detail

below, on August 3, 2019, 21 year old Patrick Crusius from Allen,

Texas, shot and killed 22 people and injured 24 others at a Walmart store

in El Paso, Texas, using a WASR-10 rifle, a semi-automatic civilian

version of the AK-47 purchased legally in Texas. As a result of that

tragedy, Walmart elected to end handgun sales, discontinue sales of

certain types of ammunition, and to ban open carry in stores. The NRA

unbelievably responded by slamming Walmart's changes to its gun

policies as "shameful" after the mass shooting. The NRA stated: "It is

shameful to see Walmart succumb to the pressure of the anti-gun elites.

Lines at Walmart will soon be replaced by lines at other retailers who are

more supportive of America's fundamental freedoms." The NRA

continued: "The truth is Walmart's actions today will not make us any

safer. Rather than place the blame on the criminal, Walmart has chosen

to victimize law-abiding Americans." Finally the NRA stated: "Our

leaders must be willing to approach the problems of crime, violence and

mental health with sincerity and honesty."

Walmart President and CEO Doug McMillon wrote, "We've also

been listening to a lot of people inside and outside our company as we

think about the role we can play in helping to make the country safer."

He continued, "It's clear to us that the status quo is unacceptable."

Walmart will no longer sell short-barrel rifle ammunition, including .223

caliber and 5.56 caliber, and it will sell only the remaining inventory of

handgun ammunition. Further, it will discontinue handgun sales in

Alaska, the last state where it has continued to sell handguns. It should be noted that Walmart stopped selling assault-style rifles in 2015 and raised the age to purchase guns from 18 to 21 in 2018.

At the end of the day, it must be remembered that the NRA is a lobbying organization for the gun industry. They can be expected to do everything they can do, within the confines of the law, to promote the economic interests of the gun manufacturers and dealers. They incessantly argue that they are out to protect the Second Amendment and the rights of gun owners under the Second Amendment. That is indirectly true. They are interested in promoting and protecting a broad interpretation of the Second Amendment, because that promotes and protects a broad market for gun and gun accessories manufacturers and dealers.

Although there was a time that the NRA had a human face and was interested in supporting and promoting common sense gun control. Those days are gone. We cannot now expect the NRA to be a helpful participant in the resolution of the firearms debate. Their absolutely uncompromising, take-no-prisoners position simply nullifies their ability to contribute to a resolution. To the contrary, their vitriolic rhetoric will simply have to be ignored if a resolution is to be reached. Similarly, the politicians who have historically accepted substantial campaign contributions from the NRA or have been the beneficiary of the activities of the NRA's political action committee, the Political Victory Fund, must be held accountable by the voters.

In the wake of the recent terrible mass shootings, the following survey posted in 2019 by the NRA on the *Rear Clear Politics* website seems telling of the current stonewall response and resolve of the NRA.

In the opinion of the author of this work, it appears clear that many of the questions posed by the NRA in the survey are based upon gross misrepresentations of the positions of firearms control advocates. The survey questions appear, to the author of this work, to be designed to grossly mischaracterize the nature of the present firearms debate, to engage readers based upon inflammatory and misleading queries, and to further harden the resolve of the hard-core NRA supporters.

NATIONAL GUN OWNERS SURVEY

Do you agree that the Second Amendment guarantees your individual right to own a firearm?
 Yes
 No
 No Opinion

Do you support the confirmation of pro-Second Amendment judges to the U.S. Supreme Court and lower federal courts?
 Yes
 No
 No Opinion

Do you support laws that protect your fundamental right to use a firearm to defend yourself and your loved ones from a violent criminal attacker?
 Yes
 No
 No Opinion

Should Congress and the states eliminate so-called "gun free zones" that leave innocent citizens defenseless against terrorists and violent criminals?
 Yes
 No
 No Opinion

Should Congress pass a law that gives law-abiding citizens the right to carry a firearm across state lines?
 Yes
 No
 No Opinion

Do you oppose any United Nations treaty that strips the U.S. of its sovereignty and gives U.N. bureaucrats the power to regulate every rifle, pistol, and shotgun you own?
 Yes
 No
 No Opinion

Do you agree that law-abiding citizens should be forced to submit to mandatory gun registration or else forfeit their guns and their freedom?
 Yes
 No
 No Opinion

Should NRA direct critical resources toward stopping anti-gun billionaires like Michael Bloomberg who are spending millions of dollars to destroy your Second Amendment freedom in states around the country?
 Yes
 No
 No Opinion

Would you vote for a politician who supports a gun-ban agenda?
 Yes
 No
 No Opinion

Would you vote for a politician who calls for the repeal of the Second Amendment?
 Yes
 No
 No Opinion

Do you believe the NRA should continue to defend your gun rights at the federal, state, and local levels?
 Yes
 No
 No Opinion

Do you trust the mainstream media to report on Second Amendment issues fairly?
 Yes
 No
 No Opinion

Do you support censorship of gun-related content on social media websites like Facebook and Twitter?
 Yes
 No
 No Opinion

Do you support laws that would require you to dismantle your guns and keep them in storage so that they are of no use to you if you are attacked by a violent criminal?
 Yes
 No
 No Opinion

Do you believe that college students, who have been trained in gun safety, should be allowed to carry a firearm on college campuses to protect themselves?
 Yes
 No
 No Opinion

Should the government limit the number of guns you are allowed to purchase?
 Yes
 No
 No Opinion

Do you believe more restrictions on law-abiding gun owners will
make our country safer?
 Yes
 No
 No Opinion

Do you support or oppose mandatory background checks to
purchase ammunition?
 Support
 Oppose
 No Opinion

Do you believe that law-abiding gun shop owners should be held
criminally responsible for the acts of violent criminals?
 Yes
 No
 No Opinion

Do you support or oppose stationing armed school resource
officers in schools to protect our children from violent criminals?
 Support
 Oppose
 No Opinion

Do you support or oppose allowing teachers who have been
trained in gun safety to carry concealed firearms to protect school
children from violent attackers?
 Support
 Oppose
 No Opinion

Do you support or oppose allowing military service men and
women to carry firearms on U.S. military bases to guard
themselves against violent criminals and radical Islamic
terrorists?
 Support
 Oppose
 No Opinion

Do you support or oppose the confiscation of firearms from law-abiding citizens without due process?
Support
Oppose
No Opinion

Do you support or oppose anti-gun politicians who refuse to prosecute convicted felons who illegally attempt to purchase a firearm?
Support
Oppose
No Opinion

Do you support or oppose an outright ban on all semi-automatic rifles, shotguns, and pistols?
Support
Oppose
No Opinion

CHAPTER 7

AUTHOR'S EXPERIENCES AND BIASES

Perhaps here is the place and now is the time to tell you more about me so you would be able to ascertain whether I have approached and whether I am capable of approaching this subject from a completely objective and unbiased viewpoint. After all, is it possible for anyone to do such a thing, especially on a matter such as gun rights?

We are all emotional creatures, some more than others. Sometimes we think more with our hearts than with our minds. I have a dear wife who has refrained since 1967 from kicking me out on the street, even though I have deserved it many times. We have six children and eleven grandchildren, and so I am naturally very concerned about the safety of children and the public in general. I must confess, thinking with my heart, that I am much more concerned about the safety of children than I am about protecting the Second Amendment. However, I am also an attorney and so, thinking with my mind, I am a very zealous advocate for individual rights and responsibilities.

I am a registered Republican and I have been a registered Republican for all but two of the Presidential election cycles since 1968. For those two cycles, I rebelled, based upon what I observed occurring in the Republican party. In the present scheme of things, I am probably more appropriately characterized as an Independent. Although I have voted more often for Republicans over my voting lifetime, more recently I have voted for more Democrats. I have two favorite Presidents of my lifetime, Ronald Reagan and Barack Obama. I also voted for and was a great admirer of Jimmy Carter and George H. W. Bush. I found them all to be dedicated and intelligent Presidents who loved America, loved

Americans, and loved freedom. Although I did not vote for Bill Clinton for either of his terms, I was much opposed to his impeachment by my Republican party for lying about an affair. It is one of the few times that I have made the effort to write to my congressman, then Chris Cannon of Utah's Fourth Congressional District, a BYU Law School classmate of mine, to express my displeasure. I registered as an Independent for one election cycle and as a Democrat for one election cycle as a result of the very undesirable changes, from my point of view, that I witnessed in the Republican Party. I was an ardent admirer of John McCain and Robert Dole. The election of 2008 was a great one because we had an outstanding candidate from each of the parties, John McCain and Barack Obama.

As I mentioned before, I grew up in a small town in rural Mississippi. Most of the people were poor but, by standard of living, would probably be considered lower middle class. We and all of the other families I knew personally had food to eat and a roof over our heads. On the other hand, at that time there were a lot of very poor African American families in my home town.

There were not a lot of activities for a growing boy except hunting, fishing and baseball. I spent a lot of time in the spring and summer playing Little League and later Pony League, and a lot of backyard baseball as well. My dad was an avid hunter and fisherman and I loved going hunting and fishing with my dad. Anything we killed hunting or caught fishing ended up in the freezer as food. We would have survived just fine without the game and the fish, so it was primarily the sport that I enjoyed with my dad. I used $5.00 a week from my pay as a bagger at a grocery store (we carried the bags of customers to their car in those days) to pay for the 16-gauge double barrel shotgun I used for quail, dove and duck hunting. I still have the 16-gauge double barrel.

A couple of events occurred which shaped my attitude toward hunting. One day when I was about 15 years old, I was hunting doves in a field behind our home. I shot a dove and retrieved it. It was still alive, and, as I held it in my hand, it started quivering. It quivered for about 15 seconds and then it died. It was probably the first time it really dawned on me that this was a beautiful living creation of a loving God whose life I had just taken to prove what a good shot I was with a shotgun. I never went dove hunting or quail hunting again.

A number of years later when I was a young married man living in Utah, I convinced myself to go deer hunting 'for the meat.' During the course of an autumn morning, a young mule deer buck stopped broadside in a clearing about 50 yards away. I took aim at him, but could not pull the trigger. He was too beautiful to shoot and did not deserve to die. I never went deer hunting again and within a few years I sold my Remington .308 semi-automatic hunting rifle. By the way, as I recall it had an internal magazine with a four or five-round capacity. I am glad to report that I never shot a deer. However, I know that there are many in the United States who depend on the meat they harvest by hunting. I might do the same if I were in their shoes. However, I have come to have a very negative attitude toward those who shoot an animal purely for sport or for a trophy to hang on a wall. Taking the life of one of God's beautiful creations for fun doesn't pass muster for me anymore.

Also, although I completely understand the disdain that sheep ranchers have for coyotes, I also believe that the practice of shooting and trapping coyotes is not the answer to the conflict. The sheep are the rancher's livelihood and we depend on wool for clothing. So, we need to develop a policy and practice that protects the sheep and the coyotes. Somehow the wild predators need to be given an opportunity to reach an equilibrium with their wild prey in the ever-shrinking space allocated to them. By shooting and trapping coyotes, we encourage larger broods and overpopulation, which results in greater, not lesser, conflicts with sheep.

Finally, I need to report that, in addition to my 16-gauge double barrel shotgun, I own four handguns for home and self-defense. They include a 9 mm semi-automatic Beretta with a 15 round detachable magazine which fits in the handle, a small 9 mm semi-automatic Ruger with a 7 round detachable magazine which also fits in the handle, an even smaller .380-auto semi-automatic Ruger with a detachable 6 round magazine which also fits in the handle, and a Smith & Wesson 38 Special 6 round revolver. I have a concealed carry permit issued by the State of Utah and I conceal carry one of the Ruger's most of the time.

I had a discussion with one of my grandsons a while ago. He is a young millennial and a college student. He has researched and written about some of the hot political issues for his college classes. He expressed disdain for the politicization of certain issues, including abortion and gun rights. He really enjoys going shooting with his friends and I believe he owns a semi-automatic assault rifle. He argued that a semi-automatic assault rifle really is just a semi-automatic hunting rifle that looks different. I quizzed him about the large detachable magazine capability difference and he responded that he did not believe it was constitutional to prohibit large magazines. He thought it was like making everyone drive 55 mph on the freeway. However, he was very supportive of universal and thorough background checks. He thought the answer was keeping guns out of the hands of the wrong people. My discussion with my grandson points up the differences in opinions of open-minded individuals who have thought a lot about a subject.

Having reported all of the foregoing, I also need to report that my research on the gun rights and gun control issues was enthusiastic and, hopefully, open minded. I confess to having enjoyed the research because I learned a lot on the subject. I hope the foregoing disclosures will help you decide how much credibility to attribute to what I have to say on the subject.

CHAPTER 8

UNIVERSAL BACKGROUND CHECKS

The gangster crime spree of the 1930's arising out of prohibition prompted public and political discussions about the need for background checks for firearms purchasers. The 1934 National Firearms Act and the 1938 Gun Control Act, the first federal gun control laws, imposed stiff regulations and heavy taxes on firearms that were associated with crime, such as sawed-off shotguns, machine guns and silencers. Gun dealers and owners were required to register with the federal government and felons were banned from owning weapons. Those federal laws were unanimously upheld by the Supreme Court in 1939 (*United States v. Miller*).

The Gun Control Act of 1968 (GCA) mandated that individual and corporate firearms dealers have a Federal Firearms License (FFL) and prohibited mail order sales of long guns. It also prohibited most felons, drug users and persons found to be mentally incompetent from buying guns. A buyer was required to answer a series of "yes/no" questions such as, "Are you a fugitive from justice?". However, the seller, even an FFL dealer, was not required to verify the buyer's answers.

It was not until after the March 1981 assassination attempt on President Ronald Reagan that intense, bipartisan support for a national background check system materialized. The event led to introduction in 1987 and the passage in 1993, during the first term of President Bill Clinton, of the Brady Handgun Violence Prevention Act (Brady Act) of 1993, named for White House press secretary, James Brady, who was seriously wounded in the assassination attempt and suffered serious permanent disabilities. The passage of the Brady Act was due in large measure to the tireless efforts of his wife, Sarah Brady. The Brady Act included an amendment to the GCA that created the National Instant Criminal Background Check System (NICS). The FBI was given the responsibility to develop and implement the NICS by 1998. At first the law applied only to handguns, but by the time the NICS was operational in 1998, it applied to all firearm purchases, including "long guns" (rifles and shotguns), obtained from FFL dealers, but only FFL dealers.

After the Brady Act was first proposed in 1987, the NRA mounted a vigorous opposition, devoting millions of dollars to attempt to defeat the bill. The Brady Act was enacted in spite of the NRA opposition, with the NRA only succeeding in getting the proposed 5-day waiting period for handgun sales removed from the bill.

After enactment of the Brady Act, the NRA initiated lawsuits in Arizona, Louisiana, Mississippi, Montana, New Mexico, North Carolina, Texas, Vermont and Wyoming, seeking to have the Brady Act declared unconstitutional. A final decision in those cases was rendered by the U.S. Supreme Court in 1997 in *Printz v. United States* discussed previously. The Court ruled that the provision of the Brady Act that compelled state and local law enforcement to perform the background checks was unconstitutional under the 10th Amendment. The 10th Amendment states simply: "The powers not delegated to the United States by the Constitution, nor prohibited by it to the States, are reserved to the States respectively, or to the people." In layman's language, it means that the Federal Government has only those powers specifically granted by the Constitution. However, the constitutionality of the overall Brady Act was upheld and states and local governments were free to continue to conduct background checks if they chose to do so, most of which have continued to do. However, just a year later in 1998, background checks for firearm purchases became mostly a federal function when the FBI brought the NICS online. As discussed above, many states continue to require state run background checks, which interface with the NICS, before a gun dealer may transfer a firearm to a buyer.

The Brady Act prohibits certain persons from shipping or transporting any firearm in interstate or foreign commerce, or receiving any firearm which has been shipped or transported in interstate or foreign commerce, or possessing any firearm in or affecting commerce. A prohibited person is one who:

1. Has been convicted in any court of a crime punishable by imprisonment for a term exceeding one year;
2. Is a fugitive from justice;
3. Is an unlawful user of or addicted to any controlled substance;
4. Has been adjudicated as a mental defective or committed to a mental institution;
5. Is an alien illegally or unlawfully in the United States;
6. Has been discharged from the Armed Forces under dishonorable conditions;
7. Having been a citizen of the United States, has renounced U.S. citizenship;
8. Is subject to a court order that restrains the person from harassing, stalking, or threatening an intimate partner or child of such intimate partner, or;
9. Has been convicted in any court of a misdemeanor crime of domestic violence.

Federally Licensed Firearms (FFL) dealers, but only FFL dealers, are required under the Brady Act to:

1.	Perform background checks on prospective firearm purchasers
2.	Maintain records of all gun sales
3.	Make those records available to law enforcement for inspection
4.	Report certain multiple sales
5.	Report the theft or loss of a firearm from the licensee's inventory

The Gun Control Act of 1968 provides that persons "engaged in the business" of dealing in firearms must be licensed. Although Congress did not originally define the term "engaged in the business," in the 1968 Act, it did so in Firearms Owners' Protection Act of 1986. That latter act defined the term "engaged in the business," as it is applied to a firearms dealer, as "a person who devotes time, attention, and labor to dealing in firearms as a regular course of trade or business with the principal objective of livelihood and profit through the repetitive purchase and resale of firearms." The troublesome part of the definition, however, is the main reason we are now having this discussion about background checks. "Engaged in the business" was defined to exclude a person who "makes occasional sales, exchanges, or purchases of firearms for the enhancement of a personal collection or for a hobby, or who sells all or part of his personal collection of firearms." This exclusion has been relied upon by nefarious unlicensed dealers who hide behind a façade of being collectors or hobbyists in an attempt to escape prosecution for trafficking firearms to felons or other prohibited persons.

To purchase a firearm from a FFL, a prospective buyer first completes an ATF form, a Firearms Transaction Record form. The FFL initiates the background check by computer or phone. The background check accesses three databases, the National Crime Information Center, the Interstate Identification Index, and the NICS Index. In at least 90% of cases, firearm background checks processed through the National Instant Criminal Background Check System (NICS) are resolved immediately. The average processing time for an electronic NICS-check is less than two minutes. If there is no match in any of the checked databases, the dealer is cleared to proceed with the transfer. It there is a match, the FBI's NICS Section must contact the appropriate judicial and/or law enforcement agencies for more information. The Brady Act requires the FBI to complete the background check and make a decision to approve or deny the transfer within three business days. If the FFL has not received the decision within that time it may legally proceed anyway. Because of the efficiency and reliability of the NCIS, background checks are easy, convenient, and impose almost no burden on law-abiding gun purchasers. The same would be true if the private sale loophole (exemption) were eliminated and a NCIS background check were required for every firearm sale or transfer transaction. Universal background checks would only increase the volume of transactions submitted to the NCIS by about 20%.

The problem is, of course, that background checks are not required under federal law for intrastate firearm transfers between private parties. Some states deal with this problem by requiring background checks for all firearm transfers or at least for gun show sales. These states either require gun sales to be processed through an FFL holder, or they require that the buyer obtain a license or permit from the state. States are permitted by the federal law to implement their own

NICS programs. Such states become the point of contact (POC) between their FFL dealers and the NICS. A few partial - POC states run FFL handgun checks, while the FBI runs long gun checks. For states without a state background check law, FFL dealers access the NICS directly through the FBI.

Updating of the NICS databases is done by the FBI. Authorized federal, state, local and tribal agencies can update the NICS Index. Also, in potential emergency situations, the NICS Section accepts calls from law enforcement departments, mental health care providers, and family members requesting the placement of individuals in the NICS Index. When such requests are made, the requester must have documentation or evidence supporting the request.

A 2017 study by researchers from Northeastern University and the Harvard School of Public Health published in the *Annals of Internal Medicine* reported that 78% of gun sales in the United States in the prior two years were made through licensed firearm dealers. The obvious downside of that statistic is that 22% of American gun owners who had obtained a gun in the previous two years did not undergo a background check before doing so. That compared to 40% of recent gun acquisitions in 1994 that were completed without a background check. The Brady Act allows people not "engaged in the business" of selling firearms to sell firearms without a license or records. That includes particularly unlicensed dealers selling guns at gun shows. This so called "gun show loophole" reportedly results in approximately 25 percent of the gun sellers at gun shows not being required to run a background check on a potential buyer. The "gun show loophole" is included in the broader "private sale loophole", also referred to as the "private sale exemption," which includes all sales or transfers not occurring through a FFL dealer.

Because of the private sale loophole, domestic abusers, people with violent criminal records, and people prohibited for mental health reasons can easily buy guns from unlicensed sellers with no background check in most states. As stated above, an estimated 22% of US gun owners acquired their most recent firearm without a background check, which translates to millions of Americans acquiring millions of guns, no questions asked, each year. In the absence of a comprehensive universal background check system, criminals and other prohibited persons will continue to routinely exploit the massive loopholes in our firearms laws. Individuals who commit crimes with firearms will continue to intentionally seek to purchase guns from sellers who are not required to run background checks. Around 80% of all firearms acquired for criminal purposes are obtained through transfers from unlicensed sellers, and 96% of inmates convicted of gun offenses who were already prohibited from possessing a firearm at the time of the offense obtained their firearm from an unlicensed seller.

Despite the serious loopholes, since the federal background check requirement of the Brady Act went in force in February, 1994, over 3 million people legally prohibited from possessing a gun have been stopped from purchasing a gun or denied a permit to purchase. More than 35% of these denials involved people convicted of felony offenses. Background check laws also help prevent guns from being diverted to the illegal gun market. States without universal background check laws export crime guns across state lines at a 30% higher rate than states that require background checks on all gun sales. This just points to the great benefit that could and would be achieved from a universal background check system.

In early 1999, at the request of President Bill Clinton, the U.S. Attorney General and the U.S. Secretary of the Treasury, who heads the Bureau of Alcohol, Tobacco, Firearms and Explosives ("ATF"), made recommendations to close the gun show loophole. After the Columbine High School massacre in April 1999, gun shows and background checks became a focus of national debate. Believe it or not considering the present NRA stonewall, but keeping in mind that the NRA was still reeling from the stinging U.S. Supreme Court defeat in 1997 in *Printz*, in May 1999, the executive vice president of the National Rifle Association (NRA) told the House Judiciary Subcommittee on Crime, "We think it is reasonable to provide mandatory, instant criminal background checks for every sale at every gun show." Those concerned about the shows believed they were a source of illegally trafficked firearms. Notwithstanding the ostensible support of the NRA, at least in 1999, and unwavering public support, efforts to eliminate the private sale loophole have been unsuccessful.

A 2008 poll conducted for Mayors Against Illegal Guns found that 83% of gun owners and 87% of the general public supported regulation, including background checks, for all private-party gun sales. A 2009 poll was conducted for the same entity, this time for regulation and background checks for gun shows only, i.e. only closing one of the non-FFL sales prongs, leaving non-gun show private party sales and transfers unregulated and without background checks. The conclusion of these two polls was that there was stronger support for the universal background check for all firearm sales and transfers than for just closing the gun show loophole and leaving private sales and transfers unregulated, without a background check of the buyer. In the August 5, 2010, issue of *The New England Journal of Medicine,* researchers Garen J. Wintemute, Anthony A. Braga, and David M. Kennedy, wrote that gun shows account for only a fraction of all U.S. gun sales and that a more effective strategy would be to make all private-party gun sales go through the screening and record-keeping processes that FFL dealers are required to do.

Following the December 14, 2012 Sandy Hook Elementary School massacre, there were numerous calls for universal background checks to close the private sale loophole. In an essay published in 2013, Wintemute said that comprehensive background checks that included private sales would result in a simple, fair framework for retail firearms commerce. In February 2014, researchers at the Johns Hopkins Center for Gun Policy and Research reported that after the 2007 repeal in Missouri of a long-standing law that required all handgun buyers to pass a background check there was a 23 percent increase in firearms homicides.

Since the 2008 poll discussed above, polls have consistently shown that the vast majority of the Americans support universal background checks on all firearm purchases and transfers. Indeed, approximately 90% of both gun owners and non-gun owners, including approximately 70% of NRA members, are in favor of universal background checks. Universal background checks for all gun sales and transfers are essential for any firearm regulation approach to prevent access to firearms by illegal purchasers, illegal gun traffickers, and persons deemed to be a high risk for mass shootings, homicides and suicides.

Even though a large majority of NRA members support universal background checks, the NRA does not. As mentioned above, even the limited background checks for FFL dealer sales provided by the Brady Act were opposed by the NRA who filed the multiple lawsuits that led to the U.S. Supreme Court decision in 1997 in *Printz*. Criticisms by the NRA and others of universal background checks include that background checks are an invasion of privacy; that "transfer" might be defined too broadly; that universal background checks would not stop crime; that the only way to properly enforce a universal system would be to require a registration database; and universal background checks disproportionally prevent poorer Americans, particularly poor minorities living in high-crime urban areas, from acquiring guns for their self-defense.

Twenty-one states and the District of Columbia have extended the background check requirement beyond federal law to at least some private sales. Twelve of those states - California, Colorado, Connecticut, Delaware, Nevada, New Jersey, New Mexico, New York, Oregon, Rhode Island, Vermont, and Washington - and the District of Columbia require universal background checks at the point of sale for all sales and transfers of all classes of firearms, whether they are purchased from a licensed dealer or an unlicensed seller. Maryland and Pennsylvania require point of sale background checks for handguns but not long guns. Instead of a point-of-sale background check, three states, Hawaii, Illinois, and Massachusetts require all firearm purchasers to obtain a permit, issued after a background check, in order to buy any firearm. New Jersey requires firearm purchasers to obtain a permit to purchase a firearm and, if the purchase is from an unlicensed seller, to conduct the transaction through a FFL dealer. Iowa, Michigan, Nebraska, and North Carolina require the purchaser to obtain a permit, which requires a background check, for the purchase of handguns, but not for long guns. Illinois also requires a point of sale background check whenever a firearm is sold at a gun show.

As you can see, approximately half of the states have additional background check requirements beyond the requirements of the Brady Act. Twelve states have implemented universal background checks for all firearm transfers, relying upon the NCIS as the principal databases for those background checks. So, we know that universal background checks for all firearm transfers are readily implementable nationwide. The method for background checking of the firearm receiving party for a private sale or transfer, could require processing though an FFL dealer or a designated law enforcement authority. States could be given the option of using either or both approaches, or a common method could be embodied in a federal statute. The most effective method would likely be requiring that all firearm transfers be conducted through licensed dealers so that background checks would more likely be reliably and correctly performed and sales or transfer records for the private sales and transfers could be readily maintained by the licensed dealers. The licensed dealers have an ongoing obligation to maintain such records for the presumably more voluminous direct sales made by the licensed dealer. This approach to universal background checks is presently used by California, Colorado, Delaware, District of Columbia, New York, Oregon, Vermont, and Washington. Rhode Island requires private sellers to conduct background checks directly through law enforcement.

Connecticut requires private sellers to conduct background checks

through licensed dealers or law enforcement. Illinois requires all sellers

to retain sales records for 10 years. Connecticut, Hawaii, Massachusetts

Report all transfers to state and local law enforcement.

Although not every study has shown a verified reduction in

firearm related homicides with the enaction of background checks, most

have shown a substantial reduction. An example is a study reported in

the *American Journal of Public Health* in 2015 which examined the

results of the first ten years of a 1995 Connecticut law which required

handgun purchasers to obtain a permit and submit to a background

check. The study found that enactment of the law had resulted in a 40

percent decline in gun homicides and a 15 percent drop in suicides. In

contrast, a study published in the *Journal of Urban Health* in 2014

regarding the 2007 repeal of a "permit-to-purchase" handgun law

in Missouri, which included the repeal of a requirement for a

background-check, was associated with a 23% increase in the firearm

homicide rate and a 15% increase in the murder rate.

A 2019 study published in the *Journal of General Internal

Medicine* completed by Michael Siegel of the Boston University School

of Public Health and David Hemenway of the Harvard T.H. Chan School

of Public Health found that state-level universal background check laws

were associated with a 14.9% reduction in homicides. However, the

authors noted that "further research is necessary to determine whether

these associations are causal ones."

However, a study jointly conducted in 2018 by the Violence

Prevention Research Program at UC Davis and the Center for Gun

Policy and Research at Johns Hopkins Bloomberg School of Public Health found no change in firearm homicide rates in the ten years following California's 1991 implementation of comprehensive background checks. What is perhaps more enlightening about the study than the primary finding, are the reasons identified by the authors for the results, including inadequate reporting of criminal records or other disqualifying information to background-check databases and a failure by sellers to conduct the required background check. Essential in the implementation of universal background checks are the availability of reliable and up-to-date databases and strict enforcement of the background check requirement.

In regard to the reliability and currency of the databases, this is probably an appropriate place for us to discuss the November 5, 2017 mass shooting perpetrated by Devin Patrick Kelley at the Sutherland Springs, Texas, First Baptist Church. Kelley killed 26 people and wounded 20 others who were attending regular Sunday church services. Kelly used a Ruger AR-556 semi-automatic assault rifle. He approached the church from the right, opening fire on and killing two people outside the church and continuing to fire on the building itself. He then entered through a right side door. He proceeded up and down the center aisle shooting churchgoers in the pews. Police found 15 empty magazines capable of holding 30 rounds each. Kelley fired an estimated 700 rounds during the massacre. Video from a camera set up at the back of the church to record regular services for uploading online shows Kelley methodically shooting the victims, pausing only to reload his rifle. This is another horrific example of the role that assault rifles and large magazines play in magnifying the deadly carnage that a mass shooter can inflict on a gathering of innocent victims.

Kelley was prohibited by federal law, the Brady Act, from purchasing or possessing firearms and ammunition. Kelley spent one year in a military jail due to a domestic violence conviction in 2014 in a court-martial while serving in the Air Force at Holloman Air Force Base, New Mexico. The Air Force failed to record the conviction in the FBI National Crime Information Center database, which, as noted above, is one of the three databases used by the NCIS.

In 2012, prior to his conviction, Kelley purchased two guns, a European American Armory Windicator .38 caliber revolver and a 9mm SIG Sauer P250 pistol from the Holloman AFB Exchange. After his release from military prison, despite his disqualification to purchase firearms, he purchased four more guns, a 9mm Glock 19 pistol, a .22-caliber Ruger SR22 pistol, a Ruger GP100 .357 Magnum revolver, and a Ruger AR-556 assault rifle, at stores in Colorado and Texas. On April 7, 2016, Kelley walked into a sporting goods store in San Antonio, Texas, and after filling out the required ATF form wherein he falsely confirmed that he did not have a disqualifying criminal history, he cleared a NCIS background check. He walked out with the Ruger AR-556 semiautomatic assault rifle that he used, a year and a half later on November 5, 2017, in the Sutherland Springs massacre. Kelley's purchase of the Ruger AR-556 assault rifle was cleared in the NCIS background check initiated by the San Antonio FFL dealer because the Air Force had not reported his conviction and imprisonment.

The Sutherland Springs shooting prompted a review of the case filing practices of the respective branches of the military. The review resulted in the determination that an average of more than 30% of the criminal cases that the four branches, the Army, Navy, Air Force and Marines were required by federal law to report to the NCIS system, were not reported. Remedial efforts are underway to bring the military in compliance.

Some additional facts about the Sutherland Springs shooting should be noted. As Kelley was exiting the church, he was confronted and fired upon by Stephen Willeford, a local resident and former NRA firearms instructor who was armed with an AR-15 semi-automatic assault rifle. Willeford, from his cover position behind a truck across the street, shot Kelley twice, once in the leg and once in the upper left torso under his bullet proof vest. Seriously wounded, Kelley fled the scene in his vehicle at a high rate of speed. Willeford was driven in pursuit of Kelley by Johnnie Langendorff, who was parked in another vehicle near the scene. After a high speed chase lasting more than 5 minutes and at times exceeding 95 mph, Kelley's loss of blood caused him to lose control of his vehicle, crash into a road sign and come to a stop in a field. When Willeford and Langendorff approached Kelley's vehicle, they found him motionless. In addition to the wounds inflicted by Willeford, Kelley had a self-inflicted gunshot wound to the head. When the police arrived a short time later, they determined that Kelley was dead. It was fortuitous that Willeford was in the vicinity with his AR-15. However, if Kelley had not been in possession of the Ruger AR-556, whether unlawfully or lawfully, Willeford would not have needed his AR-15. If Kelley had only a semiautomatic rifle with a 10-round fixed magazine, he would have been able to fire only a small fraction of the rounds he fired with the 15 detachable 30-round magazines.

Likewise, Willeford would have been adequately armed, with a semiautomatic hunting rifle having only a fixed magazine with a 10-round capacity, for the confrontation with Kelley.

In 2017, a group of 32 scholars in the fields of criminology, public health and law collaborated on a study of potential policies for prevention of firearm deaths, and they rated universal background checks as the most effective policy of the 29 possible policies considered. Although, as mentioned above, some of the studies have failed to demonstrate a clear reduction in homicides from implementation of state universal background checks. Failure to maintain accurate and updated databases, including particularly failure to report criminal cases to the NICS, and failure to comply with the law in performing a background check for all sales and transfers, are reasons given for the lack of the expected reduction.

In any event, the implementation of a federal universal background check system for all sales and transfers, including all private sales and transfers, seems to offer the best potential of any single measure to reduce firearm homicides, including most particularly mass shootings. Privacy considerations seem to be minimal since the data in the NCIS databases is confidential and is protected from release. The only feedback that a FFL dealer, or a private seller or transferor gets from the NCIS when a background check is performed, is whether the sale or transfer is approved. If the sale or transfer is not approved, the prospective buyer is given instructions or how to follow up on the rejection, if he or she considers the rejection to be in error. The prospective buyer is, however, subject to potential criminal charge if he or she enters false information on the ATF form used for the background check.

CHAPTER 9

SEMI-AUTOMATIC ASSAULT RIFLES

We have discussed previously the mass shooting at the Stockton, California Cleveland Elementary School in January 1989, where a gunman with an extensive criminal history used a semi-automatic AK-47 to kill five children and to wound thirty-one other children and a teacher. In March, 1989, in response to the attack, Republican President George H.W. Bush issued an executive order banning the import of semi-automatic rifles, which he made permanent in July, 1989.

Subsequent mass shootings, including the Luby's Cafeteria shooting in Texas in October 1991, which left 23 people dead and 27 wounded, and the July 1993 California Street shooting in San Francisco, California, where the shooter used two TEC-9 semi-automatic handguns with Hell-Fire triggers, led to strong public support for an assault weapons ban. A 1993 CNN/USA Today/Gallup Poll that found 77 percent of Americans supported a ban on the manufacture, sale, and possession of assault weapons.

An Assault Weapons Ban was included in the proposed Public Safety and Recreational Firearms Use Protection Act, which was introduced in 1993, the first year of the eight years of the Bill Clinton Administration, and enacted in 1994. Former Republican President Gerald Ford, former Democratic President Jimmy Carter, and former Republican President Ronald Reagan wrote to the United States House of Representatives in support of the Assault Weapons Ban, which undoubtedly aided its passage. The Assault Weapons Ban of 1994 had a ten-year sunset provision and it expired in September 2004, three years after the September 11, 2001 terrorist attack and two months before the

November 2004 Presidential and Congressional elections. Incumbent Republican President George W. Bush was re-elected and the Republican majorities in both houses of Congress was increased in the 2004 elections.

In 2003 as the 2004 campaign was gearing up, the September 2004 expiration date of the Assault Weapons Ban was approaching, and the political debate over assault weapons was heating up, White House spokesman Scott McClellan told reporters "[The President] supports reauthorization of the current law." Needless to say, the NRA, a staunch supporter of President Bush, was very displeased with this stated position. It should be no surprise then that the September 2004 deadline for renewing the ban came and went without an extension making it to the President's desk. The Republican majority in both houses of Congress simply declined to take up the matter.

President Bush felt serious criticism from both sides, the gun owners who felt betrayed and the gun ban proponents who felt he did not do enough to pressure Congress into passing the AWB extension. "There are a lot of gun owners who worked hard to put President Bush into office, and there are a lot of gun owners who feel betrayed by him," keepandbeararms.com publisher Angel Shamaya told the New York Times. "In a secret deal, [Bush] chose his powerful friends in the gun lobby over the police officers and families he promised to protect," said U.S. Sen. John Kerry, Bush's opponent in the looming 2004 presidential election.

In the end, not only did President George W. Bush not push for renewal of the Assault Weapons Ban, he gave the gun lobby an astounding victory. President Bush pushed for and signed happily signed into law the Protection of Lawful Commerce in Arms Act of 2005 to "prohibit civil liability actions from being brought or continued against manufacturers, distributors, dealers, or importers of firearms or ammunition for damages, injunctive or other relief resulting from the misuse of their products by others." No matter in whose hands they put assault weapons and large capacity magazines and what those persons did with them, the manufacturers, distributors, dealers, or importers of firearms or ammunition were immune to liability.

For the ten years from 1994 to 2004 that the Assault Weapons Ban was in force, new manufacturing, sales or import of firearms that met the criteria for what it defined as a "semi-automatic assault weapon", as well as magazines that met the criteria for what it defined as a "large capacity ammunition feeding device," which generally included magazines with a capacity of more than 10 rounds, were prohibited.

More or less continuous efforts have been made by members of congress since 2004 to reenact or replace the Assault Weapons Ban of 1994. In particular, the proposed Assault Weapons Ban of 2015, was introduced on December 16, 2015 to the 114th United States Congress. The bill currently has 149 co-sponsors. This proposed legislation states that its purpose is "To regulate assault weapons, to ensure that the right to keep and bear arms is not unlimited, and for other purposes." Following are excerpts of the proposed bill, with several of the long lists of specific firearms omitted and instead referred to summarily:

H. R. 4269
A BILL
(Excerpts)

To regulate assault weapons, to ensure that the right to keep and bear arms is not unlimited, and for other purposes.

Be it enacted by the Senate and House of Representatives of the United States of America in Congress assembled,

SECTION 1. SHORT TITLE.

This Act may be cited as the "Assault Weapons Ban of 2015".

SEC. 2. DEFINITIONS.

(a) IN GENERAL.—Section 921(a) of title 18, United States Code, is amended—

(1) by inserting after paragraph (29) the following:

"(30) The term 'semiautomatic pistol' means any repeating pistol that—

"(A) utilizes a portion of the energy of a firing cartridge to extract the fired cartridge case and chamber the next round; and

"(B) requires a separate pull of the trigger to fire each cartridge.

"(31) The term 'semiautomatic shotgun' means any repeating shotgun that—

"(A) utilizes a portion of the energy of a firing cartridge to extract the fired cartridge case and chamber the next round; and

"(B) requires a separate pull of the trigger to fire each cartridge."; and

(2) by adding at the end the following:

"(36) The term **'semiautomatic assault weapon'** means any of the following, regardless of country of manufacture or caliber of ammunition accepted:

"(A) A semiautomatic rifle that has the capacity to accept a detachable magazine and any 1 of the following:

"(i) A pistol grip.

"(ii) A forward grip.

"(iii) A folding, telescoping, or detachable stock.

"(iv) A grenade launcher or rocket launcher.

"(v) A barrel shroud.

"(vi) A threaded barrel.

"(B) A semiautomatic rifle that has a fixed magazine with the capacity to accept more than 10 rounds, except** for an attached tubular device designed to accept, and capable of operating only with, .22 caliber rimfire ammunition.

"(C) Any part, combination of parts, component, device, attachment, or accessory that is designed or functions to accelerate the rate of fire of a semiautomatic rifle but not convert the semiautomatic rifle into a machinegun.

"(D) A semiautomatic pistol that has the capacity to accept a detachable magazine and any 1 of the following**: "(i) A threaded barrel.

"(ii) A second pistol grip.

"(iii) A barrel shroud.

"(iv) The capacity to accept a detachable magazine at some location outside of the pistol grip.

"(v) A semiautomatic version of an automatic firearm.

"(E) A semiautomatic pistol with a fixed magazine that has the capacity to accept more than 10 rounds.

"(F) A semiautomatic shotgun that has any 1 of the following**: "(i) A folding, telescoping, or detachable stock.

"(ii) A pistol grip.

"(iii) A fixed magazine with the capacity to accept more than 5 rounds.

"(iv) The ability to accept a detachable magazine.

"(v) A forward grip.

"(vi) A grenade launcher or rocket launcher.

"(G) Any shotgun with a revolving cylinder.

"(H) All of the following rifles, copies, duplicates, variants, or altered facsimiles with the capability of any such weapon thereof:

A large number of semiautomatic rifles, including AK types, AR types and various other types and brands are listed and specifically prohibited.

"(I) All of the following pistols, copies, duplicates, variants, or altered facsimiles with the capability of any such weapon thereof:

A large number of semiautomatic pistols, including AK-47 types, AR-15 types and various other types and brands are listed and specifically prohibited.

"(J) All of the following shotguns, copies, duplicates, variants, or altered facsimiles with the capability of any such weapon thereof:
A number of semiautomatic shotguns of various types and brands are listed and specifically prohibited.

"(37) The term 'large capacity ammunition feeding device'—

"(A) means a magazine, belt, drum, feed strip, or similar device, including any such device joined or coupled with another in any manner, that has an overall capacity of, or that can be readily restored, changed, or converted to accept, **more than 10 rounds of ammunition**; and

"(B) **does not include** an attached tubular device designed to accept, and capable of operating only with, .22 caliber rimfire ammunition.".

(b) RELATED DEFINITIONS.—Section 921(a) of title 18, United States Code, as amended by this Act, is amended by adding at the end the following:

"(38) The term '**barrel shroud**'—

"(A) means a shroud that is attached to, or partially or completely encircles, the barrel of a firearm so that the shroud protects the user of the firearm from heat generated by the barrel; and

"(B) does not include—

"(i) a slide that partially or completely encloses the barrel; or

"(ii) an extension of the stock along the bottom of the barrel which does not encircle or substantially encircle the barrel.

"(39) The term '**detachable magazine**' means an ammunition feeding device that can be removed from a firearm without disassembly of the firearm action.

"(40) The term '**fixed magazine**' means an ammunition feeding device that is permanently fixed to the firearm in such a manner that it cannot be removed without disassembly of the firearm.

"(41) The term '**folding, telescoping, or detachable stock**' means a stock that folds, telescopes, detaches or otherwise operates to reduce the length, size, or any other dimension, or otherwise enhances the concealability, of a firearm.

"(42) The term '**forward grip**' means a grip located forward of the trigger that functions as a pistol grip.

"(43) The term 'rocket' means any simple or complex tubelike device containing combustibles that on being ignited liberate gases whose action propels the tube through the air and has a propellant charge of not more than 4 ounces.

"(44) The term 'grenade launcher or rocket launcher' means an attachment for use on a firearm that is designed to propel a grenade, rocket, or other similar destructive device.

"(45) The term 'permanently inoperable' means a firearm which is incapable of discharging a shot by means of an explosive and incapable of being readily restored to a firing condition.

"(46) The term '**pistol grip**' means a grip, a thumbhole stock, or any other characteristic that can function as a grip.

"(47) The term '**threaded barrel**' means a feature or characteristic that is designed in such a manner to allow for the attachment of a device such as a firearm silencer or a flash suppressor.

SEC. 3. RESTRICTIONS ON ASSAULT WEAPONS AND LARGE CAPACITY AMMUNITION FEEDING DEVICES.

(a) IN GENERAL.—Section 922 of title 18, United States Code, is amended—

(1) by inserting after subsection (u) the following:

"**(v) (1) It shall be unlawful for a person to import, sell, manufacture, transfer, or possess, in or affecting interstate or foreign commerce, a semiautomatic assault weapon.**

"(2) Paragraph (1) **shall not apply to the possession, sale, or transfer of any semiautomatic assault weapon otherwise lawfully possessed under Federal law on the date of enactment of the Assault Weapons Ban of 2015**.

"(3) Paragraph (1) shall **not apply to** any firearm that—
"(A) is manually operated by **bolt, pump, lever, or slide action.**

.   .   .   .

"**(w) (1) It shall be unlawful for a person to import, sell, manufacture, transfer, or possess, in or affecting interstate or foreign commerce, a large capacity ammunition feeding device.**

"(2) Paragraph (1) **shall not apply to the possession of any large capacity ammunition feeding device otherwise lawfully possessed on or before the date of enactment of the Assault Weapons Ban of 2015**.

Semiautomatic assault weapons and large capacity magazines "lawfully possessed under Federal law on the date of enactment of the Assault Weapons Ban of 2015" would be exempted under the proposed Act as presently drafted. However, there are restrictions in the proposed Act prohibiting transfer without a background check through the NCIS by a licensed manufacturer, dealer or importer, verifying that the intended transferee is not a prohibited person. There are also provisions requiring the owner or possessor of a grandfathered semiautomatic assault weapon to prevent the weapon from being accessed by a prohibited person.

Some of the provisions of the proposed Ban merit discussion. For a semiautomatic rifle to be classified as a semiautomatic assault weapon, it either has to have a capability for receiving a detachable magazine or has to have a fixed magazine with a capacity of more than ten rounds. Interestingly, unlike a semiautomatic rifle having a fixed magazine, a semiautomatic rifle using a detachable magazine must also have one of the following:

(i) A pistol grip.
(ii) A forward grip.
(iii) A folding, telescoping, or detachable stock.
(iv) A grenade launcher or rocket launcher.
(v) A barrel shroud.
(vi) A threaded barrel.

It appears that the proposed Ban has some glaring deficiencies, if the intended primary purpose is preventing the rapid discharge of large quantities of ammunition. A semiautomatic rifle that accepts a detachable magazine but that has none of the foregoing features, would not be classified as a semiautomatic assault weapon, whereas a semiautomatic rifle that has a fixed magazine with a greater than 10 round capacity but has none of the foregoing features would be classified as a semiautomatic assault weapon. It seems the detachable magazine rifle poses substantially greater risk of misuse than a rifle with a fixed magazine. First a legal rifle with a detachable magazine capability could be possessed and transported with relative ease, but then combined with an illegal magazine to constitute a mass injury hazard. Furthermore, even if the magazines used with the rifle have only a 10-round capacity, they could be exchanged readily and rapidly by a practiced gun user.

It is the opinion of your humble writer that semiautomatic rifles with detachable magazine capability should be classified as semiautomatic assault weapons, whether they have one of the listed features or not. Hunters and target shooters do not need to use rifles with detachable magazines. Detachable magazines are a military weapon accessory. Assault weapons are not needed for self-defense or defense of home.

Why is a pistol grip or a forward grip considered to be an assault weapon feature?
Pistol grips and forward grips are common features of military semiautomatic rifles and pistols. They increase the ability of the shooter to stabilize the firearm for rapid fire.

Why is a folding, telescoping, or detachable stock considered to be an assault weapon feature? The answer to this question is probably obvious to most readers. These features make it easier to reduce the packing, transportation or storing size of the firearm, and thereby easier to conceal for illicit use.

Why is a barrel shroud considered to be an assault weapon feature? A barrel shroud provides for protection of the shooter, as well as bystanders, from burns from a barrel superheated from repetitive shooting. It is considered to be an enabling feature for the high volume shooting associated with a mass shooting.

Why is a threaded barrel considered to be an assault weapon feature? A threaded barrel is used for the installation of a silencer. A silencer is considered to be an enabling device for a mass shooting because it prevents a warning to persons in the vicinity, who may be in danger, that a shooting is underway. It also delays notice to law enforcement and thus interdiction against the shooter.

A grenade launcher or rocket launcher feature of a rifle is obviously an assault weapons feature. It serves no purpose for hunting, target shooting or defense of person or home.

CHAPTER 10

LARGE CAPACITY MAGAZINES

The evidence seems to be convincing that the weapon of choice for mass shooters is a semi-automatic rifle with a large capacity detachable magazine, the rifle being one of many that were classified as a semi-automatic assault weapons under the Assault Weapons Ban of 1994, and would be classified as a semi-automatic assault weapons under a future assault weapons ban, and the magazines having a capacity of 30 rounds or more. As we discussed, in the Sutherland Springs massacre of 2017, the shooter used a Ruger AR-556 semi-automatic assault rifle and at least 15 detachable magazines, each with a 30 round capacity. He fired an estimated 700 rounds during the massacre. The shooter in the 2017 Las Vegas shooting of used fourteen AR-15 assault rifles and eight AR-10 assault rifles. All of the AR-15's were equipped with bump stocks and twelve of the AR-15's had 100-round magazines. The shooter fired in excess of 1100 rounds in the massacre. The shooter in the 2019 El Paso shooting used a WASR-10 rifle, a Romanian made semi-automatic civilian version of the AK-47 with multiple detachable magazines.

Excerpts from the proposed Assault Weapons Ban of 2015 dealing with large capacity magazines are repeated below.

H. R. 4269
A BILL
(Excerpts)

To regulate assault weapons, to ensure that the right to keep and bear arms is not unlimited, and for other purposes.

Be it enacted by the Senate and House of Representatives of the United States of America in Congress assembled,

SECTION 1. SHORT TITLE.

This Act may be cited as the "Assault Weapons Ban of 2015".

SEC. 2. DEFINITIONS.

(a) IN GENERAL.—Section 921(a) of title 18, United States Code, is amended—

(1) by inserting after paragraph (29) the following:

.   .   .   .   .   .

"(37) **The term 'large capacity ammunition feeding device'—**

"(A) means a magazine, belt, drum, feed strip, or similar device, including any such device joined or coupled with another in any manner, that has an overall capacity of, or that can be readily restored, changed, or converted to accept, **more than 10 rounds of ammunition**;

.   .   .   .   .   .

SEC. 3. RESTRICTIONS ON ASSAULT WEAPONS AND LARGE CAPACITY AMMUNITION FEEDING DEVICES.

(a) IN GENERAL.—Section 922 of title 18, United States Code, is amended—

(1) by inserting after subsection (u) the following:

"**(w) (1) It shall be unlawful for a person to import, sell, manufacture, transfer, or possess, in or affecting interstate or foreign commerce, a large capacity ammunition feeding device.**

"(2) Paragraph (1) **shall not apply to the possession of any large capacity ammunition feeding device otherwise lawfully possessed on or before the date of enactment of the Assault Weapons Ban of 2015.**

As we noted above, it seems that the detachable magazine rifle poses substantially greater risk of misuse than a rifle with a fixed magazine. First a legal rifle with a detachable magazine capability could be possessed and transported with relative ease, but then combined with an illegal magazine to constitute a mass injury hazard. Furthermore, even if the magazines used with the rifle have only a 10-round capacity, they could be exchanged readily and rapidly by a practiced gun user.

It is the opinion of your humble writer that semiautomatic rifles with detachable magazine capability should be classified as semiautomatic assault weapons, whether they have one of the listed assault weapon features or not. Hunters and target shooters do not need to use rifles with detachable magazines. Detachable magazines are a military weapon accessory. Assault weapons are not needed for self-defense or defense of home.

CHAPTER 11
CONCLUSIONS

How do we get the bottom line on the firearms questions that are presently energizing "the people" with a variety of severely intractable opinions on every issue? Let's break the questions down.

What was the intent of the Second Amendment?

Is the Second Amendment now superfluous since the possible need for a militia has been obviated with the passage of time?

Should the Second Amendment be repealed? Is repeal a possible solution?

What is the meaning of the Second Amendment, as determined by the U.S. Supreme Court, as it relates to the firearms questions that are central to the current debate?

What constitutional limitations are there, if any, on states and local governments within the states, as to state statutes and local ordinances regulating firearms?

What constitutional limitations are there, if any, on the U.S. Congress in enacting federal statutes regulating firearms?

What firearm law changes need to be made, if any, to address the firearm issues that precipitated the author's decision to write this book and your decision to read it?

Is a state statute approach to the present firearm controversy, wherein firearm restrictions may vary from state to state, a possible satisfactory solution?

Is a federal statutory approach to the present firearm controversy the best and necessary solution?

There are several key conclusions that the author has reached in making the journey that is documented above. Hopefully the reader has also been somewhat enlightened by the journey offered.

It appears clear that the Framers were just interested, as far as the U.S. Constitution was concerned, in protecting the right of the people to keep and bear arms for service in a militia and to enable the militia. The militia was deemed absolutely essential to protect the people and the states from the new Federal Government, particularly from any standing army established by the Federal Government. The form of the original arms provision of the proposed Bill of Rights drafted by James Madison makes abundantly clear the concern intended to be addressed by the provision.

> The right of the people to keep and bear arms shall not be infringed; a well-armed and well-regulated militia being the best security of a free country; but no person religiously scrupulous of bearing arms shall be compelled to render military service in person.

The Framers and the citizenry were very concerned about possible oppression by the new federal government, particularly with the possible development of a standing federal army. They understood the necessity of a well-armed populace at the ready to fulfill their duty as members of a militia. The concern over the need for individuals to be able to keep and bear arms for their personal defense is not expressly addressed in any version of the arms provision of the proposed Bill of Rights that ultimately became the Second Amendment. The inclusion of the clause "but no person religiously scrupulous of bearing arms shall be compelled to render military service in person" in the original draft, as well several subsequent drafts of the Bill of Rights, further elucidates the express purpose of the arms clause that became the Second Amendment.

This conclusion is further supported by the fact that, as we discussed previously, several state constitutions enacted prior to or at about the same time as the Bill of Rights passage in Congress, expressly include a guarantee of the right to bear arms "for the defense of themselves and the state." The Framers were obviously aware of those state constitutional provisions and chose not to include such a provision in the Second Amendment. The logical conclusion is that the Framers considered the right to keep and bear arms for personal defense to be a matter of common law or a matter more appropriately addressed by the states. The Framers were determined that the Federal Government would not have the authority to take weapons from the people in order to render them defenseless against an oppressive Federal Government. They had vivid recollections of the British trying to do that to the colonists, and a certain knowledge that they owed their independence and freedom to the British failure in that effort.

At the end of the day, however, the opinion of the U.S. Supreme Court is the opinion that matters on the meaning of the Second Amendment. As reported previously, the Supreme Court had decided in the 1939 case of *United States v. Miller*, 307 U.S. 174 (1939) that the "obvious purpose" of the Second Amendment was to "assure the continuation and render possible the effectiveness of" the state militia, and the Amendment "must be interpreted and applied with the end in view." The Court stated:

> In the absence of any evidence tending to show that possession or use of a "shotgun having a barrel of less than eighteen inches in

length" at this time has some reasonable relationship to the preservation or efficiency of a well-regulated militia, we cannot say that the Second Amendment guarantees the right to keep and bear such an instrument. Certainly, it is not within judicial notice that this weapon is any part of the ordinary military equipment, or that its use could contribute to the common defense. Aymette v. State, 2 Humphreys (Tenn.) 154, 158. The signification attributed to the term Militia appears from the debates in the Convention, the history and legislation of Colonies and States, and the writings of approved commentators. These show plainly enough that the Militia comprised all males physically capable of acting in concert for the common defense. 'A body of citizens enrolled for military discipline.' And further, that ordinarily when called for service these men were expected to appear bearing arms supplied by themselves and of the kind in common use at the time.

However, the Supreme Court stated 70 years later in *Heller*:

> None of the Court's precedents forecloses the Court's interpretation. Neither *United States* v. *Cruikshank*, 92 U. S. 542, 553, nor *Presser* v. *Illinois*, 116 U. S. 252, 264–265, refutes the individual rights interpretation. *United States* v. *Miller*, 307 U. S. 174, does not limit the right to keep and bear arms to militia purposes, but rather limits the type of weapon to which the right applies to those used by the militia, *i.e.*, those in common use for lawful purposes.

Notwithstanding the "militia" prefatory clause in the final passed and ratified version of the Second Amendment, the Supreme Court decided in *Heller* that the right to keep and bear arms guarantee of the Second Amendment is an individual right, and that, although there is no express supporting language in the Amendment, it guarantees the individual right to keep and bear arms for self-defense. The Supreme Court followed up the 2008 *Heller* decision with the 2010 decision in *McDonald*, wherein the Court decided that the Due Process provision of the Fourteenth Amendment, the Privileges & Immunities-Equal Protection-Due Process Amendment, resulted in the Second Amendment being applied to the States, and prohibited each State, as well as political subdivisions of each State, from abridging an individual's rights under the Second Amendment, whatever those rights may be. The Supreme Court ruled that individuals, in each of the 50 U.S. states, were therefore granted a constitutional right to keep firearms in their homes for self-protection.

It seems clear from the *Heller* and *McDonald* decisions that the Second Amendment prevents States and political subdivisions (local governments) of the States, as well as the Federal Government, from prohibiting individuals from owning, possessing and using the firearms that are reasonably needed for personal defense. The question that then arises, in view of those decisions, is what regulation by the Federal Government, the States or local governments of individual ownership, possession, and use of firearms will be allowable under the Second Amendment. What firearms may be prohibited in the home or for personal possession in public? What limits may be imposed on possession and use of non-prohibited firearms?

Perhaps the best approach to the foregoing questions is for us to consider what firearm law changes need to be made, if any, to address the contested firearm issues. We need to consider whether a state statute approach to the present firearm controversy can provide a possibly satisfactory solution. As noted above, such an approach would result in firearm restrictions varying from state to state. Could that work? Is a federal statutory approach to the present firearm controversy the best and necessary solution?

In view of all that we have considered and discussed, achieving a resolution of the firearms disputes first requires a resolution of the underlying public policy issues. We have to decide if we believe that the availability of assault firearms and large capacity magazines have been a significant contributor to the frequency or severity of mass shootings. We also have to decide if we believe that the continued availability of assault firearms and large capacity magazines amount to a significant risk for future mass shootings. Regardless of our respective opinions about what firearms restrictions are appropriate and constitutional, it seems that the obvious answer to both of the foregoing questions is "yes". The weapon of choice for mass shooters is a semi-automatic assault rifle with a large capacity magazine. The horrific Las Vegas shooting is a prime example. The shooter used fourteen AR-15 assault rifles and eight AR-10 assault rifles. All of the AR-15's were equipped with bump stocks and twelve of the AR-15's had 100-round magazines.

We will need to discuss the related public policy question, namely what limitations on firearms ownership, possession and use are we prepared to accept and enact, if any, in order to address the risk of further mass shootings, whether they be at elementary schools, night clubs, theatres, shopping centers or outdoor concerts. In that regard, we first need to discuss the two options for enacting preventative measures.

Unless the states were to cooperate in enacting uniform firearms control statutes so that a shooter could not avoid the firearms limitations of his state by traveling to another state to purchase firearms, or could not avoid the firearms limitations of a target state by transporting weapons from outside the target state, only a federal statute imposing the same limitations nationwide would work. Considering the present widely differing views from state to state regarding the necessity, appropriateness and constitutionality of firearm limitations as they relate to past mass shootings and to the risk of further mass shootings, it seems that any effective uniformity among the states is highly unlikely.

On August 3, 2019, Patrick Crusius, a 21-year-old from Allen, Texas, shot and killed 22 people and injured 24 others at a Walmart store in El Paso, Texas, using a WASR-10 rifle, a semi-automatic civilian version of the AK-47 purchased legally in Texas. A manifesto, titled *The Inconvenient Truth*, was posted by Crusius on an online message board shortly before the shooting. It identifies the type of weapon used in the attack and Crusius' name. It expressed support for the perpetrator of the Christchurch, New Zealand, mosque shootings and states similar grievances to the manifesto linked to the Christchurch attacks, alluding to "cultural and ethnic replacement", a "Hispanic invasion", and the "destruction of our planet". Apparently, he drove the 650 miles from his home is Allen, Texas, to El Paso, Texas, because, as he stated in his initial interrogation by El Paso detectives, he wanted to shoot Mexicans. The FBI classified the shooting as "domestic terrorism" and a "hate crime."

If a shooter is willing to travel 650 miles to pursue a particular ideological target, as did the El Paso shooter, or is willing to purchase and transport 15 semi-automatic assault rifles, most with bump stocks and 100 round magazines, as did the Las Vegas shooter, only uniform state statutes or a federal statute has any hope of preventing future horrific tragedies like these. Since the chance of the states cooperating in the adoption of uniform statutes is very low, the only practical solution is a federal statute.

The general approaches or concepts considered for addressing and preventing the recurrence of the horrific events being experienced over and over again in various geographical areas of the United States include:

1.	Preventing individuals considered to constitute a high risk for misuse of firearms from having access to firearms. Those individuals include most felons, certain mentally ill individuals, and drug addicts. The best approach at this point is a Universal Background Check using the NCIS.

2.	Preventing the manufacturing, sale, ownership and possession of certain firearms considered to have a high risk for use in homicides, including particularly a high risk for use in mass shootings. Those firearms include at least the semi-automatic assault weapons, namely the semi-automatic rifles, the semi-automatic pistols, and the semi-automatic shotguns characterized or specifically identified in the proposed Assault Weapons Ban of 2015.

3.	Preventing the manufacturing, sale, ownership and possession of firearm accessories considered to constitute a high risk for facilitating the use of firearms in homicides and particularly mass shootings. Those accessories include high capacity magazines, bump stocks and silencers. Silencers are a concern because of the potential for suppressing a warning to potential victims that an attack is underway and delaying law enforcement interdiction.

Measures that seem likely to pass constitutional scrutiny, allowing for personal defense as required by *Heller* and *McDonald*, while providing some measure of protection from future mass shootings and other homicides, are:

1.   Universal background checks utilizing the NCIS for all gun sales and transfers, including FFL Dealer sales, gun show sales, and private sales or transfers, with all sales or transfers not initiated with a FFL Dealer requiring that the gun show seller, private seller or private transferor engage a FFL Dealer to complete a universal background check of the purchaser or transferee for the sale or transfer.

2.   Bolt action, lever action and semi-automatic rifles with fixed magazines having a maximum capacity of 10 rounds and a maximum 45 caliber remaining legal.

3.   Rifles with detachable magazine capability being banned.

4.   Revolvers having a maximum 10 round capacity and a maximum 45 caliber remaining legal.

5.   Semiautomatic pistols with a fixed magazine having a maximum capacity of 10 rounds and a maximum 45 caliber remaining legal.

6.   Semiautomatic pistols having a maximum 45 caliber and having a detachable magazine capability for magazines having a maximum capacity of 10 rounds or less and being inserted completely in the pistol handle remaining legal.

7.   Pistols with a detachable magazine capability for magazines having a capacity exceeding 10 rounds being banned.

8.   Shotguns with a fixed magazine having a maximum capacity of 5 rounds and a maximum 10 gauge remaining legal.

9.   Revolving cylinder shotguns and shotguns with detachable magazine capability being banned.

10.   Detachable magazines and all other ammunition feeding devices, other than fixed magazines, being banned for all firearms, with the sole exception being detachable magazines for semi-automatic pistols which are insertable completely in the handle of a semi-automatic pistol of 45 caliber or less and having a capacity of 10 rounds or less.

11.   Pistol grip (rifle or shotgun); forward grip; folding, telescoping, or detachable stock; barrel shroud; threaded barrel; grenade launcher; rocket launcher and bump stock being prohibited features for any firearm or firearm accessory.

The foregoing would arguably protect the legitimate Second Amendment rights, as they are currently defined by the US Supreme Court in *Heller* and *McDonald*, as well as the hunting, target shooting, and defense of self and home needs of gun owners, while placing reasonable limits on firearms that would help stem the tide of mass shootings and other homicides. As I have stated previously, I have three handguns with detachable magazines. The foregoing provisions, if enacted into law and applied to firearms sold prior to the effective date of the law, would render one of my semiautomatic handguns, the 9 mm Beretta with a 15 round detachable magazine illegal, unless a replacement magazine having a capacity of 10 rounds or less were permitted.

The question arises, would not a handgun with a detachable magazine having a capacity of 10 rounds be a concern. Certainly, a mass shooter with a bag full of 10 round magazines could rapidly change magazines and even a 10-round magazine could become a mass shooting nightmare or a gang war facilitator. The amount of time required to change pre-loaded magazines is only a small fraction of the time that is required to reload a fixed magazine, one round at a time. So, why should a semi-automatic handgun with a 10 round magazine remain legal. Does that not jeopardize achievement of the objective? Frankly, I would support a ban on all firearms with a detachable magazine capability and a ban on all detachable magazines. However, I was repeatedly reminded by persons who kindly reviewed draft manuscripts for this work that semi-automatic handguns, most with magazines having a capacity of 10 rounds or less, are the self-defense, concealed carry weapons of choice for millions of law-abiding concealed carry permit holders. The total elimination of detachable magazines for concealed carry weapons, would require the substantial redesign or the elimination of semi-automatic pistols. Concealed carry permit holders could, of course, replace their semi-automatic pistol with a revolver. While revolvers are generally somewhat bulkier and heavier than the typical semi-automatic concealed carry pistol, I would venture to say that most concealed carry weapon owners would be willing to make the sacrifice to achieve a safer environment.

That brings us back to the foundational question, the question we need to answer individually and collectively. But first, is the question properly stated: "What is more important to us, the protection, as best we can, of our innocent fellow human beings from the horror of mass shootings and other homicides, or the protection of the right to own and use the semi-automatic weapons and large capacity magazines which were originally designed for military and law enforcement use." Or is the question more appropriately stated: "What right does government have to take away my guns. The Second Amendment says they can't do that. I am a law-abiding citizen and I have not and will not shoot anyone, unless they break into my home or try to harm me, my family or some other innocent person. I am very careful to make sure my guns are not accessed by others. Bad guys will always have guns. They always have and always will, law or no law. Don't we law abiding citizens have the right to bear arms to defend ourselves against the bad guys. Is it anybody's business if I want to hunt jack rabbits or coyotes or shoot paper targets or tin cans? Isn't that my business as long as I obey the law? I can't help it if other people misuse guns, just like I can't help it if they drive too fast on the freeway. What right do they have to take away my guns?"

Depending on how you ask the question, the obvious answer may be very different. From the point of view of a person with no interest or a limited interest in firearms, a bolt action, lever action or semiautomatic rifle with a fixed magazine of ten rounds or less; a revolver or semiautomatic pistol with a fixed magazine having a capacity of 10 rounds or less; and a pump action or semiautomatic shotgun with a fixed magazine of 5 rounds or less, should and would surely satisfy the reasonable firearm needs and desires for firearm enthusiasts.

I understand that many firearm enthusiasts greatly enjoy shooting the military style semiautomatic rifles that are referred to as assault rifles. I have been surprised at the variety of people who claim to enjoy shooting them. I rented an AR-15 at a local shooting range to sample the assault rifle experience. Although I was not particularly impressed with the experience, I could see how some gun enthusiasts would enjoy shooting it. By contrast, I really enjoy shooting my revolver and my semi-automatic pistols, including the one that would be banned under the proposals listed above.

The action we take collectively, by force of law, in regard to firearms involves the same basic policy conflict that we have to deal with over and over in many aspects of everyday life. For example, we have established speed limits for school zones, residential neighborhoods, urban streets and highways, rural highways and freeways, based upon a resolution of conflicting interests – convenience and safety. At one time, for fuel conservation concerns, the maximum highway speed was set nationwide by federal law at 55 mph. The National Maximum Speed Law (NMSL) was a provision of the 1974 Emergency Highway Energy Conservation Act that prohibited speed limits higher than 55 miles per hour. It was enacted in response to oil price increases and supply disruption crisis of 1973 and remained the law until 1995, although it was modified in 1987 and 1988 to allow up to 65 mph on certain rural roads. Prior to that time, speed limits ranged from no limits in Nevada and Montana and 75 mph in some states to lesser speeds in other states. By the way, although the projected reduction in gasoline use was 2.2%, the actual reduction achieved was only 0.5% to 1%. There was also conflicting study results on whether the NMSL resulted in any highway safety benefit. Since the law was repealed in 1995, states have generally returned to much higher highway and freeway speed limits.

Seat belts, air bags, and other vehicle crashworthiness laws were enacted over the vigorous opposition of the automobile industry and many individuals who argued they were an infringement on personal liberty. Motorcycle helmet laws, although enacted in some states, have generally been met with opposition by motorcyclists as an infringement on personal liberty. We have alcohol and drug use laws, including DUI laws, which clearly are a restriction on personal liberty, but are needed to protect public health and safety.

Considering then the many areas of everyday life where we have collectively agreed to regulate behavior and activities by law, thereby infringing on personal liberty, the only arguable difference between those activities and firearms ownership and use is the interplay of the Second Amendment. Considering the U.S. Supreme Court decisions in *Heller* and *McDonald*, and remembering that these decisions were rendered by a conservative leaning court, it seems that the Second Amendment does not come into play in the firearms regulations presently under consideration politically, and would not come into play in the consideration of the 11 potential provisions identified above by your humble writer. If there is the political will to enact any or all of the 11 potential provisions identified above, they would likely pass Second Amendment scrutiny by the Supreme Court.

As mentioned previously, the Court stated in *McDonald*:

> By the 1850's, the perceived threat that had prompted the inclusion of the Second Amendment in the Bill of Rights - the fear that the National Government would disarm the universal militia - had largely faded as a popular concern, but the right to keep and bear arms was highly valued for purposes of self-defense.

The Court further stated in *Heller*:

> III
> Like most rights, the right secured by the Second Amendment is not unlimited. From Blackstone through the 19th-century cases, commentators and courts routinely explained that the right was not a right to keep and carry any weapon whatsoever in any manner whatsoever and for whatever purpose. See, *e.g.*, *Sheldon*,

in 5 Blume 346; Rawle 123; Pomeroy 152–153; Abbott 333. For exam- ple, the majority of the 19th-century courts to consider the question held that prohibitions on carrying concealed weapons were lawful under the Second Amendment or state analogues. See, *e.g.*, *State* v. *Chandler*, 5 La. Ann., at 489–490; *Nunn* v. *State*, 1 Ga., at 251; see generally 2 Kent *340, n. 2; The American Students' Blackstone 84, n. 11 (G. Chase ed. 1884). Although we do not undertake an exhaustive historical analysis today of the full scope of the Second Amendment, nothing in our opinion should be taken to cast doubt on longstanding prohibitions on the possession of firearms by felons and the mentally ill, or laws forbidding the carrying of firearms in sensitive places such as schools and government buildings, or laws imposing conditions and qualifications on the commercial sale of arms.[26]

We also recognize another important limitation on the right to keep and carry arms. *Miller* said, as we have explained, that the sorts of weapons protected were those "in common use at the time." 307 U. S., at 179. We think that limitation is fairly supported by the historical tradition of prohibiting the carrying of "dangerous and unusual weapons." See 4 Blackstone 148–149 (1769); 3 B. Wilson, Works of the Honourable James Wilson 79 (1804); J. Dunlap, The New-York Justice 8 (1815); C. Humphreys, A Compendium of the Common Law in Force in Kentucky 482 (1822); 1 W. Russell, A Treatise on Crimes and Indict- able Misdemeanors 271–272 (1831); H. Stephen, Summary of the Criminal Law 48 (1840); E. Lewis, An Abridgment of the Criminal Law of the United States 64 (1847); F. Wharton, A Treatise on the Criminal Law of the United States 726 (1852). See also *State* v. *Langford*, 10 N. C. 381, 383–384 (1824); *O'Neill* v. *State*, 16 Ala. 65, 67 (1849); *English* v. *State*, 35 Tex. 473, 476 (1871); *State* v. *Lanier*, 71 N. C. 288, 289 (1874).

It may be objected that if weapons that are most useful in military service - M-16 rifles and the like - may be banned, then the Second Amendment right is completely detached from the prefatory clause. But as we have said, the conception of the militia at the time of the Second Amendment's ratification was the body of all citizens capable of military service, who would bring the sorts of lawful weapons that they possessed at home to militia duty. It may well be true today that a militia, to be as effective as militias in the 18th century, would require sophisticated arms that are highly unusual in society at large. Indeed, it may be true that no amount of small arms could be useful against modern-day bombers and tanks. But the fact that modern developments have limited the degree of fit between the prefatory clause and the protected right cannot change our interpretation of the right.

[26] We identify these presumptively lawful regulatory measures only as examples; our list does not purport to be exhaustive.

The Court in *Heller* seems to make it clear that "weapons that are most useful in military service - M-16 rifles and the like - may be banned" and that "It may well be true today that a militia, to be as effective as militias in the 18th century, would require sophisticated arms that are highly unusual in society at large. Indeed, it may be true that no amount of small arms could be useful against modern-day bombers and tanks." The Court further states, however, "But the fact that modern developments have limited the degree of fit between the prefatory clause and the protected right cannot change our interpretation of the right." The Court further stated, as presented previously, "The Second Amendment protects an individual right to possess a firearm unconnected with service in a militia, and to use that arm for traditionally lawful purposes, such as self-defense within the home." However, the Court further states that:

Like most rights, the Second Amendment right is not unlimited. It is not a right to keep and carry any weapon whatsoever in any manner whatsoever and for whatever purpose: For example, concealed weapons prohibitions have been upheld under the

Amendment or state analogues. The Court's opinion should not be taken to cast doubt on longstanding prohibitions on the possession of firearms by felons and the mentally ill, or laws forbidding the carrying of firearms in sensitive places such as schools and government buildings, or laws imposing conditions and qualifications on the commercial sale of arms. *Miller's* holding that the sorts of weapons protected are those "in common use at the time" finds support in the historical tradition of prohibiting the carrying of dangerous and unusual weapons.

Then, the list of 11 possible regulations or restrictions presented above would probably pass Second Amendment challenge. If they did and they were enacted into law, what about all of the weapons that are presently owned and possessed that violate these restrictions. Much discussion continues about mandatory buyback of firearms, magazines and other accessories. Are we prepared to accept the cost of buybacks in order to achieve the objectives of such restrictions? There are undoubtedly millions of firearms that would need to be subject of the buyback. It would seem that the success of such a buyback would largely depend on cooperation of the citizenry. Undoubtedly, a considerable number of gun owners would consider the forced surrender of their firearms a gross violation of their constitutional rights, whether they are compensated for them or not. However, one could hope that most gun owners would be reasonably satisfied with replacing a non-compliant firearm with a compliant one. Gun owners could still hunt and target shoot, and meet their reasonable self-defense needs, and they would probably save a considerable sum on ammunition.

In addition to the 11 regulatory items listed above, there are two additional potential measures that might be considered for reducing the likelihood of mass shootings and other homicides. These additional potential measures are the registration of all firearms and the registration of all gun owners and gun possessors. The motivation for licensing all gun owners is that a background check through the NCIS would be performed for every person owning a gun, not just every person purchasing a gun or receiving an ownership transfer for a gun after enactment of the foregoing changes. The licensing process would presumably identify prohibited persons who would then be prohibited from obtaining or possessing a firearm. The motivation for requiring the registration of all firearms is threefold, namely limiting the registration of each firearm to a person who is a licensed gun owner, limiting the registration of firearms to lawful firearms, and identifying individuals who own or possess multiple firearms. Neither laws requiring registration of firearm owners or possessors nor laws requiring registration of firearms would likely generate any Second Amendment concerns. Neither would result in any infringement on the right to bear arms by non-prohibited persons. Firearm advocates, including particularly the NRA, get up in arms, pardon the pun, over any proposal for a national firearm owner registration or a national firearm registration law. They argue that either would have a serious chilling effect on the exercise of second amendment rights and would amount to a serious invasion of personal liberty and personal privacy.

As of 2020, the states of California, Connecticut, Hawaii, Maryland, New Jersey, and New York and the District of Columbia, have various firearm registration requirements:

> California: All assault weapons and 50 caliber rifles must be registered

Connecticut: All assault weapons and large capacity magazines must be registered

Hawaii: All firearms must be registered

Maryland: All assault pistols must be registered

New Jersey: All assault weapons must be registered

New York: All handguns and assault weapons must be registered

D. Columbia: All firearms must be registered

By contrast, the states of Delaware, Florida, Georgia, Idaho, Pennsylvania, Rhode Island, South Dakota, and Vermont have state statutes prohibiting firearm registries. The remaining 36 states neither require nor prohibit firearm registries. Although firearm registration would be beneficial in achieving the objectives of reducing mass shootings and other firearm homicides, it is unlikely that there is adequate political support for such measures at this time.

The second additional measure that could be considered for reducing the likelihood of mass shootings and other homicides is a federal concealed carry law. While it seems questionable that a federal concealed carry law would contribute significantly to a reduction in mass shootings, since it deals primarily with single, smaller capacity handguns, it does seem likely that a federal concealed carry law would offer some potential for reduction in the number of other types of homicides. Again, it is unlikely that there is adequate political support for a uniform federal concealed carry law at this time.

A final question that is worth discussing is whether federal law should preempt in all areas of firearms controls. As we have already discussed, if universal background checks, assault weapon bans, and large capacity magazine bans are to be effective in reducing mass shootings and other homicides, they need to be enacted by federal law. Why then should firearms not be controlled exclusively by federal law? The answer is that what might be needed for concealed carry in New York City or Los Angeles might not be the same for Laramie, Wyoming, or Tupelo, Mississippi.   Perhaps federal law could provide for uniform minimum concealed carry regulations, but states and/or local governments could enact more stringent law. Broad Federal preemption would potentially prevent such adjustment for local conditions. Obviously, the US Congress could make it clear in any Act which areas of firearms controls are being preempted and could specifically provide for the adoption of more strict regulations by States in areas such as concealed carry and open carry.

It seems clear that preservation of the right of law abiding and mentally stable adults to own, possess and use firearms appropriate for self-defense, hunting and sport shooting is entirely compatible with the imposition of firearms controls which would substantially reduce the extent of death and injury that could be caused by a mass shooter and would substantially reduce the risk of other homicides. Semi-automatic assault weapons with large capacity, detachable magazines, namely weapons originally designed for military and law enforcement use, are not needed for self-defense, hunting or sport shooting. Semi-automatic, bolt action and lever action rifles with fixed magazines having a capacity of 10 rounds or less; revolvers or semi-automatic pistols with a fixed magazine having a capacity of 10 rounds or less; and semi-automatic or pump action shotguns with a fixed magazine having a capacity of 5 rounds or less, would fully satisfy the Second Amendment rights of law abiding and mentally stable adults.

Requiring universal background checks, banning assault weapons and large capacity detachable magazines, and banning certain firearm features or accessories, such as barrel shrouds, pistol grips, and telescoping or collapsing stocks, seems like a very small price to pay to save the lives of so many of our innocent brothers and sisters. We can only accomplish this if we vote for politicians who commit to these actions. Let's do this.

BOOK III

AMERICA THE BEAUTIFUL

When did communication, cooperation and compromise become taboo in politics? Although politics has been tough business since long before I began paying serious attention in the 1960's, it has certainly taken a turn for the worse, the much worse, since then. The divide is painful to watch and experience. The uncivil and disrespectful rhetoric and the uncompromising demagoguery are disgraceful. Partisan entrenchment and rancor are now the norm. What is the cause and what can be done about it?

As I mentioned previously, I was a devoted Republican from my first years of attention to politics in the 1960's. I persevered Richard Nixon and Watergate. I loved Ronald Reagan. From my perspective, he restored American pride and he brought down the Soviet Union and saved the world from a nuclear arms race that was spiraling out of control. Though he made some huge mistakes, and Reaganomics was a failed economic policy, he was a true patriot and he loved America and Americans. He had no difficulty working with Democrats. He had a great working relationship with Tip O'Neill, the Democratic Speaker of the House of Representatives. In that day, a true desire and a strong determination to work with members of the opposing party for the good of the country were considered desirable and admirable elements of character and integrity for statesmen politicians.

George H. W. Bush was a great man, a WWII war hero, and a President of impeccable integrity. He continued the legacy of Ronald Reagan and it was during his term that the Soviet Union finally collapsed and the Berlin Wall came down. He successfully and wisely led this country and its allies in the Gulf War - *Operation Desert Shield*, in which the Iraqi armed forces, which had invaded Kuwait at the direction of President Saddam Hussein, were rapidly and soundly defeated. When the invasion forces were decisively driven from Kuwait back into Iraq, and devastated by US and allied forces, the US and its allies retreated and did not attempt to topple Saddam Hussein. That decision, apparently contrary to the advice of US military leadership, was a tribute to the wisdom, restraint and statesmanship of President George H. W. Bush. Unfortunately, from my personal observation as a devoted Republican, it was also during his term that the Republican Party began its downward spiral into demagoguery and an ideological abyss. My observation was that he was very uncomfortable with the change in the Republican Party and was not willing or not able to make the changes that were being demanded of him. Despite the astounding accomplishments of his Presidency, he was defeated in his re-election bid.

Pro-choice Republicans and gun control Republicans have become mostly a historical footnote. At the time of the writing of this work, there are presently only three Republican Senators and no Republican members of the House of Representative who are pro-choice. The wealthy and powerful learned that they could use the Republican Party as their tool to become more wealthy and more influential, and to pass their wealth and power from generation to generation, so long as they packaged their wealth perpetuation policies with the social conservatism that would get them the votes of conservative religious groups and the other social conservatives. The Estate Tax became the Death Tax. From my perspective as a devout Republican at the time, Newt Gingrich engineered the demise of the Republican Party. I still have hope that it can be resurrected. At present, however, things are not looking good.

Things are also not looking good for the Democratic Party. During this same time period, from the beginning of the Clinton Administration, pro-life and gun rights Democrats also have mostly become a historical footnote. At the time of this writing, there are only two Democratic Senators and five Democratic members of the House of Representatives who are pro-life. As Bernie Sanders, one of the leaders for the 2020 Democratic nomination for President, exclaimed, a Democratic candidate must be decidedly pro-choice. The Democratic Party seems to have lost its direction and to be wandering in darkness. It seems that the extreme progressive elements of the party and the moderate elements of the party are in a tug of war and neither side is sure where it is trying to take the party. Never has the statement of Will Rogers, "I'm not a member of an organized political party, I'm a Democrat," been more appropriate that it is at present.

The upshot of these developments, or lack thereof, in the political parties, is that we cannot depend on either of them to generate the courage or conscience that will be necessary to resolve either the abortion or the gun rights issues. That is unless and until we force a change in the mentality of the politicians or elect new politicians. As a matter of fact, as things now sit, we can expect that they will intentionally perpetuate the divide over these issues. Recent events have only made the resolution more difficult.

Looking back a few years, in the wake of the Watergate scandal, the use of 'campaign contributions' for illegal purposes, and the resignation of President Richard Nixon on August 9, 1974, Congress passed the Federal Election Campaign Act Amendments of 1974. That Act put new limits and restrictions on contributions to campaigns. In 1978, the FEC ruled that, while the new restrictions imposed limits on donations for the direct support of candidates, they did not impose any limit on the amount donors could donate to a political party, so long as the money was used for "party building activities" such as voter registration drives. Not to be deterred by the Act or the FEC, both the Republican and Democratic parties succeeded in using those donations, lovingly referred to as "soft money," to support their candidates.

The concern, at least among certain Senators and Representatives - those statesmen of special character and integrity, those with an abiding love and concern for this amazing country of ours - regarding the influence of money and special interests in politics only intensified over the following decades. The concern transcended politics and political parties for those Senators and Representatives. In 1992, in what was certainly not his finest hour, President George H.W. Bush vetoed a bill passed by the Democratic Congress that would have, among other things, restricted the use of soft money. Unlike President George H.W. Bush, his successor, President Clinton, attempted to get a similar bill through Congress but was unsuccessful.

Republican Senator John McCain from Arizona was one of those true statesmen of great integrity who served this nation in Congress. A prisoner of war for five years and a true hero of the Vietnam War, he served two terms in the US House of Representatives and six terms in the US Senate, from 1987 until his death from brain cancer in 2018. Although he was a genuine conservative, his views and votes on campaign finance reform, as well as other issues such as LGBT rights and gun control, in which he opposed the Republican hardline position, resulted in him earning a reputation as a "maverick." It was unfortunate that his nomination for the Presidency came at the same time as Barack Obama's. It would have been great boon for the country for both Barack Obama and John McCain to have had an opportunity to serve as President.

Democratic Senator Russ Feingold from Wisconsin was another of the statesmen "mavericks" of the US Congress. He was considered a maverick because he frequently adopted an even more progressive view on issues than his democratic colleagues. A Harvard Law honors graduate, he served 10 years in the Wisconsin State Senate and then three terms in the US Senate from 1993 until 2011. He was a dedicated advocate for the protection of the rights of individuals. He was an opponent and constant critic of the Patriot Act because of civil liberties and privacy concerns. He was an ardent opponent of the authorization for President George W. Bush to wage war in Iraq and was a tireless advocate for the withdrawal of US forces from Iraq. He co-sponsored the Veterans Health Care Budget Reform and Transparency Act, which was signed into law in October 2009. He supported the Comprehensive Immigration Reform Act of 2006, an immigration reform bill that was designed to give many illegal immigrants who had been in the country for five years or more a chance to become legal citizens. For his 1998 reelection campaign for the US Senate, he vowed and kept his vow to spend only $3.8 million, $1.00 for every citizen of Wisconsin, and to allow no 'soft money' to be used in support of his campaign. Along with John McCain, he received the 1999 John F. Kennedy Profile in Courage Award.

Senator McCain and Senator Feingold jointly published an op-ed in 1995 calling for campaign finance reform. They jointly sponsored a bill that made its way to the floor of the Senate in 1998. However, the bill failed to garner the 60-vote threshold to defeat a filibuster. All 45 Senate Democrats and 6 Senate Republicans voted to invoke cloture, but the remaining 49 Republicans voted against invoking cloture. The filibuster thus resulted in the bill being tabled in 1998.

McCain's increased notoriety due to his 2000 campaign for President, and the Enron and other corporate scandals in 2001, encouraged McCain and Feingold to push the bill once again in the Senate. Chris Shays (R-CT) and Marty Meehan (D-MA) led the effort in the House of Representatives. Despite opposition by Republican leadership in both houses of Congress, the House approved the bill with a 240–189 vote and the bill passed the Senate in a 60–40 vote, the bare minimum required to overcome the filibuster. Though he had more or less ignored the Congressional battle, President George W. Bush signed the Bipartisan Campaign Reform Act of 2002, commonly referred to as the McCain–Feingold Act, into law in March 2002, despite his "reservations about the constitutionality of the broad ban on issue advertising."

In contrast to the bipartisan efforts of the dedicated statesmen of the Congress, other determined partisans readily put party and special interests and their money ahead of country. Provisions of the legislation were challenged as unconstitutional by a group of plaintiffs led by then Senate Majority Whip Mitch McConnell, a long-time opponent of the bill. In December 2003, the Supreme Court upheld most of the legislation in *McConnell v. FEC.*

However, beginning in June 2007, with the decision in *FEC v. Wisconsin Right to Life, Inc.*, 551 U.S. 449 (2007), the US Supreme Court began to whittle away at the McCain-Feingold Act. In this case, the Court found that limitations on corporate and labor union funding of broadcast ads mentioning a candidate within 30 days of a primary or caucus or 60 days of a general election were unconstitutional as applied to ads susceptible of a reasonable interpretation other than as an appeal to vote for or against a specific candidate. A much more severe blow to the Act was delivered in January 2010, in *Citizens United v. Federal Election Commission,* 558 U.S. 310 (2010). In that decision, the Supreme Court struck down sections of McCain-Feingold which limited certain activities of corporations and labor unions. The Court stated, "If the First Amendment has any force, it prohibits Congress from fining or jailing citizens, or associations of citizens, for simply engaging in political speech." Specifically, *Citizens United* struck down campaign financing laws which prohibited corporations and unions from funding the broadcast, cable or satellite transmission of "electioneering communications" (referring to a clearly identifiable federal candidate) in the 30 days before a primary or in the 60 days before a general election.

A few days later, President Barack Obama stated during his 2010 State of the Union Address, "With all due deference to separation of powers, last week the Supreme Court reversed a century of law that I believe will open the floodgates for special interests - including foreign corporations - to spend without limit in our elections. I don't think American elections should be bankrolled by America's most powerful interests, or worse, by foreign entities. They should be decided by the American people. And I'd urge Democrats and Republicans to pass a bill that helps to correct some of these problems." He went on to say that the decision was, "a major victory for big oil, Wall Street banks, health insurance companies and the other powerful interests that marshal their power every day in Washington to drown out the voices of everyday Americans."

Fortunately, at least the "Stand By Your Ad" provision of the McCain - Feingold Act, which requires candidates for federal political office, as well as interest groups and political parties supporting or opposing a candidate, to include in political advertisements on television and radio "a statement by the candidate that identifies the candidate and states that the candidate has approved the communication". Compliance typically requires a statement that "I approve," "I approved," "I authorize," or "I authorized," followed by "this ad" or "this message." The provision was intended to force political candidates to expressly associate themselves with their television and radio advertising.

The author appreciates the expressed determination of the US Supreme Court to protect the First Amendment and free speech in its 2010 decision in *Citizens United v. Federal Election Commission.* Perhaps it is a constitutionally correct decision. Perhaps we should be very grateful to the Court in this instance for its vigilance in protecting our liberties. However, this decision negated decades of deliberate effort in the Congress to reduce the inordinate influence of special interests and big money in politics. The decision has allowed unlimited election spending of "dark money" (sources and amounts unknown) by corporations and spurred the rise of Super PACs.

You may be asking, why have we gotten into a discussion of *Citizens United* here. The answer is simple. It is just a reminder, or a warning, that any efforts to reach a resolution on the firearms issues or the abortion issues by electing Senators and Representatives that are committed to a resolution, will encounter opponents supported by Super PAC's that are very well funded with "dark money."

As a lifelong Republican, the author is hopeful for a return of the Republican Party of old, the party of Gerald Ford, Ronald Reagan, George H.W. Bush, Robert Dole, Arlen Specter, and John McCain. It would be great for the party to be, once again, the party of "compassionate conservatism" spoken of by President George W. Bush. The Republican Party used to be captained by wise, tolerant, kind hearted, conservative statesmen. Until that returns or, failing that, for the few years that my sojourn on this big rock continues, I'll probably be a registered Republican voting as an Independent. Come to think of it, that is probably a really good idea anyway.

I am also hopeful for the Democratic Party to grab hold of its rudder once again. While I know many Republicans who, like me, think that Obamacare has been an improvement and that Medicare for All may be the best solution for our remaining health care woes, the Democratic Party must not succumb to the pressure exerted by certain elements in the party to drift toward the extreme left on every issue. We need moderate Democrats to take control of the party, just as we need moderate Republicans to take control of the Republican Party.

It is time for us to insist that the politicians we vote for, regardless of party affiliation, be dedicated to serve all the people, be willing to communicate civilly and respectfully with members of the opposing party, and be willing to compromise to achieve the common good and the collective will of all the people, while respecting the inalienable rights of minorities.

It is time for women, minorities and young voters to take control and to shape this country into the moderate, kind, and tolerant bastion of freedom that it could be. Old white men, like me, have made a mess of things. It's up to the rest of you to set things right. Please start with a philosophical and legal resolution of the firearms and abortion issues. Do not let the hardliners on either side of these issues tell you that it cannot be done. Do not let the special interests, extremist organizations, and Super PACS continue to have their way. It is time to take these issues off the table, time to put an end to inept politicians hiding behind these issues, and time to remove the camouflage from the wealth and power perpetuation objectives of the rich and powerful. You young voters need to decide what kind of world you want to live in. It's up to you.

END

BIBLIOGRAPHY

COURT CASES CITED - CHRONOLOGICAL ORDER

Nunn v. State, 1 Ga. 243, 251 (1846)

Dred Scott v. Sandford, 60 U.S. 393 (1857)

United States v. Cruikshank, 92 U.S. 542 (1875)

Presser v. Illinois, 116 U.S. 252 (1886)

United States v. Miller, 307 U.S. 174 (1939)

Duncan v. Louisiana, 391 U.S. 145 (1968)

Swann v. Charlotte-Mecklenburg Board of Education, 402 U.S. 1 (1971)

Roe v. Wade, 410 U.S. 113, 164 (1973)

Milliken v. Bradley, 418 U.S. 717 (1974)

Lewis v. United States, 445 U.S. 55 (1980)

United States v. Verdugo-Urquidez, 494 U.S. 259 (1990)

Farmer v. Higgins, 907 F.2d 1041 (11th Cir. 1990), cert. denied, 498 U.S. 1047 (1991)

United States v. Rock Island Armory, 773 F. Supp. 117 (C.D. Ill. 1991)

United States v. Warner, 5 F.3d 1378 (10th Cir. 1993)

United States v. Lopez, 514 U.S. 549 (1995)

United States v. Rybar, 103 F.3d 273 (3d Cir. 1996)

Printz v. United States, 521 U.S. 898 (1997)

Navegar Inc. v. United States, 192 F.3d 1050 (D.C. Cir. 1999)

United States v. Emerson, 270 F.3d 203 (5th Cir. 2001), cert. denied, 536 U.S. 907 (2002)

Silveira v. Lockyer, 312 F.3d 1052 (9th Cir. 2002)

United States v. Stewart, 348 F.3d 1132 (2003) and 451 F.3d 1071 (2006)

FEC v. Wisconsin Right to Life, Inc., 551 U.S. 449 (2007)

District of Columbia v. Heller, 554 U.S. 570 (2008)

McDonald v. Chicago, 561 U.S. 742 (2010)

Citizens United v. Federal Election Commission, 558 U.S. 310 (2010)

Nordyke v. King, 644 F.3d 776 (9th Cir. 2011)

People v. Aguilar, 2 N.E. 3d 321 (Ill. 2013)

Henderson v. United States, 135 S. Ct. 1780 (2015)

Caetano v. Massachusetts, 136 S. Ct. 1027 (2016)

New York State Rifle & Pistol Association Inc. v. City of New York, 590 U.S. ___ (2020)

<u>REFERENCED ARTICLES</u>

Acevedo, Z. "Abortion in Early America." *Women Health.* (1979)

"Abortion and Christianity." Wikipedia. https://en.wikipedia.org/wiki/abortion_and_christianity.

"Abortion in India." Wikipedia. https://en.wikepedia.org/wiki/abortion-india#p-search

"Abortion in Mississippi." Wikipedia.
htpps://en.m.wikipedia.org/wiki/Abortion_in_Mississippi.

"Abortion in the Republic of Ireland." Wikipedia.
htpp://en.m.wikipedia.org/wiki/Abortion_in_the_ Republic_ of_ Ireland.

"Abortion in the United States." Wikipedia.
https://en.m.wkipedia.org/wiki/Abortion_in_the_United_States.

"Abortion Law." Wikipedia.
htpps://en.m.wikipedia.org/wiki/Abortion_law

"Abortion statistics in the United States." Wikipedia.
https://en.wikepedia.org/wiki/abortion_statistics_in_the_united_states#p-search.

ABORT73. "Facts and Figures relating to the frequency of abortion in the United States." http.//ABORT73.com.

Affir, Erfani. "Abortion in Iran: What Do We Know?" PSC Discussion Papers Series.
Volume 22, Issue 1. University of Western Ontario. (Jan. 2008).

American College of Pediatricians. "When Life Begins." (March 2017)

American Life League, Inc. "Abortion Statistics." (2020)

"American Revolutionary War." Wikipedia.
https://en.m.wikipedia.org./wiki/American_Revolutionary_War.

"American Revolution Boston Massacre."
https://www.duckster.com/history/american_revolution.php

"American Revolution Timeline."
https://www.ducksters.com/history/revolutionarywartimeline.php.

"Ambrose Burnside." Wikipedia.
https://en.m.wikipedia.org/wiki/Ambrose_Burnside

"Anglican Church in North America." Wikipedia.
https://en.m.wikipedia.org/wiki/Anglican_Church_in_North_America.

A1F Daily Staff. "The Truth Behind the proposed New Assault Weapons Ban." (Jan. 7, 2016)

"Arming America." Wikipedia.
https://en.m.wikipedia.org/wiki/Arming_America.

"Articles of Confederation" Wikipedia.
https://en.m.wikipedia.org/wiki/Articles_of_Confederation.

Assault Rifle, "Assault Weapons." Wikipedia.
https://en.m.wikipedia.org/wiki/Assault_Weapons.

"Assault Weapon Legislation in the United States." Wikipedia.
https://en.m.wikipedia.org/wiki/Assault_Weapon_
Legislation_in_the_United_States.

Baron, Dennis. "Antonin Scalia was wrong about the meaning of ' bear arms.'" (May 21, 2018)

BBC. "Buddhism and Abortion."
http://www.bbc.co/.uk/religion/buddhistethics/abortion.sthm/.

BBC. "Sanctity of Life." (2014)

Beale, Stephen. "Just How Many Protestant Denominations Are There?"

Beckwith, Francis J. "Answering the Arguments for Abortion Rights (Part Four): When Does a Human Become a Person." CRI, Charlottes, NC. www.equip.org/PDF/DA020-4.PDF

Beckwith, Francis J. "Viability: Is a Fetus a Person Once it Can Live Outside the   Mother's Womb?" (March 26, 2009)
htps://www.equip.org/articles/viability-is-a - fetus-a-person-once-it-can-live-outside-a-mothes-r,-s-womb.

Berry, Zoe. "What Abortion Looks Like in Mississippi." *The New York Times*. (June 13, 2019)

"Bipartisan Campaign Reform Act." Wikipedia. https://en.wikipedia.org/wiki/bipartisan_campaign_reform_act#p-search.

Buck, Stephanie. "After one Georgia gun lover wanted to build his own machine gun, the NRA got its worst defeat ever." Timeline.com. (Oct. 11, 2017)

"Bump Fire." Wikipedia. https://en.wikipedia/wiki/bump-fire.

"Bushmaser XM-15" Wikipedia. https://en.wikipedia/wiki/bushmaser_xm-15.

Carter, Joe. "5 facts about Reformation Day." *Free weekly Acton Newsletter.*

Libreria Editrice Vaticana. *Catechism of the Catholic Church, Second Edition.* (2019).

CBS News. "Texas shooter evaded background check by purchasing weapon in private sale." (Sept.3, 2019)

CDC. "Abortion Surveillance System FAQ's" (2016)

"Citizens United." Wikipedia. https://en.wikipedia.org/wiki/citizens_united_v._fec.

Classes of Offenses Under United States Federal Law. https://en.wikipedia.org/wiki/classes_of_offenses_under_united_states_federal_law#m.w-head

"Clayton Cramer." Wikipedia. https://en.wikipedia.org/wiki/clayton_cramer

Cleveland Clinic. "Fetal Development: Stages of Growth"

Clowes, Brian, Ph.D. "The Miracle of Fetal Development." https://www.hli.org/resources/miracle-fetal-development.

Coleman, Arica L. "When the NRA Supported Gun Control" *TIME History newsletter.*   (July 29, 2016)

Collins, Eliza. "Poll: Support for assault weapons ban drops to lowest in 20 years." (Dec.16, 2015)

"Concealed Carry in the United States" Wikipedia. https://en.wikipedia.org/wiki/concealed_carry_in_the_united_states

Congress of the United States. "Concerning Bill of Rights." (September 25, 1789)

"Constitution of the United States" Wikipedia. https://en.wikipedia.org/wiki/constitution_of_the_united_states.

Cramer, Clayton E.& Olson, Joseph Edward. "What Did "Bear Arms" Mean in the Second Amendment?" Georgetown Journal of Law & Public Policy, Vol.6, No.2, (2008)

Crary, David. "Number of abortions in US falls to lowest since 1973." (Sept.17, 2019)

Danner, Chas. "Everything We Know About the El Paso Walmart Massacre."

Davies, Mathew, Shea, Maureen. "Episcopalians show support for reproductive freedom at march." (April 26, 2004)

DenHoed, Andrea. "Forgotten Lessons of the American Eugenics Movement." (April 27, 2019)

"Dennis Baron." Wikipedia. https://en.wikipedia.org/wiki/dennis_Baron.

Drazin, Israel. "Who was the Jewish philosopher Philo." *Book Review of "Rediscovering Philo of Alexandria." (*Aug. 28, 2016)

"Dred Scott v. Sanford." JUSTICIA Supreme Court. https://supreme.justia.com/cases/federal/us/60/393/ (2020)

"Dred Scott v. Sanford." Wikipedia.
https://en.wikipedia.org/wiki/Dred_Scott_v._Sandford.

"Ensoulment." Wikipedia. https://en.wikipedia.org/wiki/ensoulment.

ER Services. "Module 4: The Cardiovascular System: Blood Vessels
and Circulation. *Anatomy and Physiology II.*

"Federal Assault Weapons Ban." Wikipedia.
https://en.wikipedia.org/wiki/federal_assault_weapons_ban

"Federal preemption." Wikipedia.
https://en.wikipedia.org/wiki/federal_preemption.

Ferguson, Maureen. "Why Abortion Is Antithetical to Women's
Empowerment." *Real Clear Politics.* (Jan.18, 2020)

"Fetal circulation." Wikipedia.
https://en.wikipedia.org/wiki/fetal_circulation.

"Fetal Development." MedlinePlus. https://medlineplus.html

"Fetal viability." Wikipedia.
https://en.wikipedia.org/wiki/fetal_circulation.

"Firearm Owners Protection Act of 1986," aka "The Peaceable Journey
Law."

"A Declaration of the Rights of the Inhabitants of the Commonwealth,
Or State of Pennsylvania." *The Pennsylvania Constitution.*

"Firearm Owners' Protection Act 1986. "Wikipedia.
https://en.wikipedia.org/wiki/firearm_owners'_protection-act.

"Firearm registration requirements by state." Wikipedia.
https://en.wikipedia.org/wiki/firearm_registration_requirements_by_state
.

"Fire preemption conflicts between state and local governments."
https://Ballotpedia.governments.org/Preemption_conflicts_between_state
_and_local_governments.

"First Continental Congress." Wikipedia.
https://en.wikipedia.org/wiki/first_continental_congress.

"First Trimester Ultrasound-Normal." Ultrasoundpaedia
https://www.ultrasoundpaedia.com/normal-1sttrimester/#protocol

Foe, Franklin. "Fetal Viability." (May 25, 1997)

"Founding Fathers of the United States."
https://en.wikipedia.org/wiki/founding_fathers_of_the_united_states.

Frazin, Rachel. "NRA slams Walmart's 'shameful' change to gun
policies." (Sept. 13, 2019)

Frum, David. "The Lost History of the NRA." (Jan. 15, 2013) *The
Daily Beast.*

Gazzaniga, Michael S. *'The Ethical Brain', Chapter one.* (June 19,
2005) https://www.nytimes.com/2005/06/19/books/chapters/the-ethical-
brain.html#story-continues-1.

General Board of American Baptist Churches in the U.S.A., The.
"American Baptist Resolution Concerning Abortion and Ministry In The
Local Church." (May 12, 1987)

"George Wallace." Wikipedia.
https://en.wikipedia.org/wiki/george_wallace_(disambiguation)

"George Washington." Wikipedia.
https://en.wikipedia.org/wiki/George_washington

Giffords Law Center to Prevent Gun Violence. "NICS & Reporting
Procedures."
https://lawcenter.giffords.org/gun-laws/policy-areas/background-
checks/nics-reporting-procedures/. (2018)

Giffords Law Center to Prevent Gun Violence. "Universal Background Checks."
https://lawcenter.giffords.org/gun-laws/policy-areas/background-checks/universal-background-checks/#state. (2018)

Gordon, Tim. "Why are pistol grips so deadly."

Graham, Ruth. "This Could Be The End of The Road for Pro-Life Democrats in Congress: With Joe Donnely's Loss, The Coalition Looks Shakier Than Ever. (Nov. 07, 2018)

"Gun Control Act 1968." Wikipedia.
https://en.wikipedia.org/wiki/gun_control_act_1968.

"Gun laws in the United States by state." Wikipedia.
https://en.wikipedia.org/wiki/gun_laws_in_the_united_states_by_state.

Guttmacher Institute. "Induced Abortion in the United States." (Sept. 2020)

"Hadith." Wikipedia.
https://en.wikipedia/wiki/hadith.

Hanegraaf, Hank. "Pro-Life vs. Pro-Choice: Annihilating the Abortion Argument."

Hanna H. Grey (Judson Distinguished Professor of History Emeritus, University of Chicago)

Hedarat, KM, Shooshtarizadeh, P, Raza, M. "Therapeutic abortion in Islam: Contemporary Views of Muslim Shiite Scholars and effect of recent Iranian Legislation." J Med Ethics, Nov. 2006.
https://www.ncbi.hlm.nih.gov/pmc/articles/PMC2563289.

"Hell-Fire trigger." Wikipedia.
https://en.wikipedia.org/hell_fire_trigger.

Hernandez, Clementine "Little Hawk." "Indians for Life."
https://www.nrlc.org/outreach/ifl

"High-capacity magazine ban." Wikipedia.
https://en.wikipedia.org/wiki/high_capacity_magazine_ban

"Hinduism." Wikipedia. https://en.wikipedia.org/wiki/Hinduism.

"Hinduism and Abortion."
https://www.patheos.com/blogs/whitehindu/2013/04/Hinduism-and-abortion

History.com editors. "Battles of Lexington and Concord." Originally Published: Dec.2, 2009. Access Date: June 10th, 2009.

History.com editors. "Dred Scott Case." Originally Published: Nov. 4, 2019. Access Date: Feb. 10, 2020.

"History of Christian thought on abortion." Wikipedia.
https://en.wikipedia.org/wiki/history_of_christian_thought_on_abortion.

Hooten, Kyle. "New Zealand Gun Buyback Was An 'Unmitigated Failure'." *Daily Caller.* (Dec.22, 2019)

Humphreys, Kenneth. "Jesus Never Existed." (Nov11, 2011)

"Is a Baby Human from the Beginning?' *Zaber's Cyclopedic Medical Dictionary*, "Fetal Development."

"Islam and abortion." Wikipedia.
https://en.wikipedia.org/wiki/islam_and_abortion#p-search.

"Islamic View on Abortion."
http://search.ebscohost.com/login.aspt?direct=true&db=rlh&AN=34908761&site=ehost-live.

"James Madison." Wikipedia.
https://en.wikipedia.org/wiki/james_madison.

"James Monroe." Wikipedia.
https://en.wikipedia.org./wiki/james_monroe.

"John McCain." Wikipedia. https://en.wikipedia.org/wiki/john_mccain.

"Joseph Warren." Wikipedia.
https://en.wikipedia.org/wiki/joseph_warren.

Junger, Peter D. "The Original Plain Meaning of the Right to Bear Arms." Case Research Paper in Legal Studies, School of Law, Case Western Reserve University, 2013.

Junger, Peter J. "The Original Meaning of The Right to Bear Arms." (Jan., 2013) https://ssrn.com/abstract=1082417

Katz, Stanley N. Chair (Professor of Public and International Affairs, Princeton University.) "BBC-Religions-Islam: Abortion"

Kenyon Edwin. *The Dilemma of Abortion. Edwin Burn Trowbridge Wilshire,* 1986.

King James Bible. (1611)

Kilgore, Ed. "The Near-Extinction of Pro-Choice Republicans in Congress. June 28, 2018.

Koch, Christoph. "When Does Consciousness Arise in Human Babies." (Sept 12, 2009) *Scientific America, Division of Springer Nature America, Inc.* (2019)

Kraft, Brooks. "Gun Rights Under President George W. Bush: A Relaxation of the Clinton Era Gun Restrictions." Updated (July 3, 2019)

"Latest Election Polls." *RealClearPolitics-2020.*
https://www.realclearpolitics.com/epolls/latest_polls/elections.

Laurel Thatcher Ulrich (James Duncan Phillips Professor of History, Harvard University)

Lewis, Danny. "1873 Colfax Massacre Crippled the Reconstruction Era." Smithsonianmag.com. (Apr. 13, 2016).

Lion's Roar Staff. "Ask the Teachers: As a Buddhist Should I support the pro-choice view on abortion?" (July 9, 2015.)

"Lists of Christian denominations by number of members." Wikipedia. https://en.wikipedia/wiki/list_of_christian denominations_by_number_of_members.

"List of firearm court cases in the United States." Wikipedia. htps://en.wikipedia.org/wiki/list_of_firearms_cases_in_the_united_states
.

"List of infantry weapons in the American Revolution." Wikipedia. https://en.wikipedia.org/wiki/list_of_infantry_weapons_in_the_american _revolution.

Litidayat, KM, Shooshtarizaden, P and Raza, M. "Therapeutic abortion in Islam: contemporary views of Muslim Shiite scholars and effect of recent Iranian legislation." (Nov.23, 2006)

McGary, Patsy. "Catholic Church teaching on abortion dates from 1869." (July 1, 2013)

MedlinePlus. "Fetal Development,"
https://medlineplus.gov/pregnancy.html

MedlinePlus. "5 Weeks Pregnant."
https://medlineplus.gov/pregnancy.html

MedlinePlus. "8 Weeks Pregnant."
https://medlineplus.gov/pregnancy.html

MedlinePlus. "18 Weeks Pregnant."
https://medlineplus.gov/pregnancy.html

MedlinePlus. "23 Weeks Pregnant."
https://medlineplus.gov/pregnancy.html

MedlinePlus. "24 Weeks Pregnant."
https://medlineplus.gov/pregnancy.html

Morgan, Thad. "Even The NRA Supported Taking Away Gun When The Black Panthers Had Them" (August 30, 2018)

Mount Vernon Ladies' Association. "6 Key Players At The Constitutional Convention." Mount Vernon Ladies' Association. (2019)

Mount Vernon's Ladies' Association. "Timeline of Revolutionary War." Mt. Vernon's Ladies' Association.

Mohammad, Khaleel, San Diego University. "Islam and Reproductive Choice."   *Religious Coalition for Reproductive Choice.* (2017)

Mufti Muhammad ibn Adam al-Kawthari. "When Does the Soul Enter the Fetus."

Nash, Elizabeth, Drewexe, Joerg. "The U.S. Abortion Rate Continues to Drop: Once Again, State Abortion Restrictions Are Not the Main Driver." *Gutmacher Institute.* (Sept. 18, 2019)

"National Firearms Act of 1934." Wikipedia. https://en.wikipedia.org/wiki/national_firearms_act.

"National Instant Criminal Background Check System." Wikipedia. https://en.wikipedia.org/wiki/national_instant-criminal-background-check_system.

The National Rifle Association. "National Gun Owners Survey." (2019)

"National Rifle Association." Wikipedia. https://en.wikipedia.org/wiki/national_rifle_association.

New American Bible. (1970)

New American Bible, Revised Edition. (2011)

Newman, Amie. "What the Standing Rock Resistance Can Teach Us About Reproductive Justice for Native American Women." (Dec.8, 2016)

New South Wales Jewish Board of Deputees. "Judaism And Abortion,"
2009.
https://www.nswjbd.org/What-is-the-Jewish-veiw-on-abortion-
/default.aspx.

New Testament. Encyclopedia Brittanica.
https://www.britannica.com/topic/new-testament# accordion-article-
history.

New Testament. Wikipedia.
https://en.wikipedia.org/wiki/new_testament.

"New York State Rifle & Pistol Association v. City of New York."
Wikipedia.
https://en.wikipedia.org/wiki/new_york_state_rifle_association_v._city_
of_new_york.

"1960 Presidential Election."
https://www.270towin.com/1960_Election/.

"1960 Presidential Election Map." Wikipedia.
https://en.wikepedia.org/wiki/1960

"Nirvana." https://www.thesaurus.com/blows/nirvana.

https://www.leagle.com/decision/infco2011502123.
O'Brien, Barbara. "Precepts of Buddahism." Aug.26, 2018.

114th Congress 1st Session. "Assault Weapons Ban." (December 16,
2015)

103rd United States Congress. "Brady Handgun Violence Prevention
Act." (date effective: Feb 28,1994)

Peck, Sarah: "Post- Second Amendment Jurisprudence." Congressional
Research Services. https://crsreports.congress.gov. R44618.

Perry, Nick. "New Zealanders hand in 50,000 guns after assault weapon
ban." *Associated Press.* (Dec.20, 2019)

"Philo ." Wikipedia. https://en.wikipedia.org/wiki/philo.

"Pistol Grip." Wikipedia. https.//en.wikipedia.org/wiki/pistol_grip.

Pius XI. "Casti Connubi." (Dec 31, 1930)

"Protection of Lawful Commerce in Arms Act." Wikipedia. https://en.wikipedia.org/wiki/protection_of_lawful_commerce_in_arms_act.

"QURAN IN ENGLISH." *Clear Quran,* Talil Itani, translator. www.clearquran.com

Ramsey, Michael. "Dennis Baron on Scalia, Heller, and Corpus Linguistics." (May 23, 2018)

"Report of the Investigative Committee in the matter of Professor Michael Bellesiles" (July 10, 2002)

"Resolutions Regarding Abortion." *The Archives of the Episcopal Church.*

Rettner, Rachael. "Is a 'Fetal Heartbeat' Really a Heartbeat at 6 Weeks?" *Live Science.*

"Roberti-Roos Assault Weapons Control Act of 1989." Wikipedia. https://en.wikipedia.org/wiki/roberti-roos_assault_weapons_control_act_of_1989.

"Robert Spitzer (political scientist.) Wikipedia. https:/econd/en.wikipedia.org./wiki/robert_spitzer_(political_scientist).

"Roe v. Wade." Wikipedia. https//:en.wikipedia.org/wiki/roe_v._wade.

Rogers, Adam. "'Heartbeat' Bills Get the Science of Fetal Heartbeats All Wrong." Published by: WIRED

"Russ Feingold." Wikipedia. https://en.wikipedia.org/wiki/russ_feingold#p-search.

"Sandy Hook Elementary School shooting." Wikipedia.
https://en.wikipedia.org/wiki/sandy_hook_elementary_school_shooting.

Savage, David G. "Supreme Court Lets Stand Ban on Machine Gun
Ownership." *Los Angeles Times*, 2019.

"Second Amendment to the United States Constitution." Wikipedia.
https://en.wikipedia.org/wiki/second_amendment_to_the_united_states_
of_america.

Selk, Avi. "A gunmaker tried to reform itself. The NRA nearly
destroyed it." Published by: Hillery Smith Garrison/Associated Press.

Sh. G.F. Haddad. "Hadiths On The Formation Of Human Life."
https://www.livingislam.org/n/hfhl_e.html

Sifert, Maria. "Republican-lawmakers-Amicus filing-filing-to-Supreme-
Court-on-Louisiana Abortion Case."

Soodlater, Ron. "Cannons of the Armed Forces." *MHQ Magazine*
(Feb.6, 2017)

Tawia, Susan. "When is the Capacity for Sentience Aquired During
Human Fetal development?" (July 7, 2009)

Theodore Sedgwick." Wikipedia.
https://en.wikipedia.org/wiki/theodore_sedgwick.

Quran In English. Translated by Talal Itani. ClearQuran.com.

The Twelve Disciples. Wikipedia.
https://en.wikipedia.org/wiki/the_twelve_disciples.

"Thomas M. Cooley." Wikipedia.
htps;//en.wikipedia.org/wiki/Thomas_m._cooley

Tworkoy, Helen. "Anti-Abortion/Pro-Choice; Taking Both Sides."
(1992)

"2017 Las Vegas Shooting." Wikipedia.
https://en.wikipedia.org/wiki/2017_las-vegas_shooting.

"2019 El Paso shooting." Wikipedia.
https://en.wikipedia.org/wiki/2019_el_paso_shooting.

"Unitarian Universalism." Wikipedia.
https://en.wikipedia.org/wiki/unitarian_universalism.

"Unitarian Universalist Association." Wikipedia.
https://en.wikipedia.org/wiki/unitarian-universalist_association.

United States Code. 18 U.S.C. Title 18. PART 1. CHAPTER 44-
FIREARMS. U.S. Government Publishing Office. (2009)

United States Code. 18 U.S. Code§ 922. Unlawful Acts.
https://www.law.cornell.edu/uscode/text/18/922#tab_default_1

"United States v. Emerson". Wikipedia.
https://en.wikipedia.org./wiki/united_states_v._emerson

"Universal background check." Wikipedia.
https:/en./Wikipedia.org/wiki/universal_background_check.

Upanishad, Garbha. Wikipedia.
https://en.wikipedia.org/wiki/garbha_upanishad.

US Abortion Clock.org. "Number of Abortion-Abortion Counters."
www.usabortionclock.org.

U.S. Congress. "Declaration of Independence: A Transcription." (July 4,
1776)

U.S. Congress. "Declaration of Independence" (July 4, 1776)

U.S. Congress. "Fourteenth Amendment."

U.S. Congress. "The first Continental Congress of the United States."

"Vertical forward grip." Wikipedia.
https://en.wikipedia.org/vertical_forward_grip.

Volokh, Eugene. The Volokh Conspiracy. "Do Pistol Grips Make Semi-Automatic Rifles More Dangerous, Because They "Aid Shooters when 'Spray Firing' from the Hip"?"
http://volokh.com/2014/01/02/pistol-grips-make-semi-automatic-rifles-dangerous-aid-shooters-spray-firing-hip/. (Jan. 2, 2014).

Volokh, Eugene, Prof, UCLA Law School. "18th and 19th Century Commentary on the Right to Keep and Bear Arms."
www2.law.ucla.edu/Volokh/beararms/comments.htm

White, Theodore H. *The Making of the President 1968.* Harper Collins. (Oct. 5, 2010)

"William Blackstone." Wikipedia.
https://en.wikipedia.org/wiki/William_blackstone.

Winningham, April L. "Gestational age."
https://www.britannica.com/science/gestational-age.

"Your Baby at Week 12."
https://www.whattoexpect.com/pregnancy/week_by_week/week-12

Yuhas, Alan. "The right to bear arms: what does the second amendment really mean?" (Oct. 5, 2017) Printed by: The Guardian, 2017.

Zero to Three: Early Connections Last a Lifetime. "When Does the Fetus's Brain Begin to Work?"